Learn

Pascal

Sam A. Abolrous

Wordware Publishing, Inc.

Library of Congress Cataloging-in-Publication Data

Abolrous, Sam A.
    Learn Pascal / by Sam A. Abolrous.
    p. cm.
    ISBN 1-55622-706-X (pb)
    1. Pascal. I. Title.

    QA76.73.P2 A248 2000
    005.13'3--dc21
                              99-088051
                                CIP

ISBN 1-55622-706-X
10 9 8 7 6 5 4 3 2 1
0002

All inquiries for volume purchases of this book should be addressed to Wordware Publishing, Inc., at the above
address. Telephone inquiries may be made by calling:

(972) 423-0090

Contents

Contents

Contents

Contents

Preface

This book is intended for both beginners and advanced users. As a beginner, you can learn the Pascal language through examples and step-by-step procedures. You start with simple programs that crunch numbers and end up with structured programs and advanced problem-solving algorithms. As an experienced programmer, you can use the book as a complete reference that covers the language and the advanced programming techniques.

Historically, Pascal was developed by Niklaus Wirth (a Swiss computer scientist) in the early 1970s and was named after the French mathematician Blaise Pascal (1623-1662). A recent standard for the language was formulated in 1983 and approved by the Institute of Electrical and Electronics Engineers (IEEE) and the American National Standards Institute (ANSI). With the growing use of microcomputers, extensions and variations have been added to the language. The most popular of these variations are UCSD Pascal (developed by University of California at San Diego) and Turbo Pascal (developed by Borland International).

The goal of this book is to teach you how to write a portable program in Pascal regardless of the computer you use. Mainly the standard IEEE/ANSI language is used, but the new features are discussed and their origins referred to. This book is not intended to go into the details of the nonportable areas of the language (such as graphics), but rather to make use of the powerful features of the modern implementations that help in data processing. The programs included in this book were compiled using Turbo Pascal, but you can use any compiler to run them. In a few places you may need to make minor modifications, which will be referenced. If you are using a Windows-based compiler (such as Delphi), you have to use the console mode to compile the examples of this book. For your convenience, both the source files and the executable files are included on the companion CD. Therefore, you have the option to either compile the source files or take a sneak peek at the programs' results without compiling them.

Sam A. Abolrous

Acknowledgment

I would like to thank my daughter, Sally Abolrous, for her help with editing this book.

Chapter 1

Getting Started with Pascal

- **Program structure**
- **Evaluating numeric expressions**
- **Arithmetic operators**
- **Using variables and named constants**
- **Reading input from the keyboard**
- **Displaying and formatting output**

1-1 The Pascal Version of "Hello World!"

Let us start with the smallest Pascal program, which is shown in the following example. It displays on your screen the phrase "Hello World!"

```
{ ---------------------------- Example 1-1 ---------------------------- }
PROGRAM FirstProgram(OUTPUT);
BEGIN
   WRITELN('Hello World!')
END.
{ -------------------------------------------------------------------- }
```

Whether the Pascal program is small or large, it must have a specific structure. This program consists mainly of one statement, WRITELN, which does the actual work here, as it displays whatever comes between the parentheses. The statement is included inside a frame starting with the keyword BEGIN and ending with the keyword END. This is called the *program main body* (or the *program block*) and usually contains the main logic of data processing. The Pascal program may also contain other building blocks called *procedures* and *functions*, which are explained in Chapter 7.

Comments

Consider the first line in the program:

```
{ -------------------------- Example 1-1 ---------------------------- }
```

This is a *comment* and is totally ignored by the compiler. Comments can appear anywhere in the Pascal program between two braces ({}) or between the two symbols (* and *) like this:

```
(* This is a comment *)
```

The Program Heading

The second line is called the *program heading*. It starts with the keyword PROGRAM, followed by a space, followed by the program name (FirstProgram). The program name is a user-invented word. User-invented words are classified in Pascal as *identifiers*. An identifier must begin with a letter and may contain any number of letters or digits (in Turbo Pascal it may contain underscores as well). You are free to choose any meaningful name for your program, but do not expect a program name like BEGIN or PROGRAM to be accepted. These words are called *reserved words*, and they are only used in the proper place in the program. Pascal's reserved words are summarized in Appendix B.

The program name is followed by the word OUTPUT contained in parentheses and terminated with a semicolon:

```
PROGRAM FirstProgram(OUTPUT);
```

The keyword OUTPUT tells the compiler that this program is going to produce output (such as writing to the screen), which is the counterpart of INPUT (such as reading from the keyboard). The words OUTPUT and INPUT are called *file parameters*. The program may perform both input and output, in which case the file parameters take the form:

```
PROGRAM FirstProgram(INPUT,OUTPUT);
```

In Turbo Pascal the program heading is optional. You may skip the whole line and start your program with the word BEGIN, or you may use the program name without parameters, like this:

```
PROGRAM FirstProgram;
```

Syntax and Conventions

The most important syntax is the semicolon after the program heading (which is used as a separator) and the period after the word END (which terminates the program).

A common convention is to write Pascal keywords in uppercase and the user-invented names (identifiers) in lowercase with the first letter capitalized. If the name consists of more than one word (which is the case in this program), the first letter in each word is capitalized. So, in Pascal programs you may see identifiers like:

Wages
Payroll
HoursWorkedPerWeek

This is just a convention to make your program readable, but Pascal compilers are not case-sensitive. This means that you can write the entire program in lowercase as in Example 1-2, or in uppercase as in Example 1-3. All three versions of the program will compile and run.

```
{ --------------------------- Example 1-2 --------------------------- }
program firstprogram(output);
begin
   writeln('Hello World!')
end.
{ ------------------------------------------------------------------- }

{ --------------------------- Example 1-3 --------------------------- }
PROGRAM FIRSTPROGRAM(OUTPUT);
BEGIN
   WRITELN('Hello World!')
END.
{ ------------------------------------------------------------------- }
```

All blank lines, indentation, and spaces (except those following the Pascal keywords) are optional, but it is a good programming habit to use this method to make your program well-organized and readable.

1-2 Displaying Output: WRITELN, WRITE

To display several lines of text you need a WRITELN statement for each line, as in the following program in Example 1-4.

```
{ --------------------------- Example 1-4 --------------------------- }
PROGRAM LinesOfText(OUTPUT);
BEGIN
   WRITELN('Hi there.');
   WRITELN('How are you today?');
   WRITELN('Are you ready for Pascal?')
END.
{ ------------------------------------------------------------------- }
```

Now the program contains more than one statement. Each statement must be separated from the next one with a semicolon. This is the only way the compiler can recognize the end of a statement. However, for the last statement in the program block, you may skip the semicolon.

When you compile this program it will give the following output:

```
Hi there.
How are you today?
Are you ready for Pascal?
```

The WRITELN statement displays a line of text followed by a new line (a line feed and a carriage return). If you wish to display two strings on the same line, you need to use the WRITE statement as shown in the following program.

```
{ --------------------------- Example 1-5 --------------------------- }
PROGRAM TwoLines(OUTPUT);
BEGIN
   WRITE('Hi there. ');
   WRITELN('How are you today?');
   WRITELN('Are you ready for Pascal?')
END.
{ ------------------------------------------------------------------- }
```

Output:

```
Hi there. How are you today?
Are you ready for Pascal?
```

As you can see in the program output, the second string is written on the same line as the first string as a result of using the WRITE statement to display the first string. This is the only difference between the two output statements WRITE and WRITELN.

If you want to display a blank line, you only need the statement:

```
WRITELN;
```

Drill 1-1

Write a Pascal program to display the following text on the screen:

```
Wordware Publishing, Inc.
-------------------------
2320 Los Rios Boulevard
Plano, Texas 75074
```

1-3 Working with Numbers

The easiest task for any program is to crunch numbers. The statement WRITELN (or WRITE) can be used to both display numbers and evaluate numerical expressions. You can build up arithmetic expressions using the following *arithmetic operators*:

+   for addition
−   for subtraction
*   for multiplication
/   for division

Take a look at these examples:

```
WRITELN(123);
WRITELN(1.23 * 4);
```

The first example displays the number in the parentheses (123). The second example performs multiplication of two numbers and displays the result. Notice that for numeric values, unlike text strings, you don't use quotes.

You may use WRITELN to display text and numbers in the same statement by using the comma as a separator like this:

```
WRITELN('The result is=', 125 * 1.75);
```

The following program is used to evaluate two numeric expressions (multiplication and division) and display the results preceded by the proper text.

```
{ --------------------------- Example 1-6 --------------------------- }
PROGRAM CrunchNumbers(OUTPUT);
BEGIN
   WRITELN('I can easily crunch numbers.');
   WRITELN('Here is multiplication of 50x4:',50*4);
   WRITELN('..and here is division of 2400/8:',2400/8)
END.
{ ------------------------------------------------------------------- }
```

Output:

```
I can easily crunch numbers.
Here is multiplication of 50x4:200
..and here is division of 2400/8: 3.0000000000E+02
```

The multiplication is done as expected. The two operands (50 and 4) are integers (whole numbers) and the result (200) is an integer too. The format of the division result, however, needs some explanation.

Real Division: /

The division performed with the / operator is called *real division* and always produces a real number as its result . Real numbers may be written in fixed-point notation (such as 300.0) or in scientific (exponential) notation (such as 3.0E+02), but in Pascal, real number output will always be represented in scientific notation by default. A number written in scientific notation is made up of two parts divided by the letter E (or e). The left part is called the *mantissa* and indicates the significant digits, while the right part is called the *exponent*. The exponent is a power of ten that determines the position of the decimal point. So, in this example the number:

3.0000000000E+02

is the same as the number:

3×10^2

The same number, when expressed in fixed-point format, becomes:

300.0

If the exponent is preceded by a minus sign as in:

3.124E–02

then the decimal point is shifted two positions to the left. This number, then, is the same as:

0.03124

If the number is negative, the minus sign should precede the mantissa:

–0.0124E–02

If the number is positive, you may omit the sign for either the mantissa or the exponent:

1.23E02

The division operator (/) is called the *real division operator*, because the result always appears as a real number regardless of the type of the operands.

Integer Division: DIV

For *integer division* use the DIV operator as in the example:

```
WRITELN(2400 DIV 8);
```

This will produce the output 300.

With integer division, any fraction in the result will be truncated, as in this example:

```
WRITELN(9 DIV 4);              {Produces the output 2.}
```

Remainder of the Integer Division: MOD

Another important operator, MOD, is used to get the remainder of integer division (modulo), as in these examples:

```
WRITELN(9 MOD 4);             {Produces the output 1.}
WRITELN(3 MOD 4);             {Produces the output 3.}
```

The DIV and MOD operators take only integer operands and produce integer output.

For the other operators (+, –, and *), if either one of the operands is real, the result will be real.

Drill 1-2

Evaluate the following expressions and write the result either as an integer (if integer), or as a fixed-point real number (if real):

A.   144 / 12
B.   144 DIV 12
C.   17 MOD 5
D.   3 MOD 5
E.   3e+02 + 3
F.   345E–01 – 1

Operator Precedence in Arithmetic Expressions

When you build more complicated arithmetic expressions, you have to watch the priority of each operator involved in the expression. Take a look at these two expressions:

```
2 + 10 / 2
(2 + 10) / 2
```

Although the two expressions use the same numbers and operators, the first expression is evaluated as 7, while the second is evaluated as 6. This is because in the first expression the division is evaluated before the addition, while in the second expression the parentheses are used to change the order of evaluation, in which case the expression inside the parentheses is evaluated first. In general, the arithmetic operators in Pascal have two levels of precedence: *high* and *low*.

The + and – have low precedence, while all other operators have high precedence.

If an expression contains two operators of the same precedence level, they are evaluated from left to right. Consider this example:

```
5 + 3 * 2 - 6 DIV 2
```

The first operation to be performed is the multiplication:

```
5 + 6 - 6 DIV 2
```

The second operation, of next highest priority, is the division:

```
5 + 6 - 3
```

This leaves two operations of equal priority. They are evaluated from left to right resulting in:

```
8
```

When parentheses are used to alter the order of evaluation, they form subexpressions which are evaluated first. If parentheses are nested, the innermost subexpressions are evaluated first. Consider the same example with nested parentheses:

```
((5 + 3) * 2 - 6) DIV 2
```

This expression is evaluated according to the following steps:

```
(8 * 2 - 6) DIV 2
(16 - 6) DIV 2
10 DIV 2
5
```

Arithmetic operators are summarized in Table 1-1, along with their precedence and properties.

The + and – signs are also used as *unary operators* (to signify positive and negative). The unary operators are of the same low priority as the binary operators + and –. If a binary operator precedes the unary operator such as 5 * – 4, you must enclose the unary operator and its number in parentheses: 5 * (–4). The first form may be accepted by some compilers, but do not try it.

Table 1-1: Arithmetic operators

Operator	Arithmetic Operation	Operands	Result	Precedence
+	Addition	REAL/INTEGER	REAL/INTEGER	Low
−	Subtraction	REAL/INTEGER	REAL/INTEGER	Low
*	Multiplication	REAL/INTEGER	REAL/INTEGER	High
/	Real division	REAL/INTEGER	REAL	High
DIV	Integer division	INTEGER	INTEGER	High
MOD	Remainder of integer division	INTEGER	INTEGER	High

Drill 1-3

Evaluate the following expressions and write the result either as an integer (if integer), or as a fixed point real number (if real):

A.   15 − 15 DIV 15
B.   22 + 10 / 2
C.   (22 + 10) / 2
D.   50 * 10 − 4 MOD 3 * 5 + 80

1-4 Variables

Data are stored in the memory locations at specific addresses. Programmers, however, refer to these locations using variables. When variables are used in a program, they are associated with the specific memory locations. The value of a variable is actually the contents of its memory location. As data are processed by the program, the contents of any location may change, and so does the value of the associated variable. Variables are given names (identifiers) according to the rules mentioned earlier.

Variable Declaration

Before using a variable in a Pascal program, its name and *type* must be declared in a special part of the program called the *declaration part*. This part starts with the keyword VAR, as in the following example:

```
VAR
    a :INTEGER;
    x :REAL;
```

The variable a is of the type INTEGER, which means that it can hold only integer numbers such as 4, 556, and 32145. The variable x is declared as of the type REAL and can hold real numbers such as 3.14, 44.567, and 3.5E+02.

If you want to declare more than one variable of the same type, you may declare each on a separate line:

```
VAR
      a :INTEGER;
      b :INTEGER;
      c :INTEGER;
      x :REAL;
      y :REAL;
```

or, you may also declare all variables of the same type as a list like this:

```
VAR
      a, b, c     :INTEGER;
      x, y        :REAL;
```

The keywords INTEGER and REAL are classified as *standard identifiers*, which are predefined in Pascal. The standard identifiers can be redefined by the programmer, but this is not recommended. Standard identifiers are listed in Appendix B.

In the following program three variables are declared: a and b are integers, while x is real. The contents of each one are displayed using the WRITELN statement.

```
{ --------------------------- Example 1-7 ---------------------------- }
PROGRAM Variables(OUTPUT);
{ Variable Declarations }
VAR
   a, b :INTEGER;
   x    :REAL;
{ Program Block }
BEGIN
   WRITELN('Contents of a=',a);
   WRITELN('Contents of b=',b);
   WRITELN('Contents of x=',x)
END.
{ ------------------------------------------------------------------ }
```

Output:

```
      Contents of a=0
      Contents of b=631
      Contents of x= 2.7216107254E-26
```

Note that the contents of a and b are displayed as integers while the contents of x are displayed in real format. However, the output numbers are just garbage because no values were actually stored in those variables. Unless you store data values in your variables, they will contain whatever was last left in those memory locations.

The Assignment Statement

To store a value in a variable you can use the *assignment operator* (:=) as in the following examples:

```
a := 55;
x := 1.5;
y := 2.3E+02;
```

Caution: Do not use a real number like this:

```
.1234
```

A legal real number in Pascal must have a digit to the left of the decimal point, like this:

```
0.1234
```

Also, the number:

```
123.
```

may be rejected by some compilers. It would be better to use the legal form:

```
123.0
```

In the following program, two integers a and b are declared in the declaration part, then assigned integer values in the program block. The WRITELN statement is then used to evaluate and display the results of different arithmetic operations performed on those variables.

```
{ ---------------------------- Example 1-8 --------------------------- }
PROGRAM Arithmetic(OUTPUT);
{ Variable Declarations }
VAR
   a, b :INTEGER;
{ Program block }
BEGIN
   a := 25;
   b := 2;
   WRITELN('a=',a);
   WRITELN('b=',b);
   WRITELN('a+b=',a+b);
   WRITELN('a-b=',a-b);
   WRITELN('a*b=',a*b);
   WRITELN('a/b=',a/b);
   WRITELN('a div b=',a DIV b);          {used with integers only}
   WRITELN('a mod b=',a MOD b)           {used with integers only}
END.
{ --------------------------------------------------------------------- }
```

Output:

```
a=25
b=2
a+b=27
a-b=23
a*b=50
a/b= 1.2500000000E+01          → Real division
a div b=12                     → Integer division
a mod b=1                      → Remainder of integer division
```

You may assign one variable to another:

```
x := y;
```

In this case, the contents of the variable y are copied to the variable x. You may also assign an arithmetic expression to a variable, like this:

```
z := a + b - 2;
GrossPay := PayRate * HoursWorked;
```

In these statements the value of the expression to the right of the assignment operator is calculated and stored in the variable to the left of the assignment operator (z or GrossPay).

Drill 1-4

Write a Pascal program to do the following:

A. Assign the value 2 to a variable a, and the value 9 to a variable b.

B. Display the values of the expressions:

```
a + b DIV 2
(a + b) DIV 2
```

1-5 Constants

Data values (in many languages including Pascal) are called *constants*, as they never change during the program execution. In Pascal there are two types of constants:

- Literal constants
- Named constants

Literal constants are data values such as explicit numbers and text strings, while a named constant is a *constant variable*. The difference between a named constant and a variable is that the value of the named constant does not change during the program. Like variables, a named constant is given a name and has to be declared in the declaration part. Actually, the declaration part is divided into two sections, CONST and VAR;

the CONST section comes before the VAR section. Suppose that you would like to use the value 3.14159 (a numerical constant known as Pi) many times in your calculations. It would be more convenient to give it a name and use the name in your code. You can declare named constants as in the following example:

```
CONST
    Pi = 3.14159;
    ThisYear = 1992;
    Department= 'OtoRhinoLaryngology';
```

Some constants are predefined in Pascal as standard identifiers. One useful predefined named constant is MAXINT, which gives the maximum value an integer can possess. The value depends on the computer used. If you want to know the value of MAXINT in your computer, use the statement:

```
WRITELN(MAXINT);
```

A typical value is 32767 (two bytes).

In the following program, the perimeter of a circle is calculated using the named constant Pi.

```
{ ----------------------------- Example 1-9 --------------------------- }
PROGRAM Constants(OUTPUT);
{ Constant Declarations }
CONST
    Pi = 3.14159;
{ Variable Declarations }
VAR
    Radius, Perimeter  :REAL;
{ Program block }
BEGIN
    Radius := 4.9;
    Perimeter := 2 * Pi * Radius;
    WRITELN('Perimeter=', Perimeter)
END.
{ ------------------------------------------------------------------- }
```

Output:

```
    Perimeter= 3.0787582000E+01
```

Note: If you are using Turbo Pascal, you do not need to redefine the constant Pi, as it is predefined as a standard identifier.

1-6 Type Conversion: ROUND, TRUNC

You can assign an integer to a variable of the type REAL, but the opposite is not permitted. The reason for this is because the storage size allocated for an integer is smaller than that allocated for a real number. If this were permitted, data could be lost or corrupted when a large number was moved to a smaller location in which it did not fit. You can, however, perform the conversion with one of two functions:

> **ROUND**(n) rounds n to the closest integer
> **TRUNC**(n) truncates the fraction part of n

where:

> n is a real variable or expression.

Consider these examples:

```
ROUND(8.4)    returns 8
ROUND(8.5)    returns 9
TRUNC(8.4)    returns 8
TRUNC(8.5)    returns 8
```

As you can see in the examples, the two functions may or may not return the same integer value for the same argument.

In the following program the two functions are used to get the rounded and the truncated integer values of the real variable Perimeter.

```
{ --------------------------- Example 1-10 -------------------------- }
PROGRAM Functions1(OUTPUT);
{ Constant Declarations }
CONST
   Pi = 3.14159;
{ Variable Declarations }
VAR
   Perimeter, Radius                      :REAL;
   RoundedPerimeter, TruncatedPerimeter   :INTEGER;
{ Program block }
BEGIN
   Radius := 4.9;
   Perimeter := 2*Pi*Radius;
   RoundedPerimeter := ROUND(Perimeter);
   TruncatedPerimeter := TRUNC(Perimeter);
   WRITELN('Perimeter=', Perimeter);
   WRITELN('Perimeter (rounded)=', RoundedPerimeter);
   WRITELN('Perimeter (truncated)=', TruncatedPerimeter)
END.
{ ------------------------------------------------------------------- }
```

Output:

```
Perimeter= 3.0772000000E+01          → The actual result
Perimeter (rounded)=31               → Rounded result
Perimeter (truncated)=30             → Truncated result
```

1-7 Reading from the Keyboard: READLN, READ

The previous program is used to calculate the perimeter for a given radius, hardcoded in the program. A more useful program would accept the radius from the user, do the calculations, then display the result. You can use either READLN or READ to make the program pause and wait for user input. The READLN statement is used to read the value of one or more variables. It takes the general form:

READLN(variable-list);

To read the value of a variable x from the keyboard, you can use the statement:

```
READLN(x);
```

To read the values of the three variables x, y, and z, use the statement:

```
READLN(x, y, z);
```

When you enter the values of more than one variable (such as x, y, and z), they should be separated by one or more blanks or by pressing the Enter key.

Replace the assignment statement in the previous program with a READLN statement as follows:

```
READLN(Radius);
```

If you try the program now, it will pause until you type a number and press Enter; it then resumes execution and displays the results. Unfortunately, you cannot use the READLN statement to display a user prompt when the program is waiting for input. This must be done using a WRITE (or WRITELN) statement such as:

```
WRITE('Please enter the radius:');
```

Here is the program in its new shape:

```
{ -------------------------- Example 1-11 -------------------------- }
PROGRAM KeyboardInput(OUTPUT);
{ Constant Declarations }
CONST
   Pi = 3.14159;
{ Variable Declarations }
VAR
   Perimeter, Radius                      :REAL;
   RoundedPerimeter, TruncatedPerimeter   :INTEGER;
{ Program block }
```

```
BEGIN
   WRITE('Please enter the radius:');
   READLN(Radius);
   Perimeter := 2*Pi*Radius;
   RoundedPerimeter := ROUND(Perimeter);
   TruncatedPerimeter := TRUNC(Perimeter);
   WRITELN('Perimeter=', Perimeter);
   WRITELN('Perimeter (rounded)=', RoundedPerimeter);
   WRITELN('Perimeter (truncated)=', TruncatedPerimeter)
END.
{ ------------------------------------------------------------------- }
```

Sample Run:

```
Please enter the radius:4.9                    → Type the number and press Enter
Perimeter= 3.0787582000E+01
Perimeter (rounded)=31
Perimeter (truncated)=30
```

Note: At this stage you can use either READ or READLN for keyboard input as the difference between them is not noticeable in our applications so far.

1-8 Formatting Output

You have probably thought that scientific notation is not the best format for output, especially with business and money figures. You're right. Scientific notation is useful only with very large or very small numbers, where the power of ten represents an order of magnitude of the number.

Whenever you want to see your results in fixed-point notation, use the *format descriptors* as in this example:

```
WRITELN(Wages :6:2);
```

The format :6:2 determines a field width of 6 positions, including 2 decimal places. So, if the value of the variable Wages is 45.5 it will be displayed as:

```
B45.50
```

where the letter B refers to a blank space. If the output digits are less than the field width, which is the case in this example, the result will be shifted right. If the number is larger than the field width, then the field will be automatically enlarged and the entire number printed.

You can add a character (such as the dollar sign) to the left of the number as follows:

```
WRITELN('$',Wages :6:2);
```

This will produce the output:

```
$ 45.50
```

By using a smaller field width, you can have the number shifted to the left and the dollar sign attached to the first significant digit:

```
WRITELN('$',Wages :0:2);
```

This will produce:

```
$45.50
```

You can format any type of data using the same method. The only difference is that with integers or strings you specify the width field without decimal places.

In the following program different types of data are formatted to fit into specific fields, as shown in the output.

```
{ --------------------------- Example 1-12 --------------------------- }
PROGRAM Format(OUTPUT);
{ Variable Declarations }
VAR
    a    :INTEGER;
    b    :REAL;
{ Program Block }
BEGIN
    b := 1.2e+02;
    a := 320;
    WRITELN('I am a text string starting from position 1.');
    WRITELN('I am now shifted to the right end of the field.':50);
    WRITELN('I am an unformatted integer:', a);
    WRITELN('I am an integer written in a field 6 characters wide:', a:6);
    WRITELN('I am a money amount written in 8 positions:$',b:8:2);
    WRITELN('I am a money amount shifted to the left:$',b:0:2)
END.
{ -------------------------------------------------------------------- }
```

Output:

```
I am a text string starting from position 1.
    I am now shifted to the right end of the field.
I am an unformatted integer:320
I am an integer written in a field 6 characters wide:   320
I am a money amount written in 8 positions:$  120.00
I am a money amount shifted to the left:$120.00
```

If you display the numeric variables alone (without text), they will appear as follows:

```
320
   320
$   120.00
$120.00
```

Drill 1-5

Write a program to calculate employee wages according to the formula:

```
Wages := HoursWorked * PayRate;
```

Accept the HoursWorked and the PayRate from the keyboard and display the Wages in fixed-point notation preceded by a dollar sign.

Summary

In this chapter you were introduced to the most important tools in Pascal programming.

1. You are now familiar with the Pascal program structure:
   - The program heading
   - The declaration part
   - The CONST section
   - The VAR section
   - The program main body between BEGIN and END.

2. You know two important data types, INTEGER and REAL, and how to express and evaluate arithmetic expressions using both types.

3. You know the arithmetic operators in Pascal, their properties, and their precedence:

   + − * / DIV MOD

4. You know how to declare variables of both types, how to name them using identifiers, how to store values in them whether by assignment (:=) or by entering values from the keyboard, and how to display their values on the screen.

5. You learned how to use the following conversion functions to truncate and round real expressions:

   TRUNC(*n*)   truncates the fraction part of *n*.
   ROUND(*n*)   rounds *n* to the closest integer.

6. You know as well how to declare named constants and use them in the program.

7. During your first tour of Pascal, you learned the following output statements to display both variables and numeric or string literal constants:

   WRITELN
   WRITE

   Also, you learned the following input statements to read variable values from the keyboard:

   READLN
   READ

8. Finally, you learned how to format your numeric or string output to have the results in the desired form.

Exercises

1. What is the difference between a variable and a named constant?

2. Write declarations using suitable variable names and types to store the following items:
   - Price plus tax
   - Total number of employees in a company
   - The root mean square of electric voltage
   - The average of a student's grades

3. Write Pascal expressions to calculate the following:
   - The surface area of a rectangle (given the width and the length)
   - The surface area of a cylinder (given the radius and the height)
   - The mathematical expression $2x^2 + 4y + 2$

4. Evaluate the following expressions:
   a. $4 + 3 * 2 - 6 / 2$
   b. $(4 + 3) * 2 - 6 / 2$
   c. $(4 + 3 * 2 - 6) / 2$
   d. $((4 + 3) * 2 - 6) / 2$

5. Given the values:

   $A = 3.0, B = 4.0, J = 4, I = 3,$

   evaluate the following expressions and print the results using the fixed-point notation:
   a. A / B
   b. A / J
   c. I / B
   d. I DIV J
   e. I MOD J

    f. B / I

    g. ROUND(B / I)

6. Write a Pascal program to display the following figure:

7. Write a Pascal program to display the user menu for a telephone database that gives the following options:

- Enter a new phone number
- Get a phone number
- Save new records
- Remove records
- End the program

Answers

4. a. 7.00, b. 11.00, c. 2.00, d. 4.00

5. a. 0.75, b. 0.75, c. 0.75, d. 0, e. 3, f. 1.33, g. 1

Chapter 2

Data Types

Chapter Topics:

- Numeric data types
- Character data types
- Boolean data types
- String storage in standard Pascal and in modern implementations of the language
- Standard functions and operators for processing different data types
- Additional Turbo Pascal types, operators, and functions

2-1 Overview of Data Types

You have already used the INTEGER and REAL types as both numeric constants and variables. You have also already used arithmetic operators with variables and constants to build arithmetic expressions, and you have tasted the flavor of some functions such as ROUND and TRUNC. The data processed by any program may also contain single characters, strings of text, and logical quantities. Each data type is stored and manipulated differently. Pascal provides the following standard data types (also referred to as simple or *scalar* data types):

INTEGER
REAL

       CHAR
       BOOLEAN

This chapter introduces the whole picture of numeric data types and related functions and expressions. It also introduces the type CHAR which is used to represent single characters, and the type BOOLEAN to represent logical values. The discussion of the single character type contains an overview of how strings were represented in standard Pascal and also how they are represented in the modern implementations such as Turbo Pascal and UCSD Pascal (using the type STRING).

2-2 Numeric Types

The range of numbers that may be represented as integers (or as reals) depends on the implementation. For the type INTEGER it is determined by the following limits:

MAXINT	the maximum positive integer
–(**MAXINT**+1)	the maximum negative integer

Again, the value of MAXINT depends on the implementation.

Real numbers are generally stored in a larger number of bytes than are integers, but they are of limited precision. Fractions such as 0.333333 and 0.666666 can never be as precise as the exact values 1/3 and 2/3, regardless of how many digits are used to represent the number. For this reason, it is not recommended to test two real numbers for equality. Instead, it would be better to test to see if the difference between the two numbers is less than some specific small amount.

In Turbo Pascal, there are additional numeric types, which are introduced in the following section.

Numeric Types in Turbo Pascal

There are additional integer types (including the type INTEGER) in Turbo Pascal. They are shown in Table 2-1 along with their storage sizes and the maximum range of values that can be represented in each.

In one byte, you can store either a SHORTINT or a BYTE. The BYTE is actually an unsigned SHORTINT, which means that it can hold only positive numbers. As you can see in the table, the maximum range of values for a type is doubled when the sign is not used. The same applies to the types INTEGER and WORD, as the WORD is a positive integer of doubled maximum range.

Table 2-1: Turbo Pascal integer types

Data Type	Size (in bytes)	Range
SHORTINT	1	from −128 to +127
BYTE	1	from 0 to 255
INTEGER	2	from −32768 to +32767
WORD	2	from 0 to 65535
LONGINT	4	from −2,147,483,648 to +2,147,483,647

The LONGINT is the largest integer that can be represented in Turbo Pascal. You can test its value by displaying the value of the predefined constant MAXLONGINT as follows:

```
WRITELN(MAXLONGINT);
```

Notice that the negative range of any signed type exceeds the positive range by one (e.g., +127 and −128). This is because zero is counted with the positive numbers.

Caution: The commas used here to express large numbers are used only for readability. You will neither see them in the output of a program, nor are they accepted as a part of literal constants. So, the number 2,147,483,647 must be used as 2147483647.

In Turbo Pascal, there are also additional real types (including the type REAL) as shown in Table 2-2. For real numbers, a new column is added to the table to describe the accuracy of a number as the maximum number of precise digits.

Table 2-2: Turbo Pascal real types

Data Type	Size (in bytes)	Precision (up to)	Range
SINGLE	4	7 digits	from 0.71E−45 to 3.4E+38
REAL	6	11 digits	from 2.94E−39 to 1.7E+38
DOUBLE	8	15 digits	from 4.94E−324 to 1.79E+308
EXTENDED	10	19 digits	from 3.3E−4932 to 1.18E+4932
COMP	8	integers only	±9.2E+18

If you examine the range of the type SINGLE, you will find that it is pretty close to that of the type REAL, especially in the area of the very large numbers. The main difference between the two lies in the economical storage of the SINGLE type (4 bytes compared to 6), which comes at the expense of precision (7 digits compared to 11). Real number types other than REAL are not available unless a math coprocessor is used. The type COMP actually belongs to the set of integers, as it does not accept fractions, but it is usually mentioned among reals as it requires the use of a math coprocessor.

2-3 Arithmetic Functions

Pascal includes a large number of predefined functions that may be used in expressions among constants and variables. Table 2-3 shows the standard arithmetic functions divided into three groups:

- Conversion functions
- Trigonometric functions
- Miscellaneous functions

Any function operates on the parameter that is presented inside its parentheses. The parameter is an expression of a specific type (notice that the expression may be a single variable or constant). Before using any of these functions, you must know the type of parameter the function uses and the type of the returned value (which is also the type of the function). The conversion functions, for instance, take real parameters and return integer results. Other functions use either integer or real parameters and produce different types. The type of the returned value is important when you assign the function to a variable.

Table 2-3: Standard arithmetic functions

Function Format	Returned Value	Parameter Type	Result Type
CONVERSION FUNCTIONS:			
ROUND(x)	x rounded to the nearest integer	REAL	INTEGER
TRUNC(x)	x with the fraction part truncated	REAL	INTEGER
*TRIGONOMETRIC FUNCTIONS:			
ARCTAN(x)	The arctangent of x	REAL/INTEGER	REAL
COS(x)	Cosine of x	REAL/INTEGER	REAL
SIN(x)	Sine of x	REAL/INTEGER	REAL
MISCELLANEOUS FUNCTIONS:			
ABS(x)	The absolute value of x	REAL/INTEGER	REAL/INTEGER
EXP(x)	The exponential function of x (ex)	REAL/INTEGER	REAL
LN(x)	The natural logarithm of x	REAL/INTEGER	REAL
SQR(x)	The square of x (x^2)	REAL/INTEGER	REAL/INTEGER
SQRT(x)	The square root of x ($\sqrt{x}$)	REAL/INTEGER	REAL
* All angles must be expressed in radians.			

Look at these examples:

```
SQR(3)=9
SQR(2.5)=6.25
SQRT(9)=3.00
ABS(-28.55)=28.55
LN(EXP(1))=1.00
ARCTAN(1)=45 degrees
```

Note that the type of result returned by the function SQR is the same as the type of the parameter, but the function SQRT returns a real number regardless of the parameter type. Notice also that the parameter of any function may contain another function, such as LN(EXP(1)).

The output returned from the last function (ARCTAN) is converted to degrees here but will be returned in radians if not converted. The program which produced these results is shown in Example 2-1. Pay attention to the format descriptors, which are used to produce the output in these formats.

```
{ ---------------------------- Example 2-1 ---------------------------
}
{ Arithmetic Standard Functions }
PROGRAM FunctionDemo(OUTPUT);
CONST
   Pi = 3.14159;                        {No need for this part in Turbo Pascal}
BEGIN
   WRITELN('SQR(3)=',SQR(3));
   WRITELN('SQR(2.5)=',SQR(2.5):0:2);                {Notice the format}
   WRITELN('SQRT(9)=',SQRT(9):0:2);
   WRITELN('ABS(-28.55)=',ABS(-28.55):0:2);
   WRITELN('LN(EXP(1))=',LN(EXP(1)):0:2);
   WRITELN('ARCTAN(1)=',ARCTAN(1)* 180/Pi:0:0,' degrees') {Notice the
                                              conversion and the format}
END.
{ -------------------------------------------------------------------
}
```

The Power Function

The power operator does not exist in Pascal as it does in some other languages (such as Fortran and Basic), but you can make one using arithmetic functions. You can, of course, use the function SQR to produce small powers, thus:

SQR(x)	power 2
SQR(x) * x	power 3
SQR(SQR(x))	power 4

You can also make use of the following mathematical relationship to express any power:

$$x^y = \text{EXP}(\text{LN}(x) * y)$$

In the following program this expression is used to raise a number to any power. The program asks you to enter both the base x and the exponent y, then displays the formatted result.

```
{ --------------------------- Example 2-2 ---------------------------- }
{ Arithmetic Standard Functions }
PROGRAM PowerOperator(INPUT,OUTPUT);
VAR
   a, b :REAL;
BEGIN
   WRITE('Enter the base and the exponent separated by a space: ');
   READLN(a,b);
   WRITELN('The value of ',a:0:2,' raised to the power ',b:0:2,' is ',
           EXP(LN(a)*b):0:2)
END.
{ ------------------------------------------------------------------- }
```

Sample Run:

```
Enter the base and the exponent separated by a space: 2 10
The value of 2.00 raised to the power 10.00 is 1024.00
```

Application: Grocery Store

In a grocery store a fast calculation is needed to count the number and type of coins that make up the change remaining from a dollar, so it is a great help to have this logic programmed into the cash register. The following program accepts from the keyboard the price of the purchase (for the sake of simplicity, this is assumed to be less than one dollar) and produces as output the number of quarters, dimes, nickels, and pennies remaining from a dollar bill. The program is an application of the integer operators DIV and MOD.

```
{ --------------------------- Example 2-3 ---------------------------- }
{ Grocery Store }
PROGRAM Grocery(INPUT,OUTPUT);
VAR
   Change, TotalPrice,
   Dollars, Quarters, Dimes, Nickels, Cents :INTEGER;
BEGIN
   WRITE('Enter the total-price in cents: ');
   READLN(TotalPrice);
   Change := 100 - TotalPrice;
   { Quarters }
     Quarters := Change DIV 25;
     Change := Change MOD 25;
   { Dimes }
     Dimes    := Change DIV 10;
     Change   := Change MOD 10;
```

```
    { Nickels }
      Nickels := Change DIV 5;
      Change  := Change MOD 5;
    { Cents }
      Cents   := Change;
    WRITELN('The change is:');
    WRITELN(Quarters,' Quarters');
    WRITELN(Dimes,   ' Dimes');
    WRITELN(Nickels, ' Nickels');
    WRITELN(Cents,   ' Cents')
END.
{ ------------------------------------------------------------------- }
```

Sample Run:

```
    Enter the total-price in cents: 22          → Type 22 and press Enter
    The change is:
    3 Quarters
    0 Dimes
    0 Nickels
    3 Cents
```

Drill 2-1

Modify the above program to accept any amount of money as total-price (including fractions of a dollar) and any amount of cash as amount-paid. The program should read the amount-paid and the total-price, and display the change in bills of different denominations, quarters, dimes, nickels, and cents.

Turbo Pascal Additional Arithmetic Functions

Turbo Pascal has a considerable number of additional arithmetic functions. Of these functions, you will especially need two of them:

FRAC(n)   returns the fractional portion of the real number n

INT(n)   returns the integer portion of the real number n

For example:

```
    WRITELN(FRAC(8.22):2:2);       produces 0.22
    WRITELN(INT(8.22)2:2);         produces 8.00
```

Both functions return real numbers.

You can make use of these functions in Drill 2-1.

Another couple of functions are used to generate random numbers:

RANDOM(*n*)   returns a random integer between 0 and the integer *n* (the zero is included)

RANDOM   returns a real random number between 0 and 1 (the zero is included)

Try these two statements:

```
WRITELN(RANDOM:2:2);
WRITELN(RANDOM(n));
```

where *n* is an integer variable readout from the keyboard.

Use the two statements in a program and look at the results for several runs. They should be different in each run.

Drill 2-2

Write the Pascal expressions for the following:

1.   The quadratic equation: $Ax^2 + Bx + C$

2.   The determinant: $B^2 - 4AC$

3.   The square root of the determinant

4.   The absolute value of the determinant

Then, write a program to produce the roots of the equation according to the input values of A, B, and C. Use test values for A, B, and C that give real roots. Typical values are:

A=1, B=2, C=1, give the solution: X1= X2= –1.00

A=1, B=4, C=2, give the solution: X1= –0.59, X2= –3.41

2-4 The CHAR Type

The CHAR type is used to store a single character in Pascal. You can declare a variable of the type CHAR as in the following example:

```
VAR
      SingleLetter : CHAR;
```

In the main body of the program (between BEGIN and END.) you may assign a single character to the variable SingleLetter like this:

```
SingleLetter := 'A';
```

As is clear from this example, a constant literal of the type CHAR must be exactly one character, included in single quotes:

'A' '3' '*' '$' ' '

In order to represent a single quotation (or apostrophe) as a character constant, use two single quotes like this:

''''

You can use the output statements WRITELN or WRITE to display a character constant or a character variable:

```
WRITELN('A');
WRITELN(SingleLetter);
```

The character set is internally represented by a one-byte integer code. The universally used code for small computers is the ASCII code (American Standard Code for Information Interchange). The ASCII code includes 256 characters from 0 to 255 (see Appendix A). The first half of the ASCII code (from 0 to 127) is standard on all personal computers. It includes the following characters:

■ The uppercase letters (A-Z): ASCII 65 to 90

■ The lowercase letters (a-z): ASCII 97 to 122

■ The digits (0-9): ASCII 48 to 57

The code also contains punctuation characters and control characters.

The second half of the ASCII code is not standard and is implemented differently on different machines.

The relative sequence of a character in the ASCII set is called the *ordinal number.*

Standard Functions for Characters

There are four standard functions that handle character operations:

ORD(c)   returns the ordinal number of the character c

CHR(n)   returns the character represented by the ordinal number n

PRED(c)   returns the character preceding c in the ordinal sequence

SUCC(c)   returns the next character after c in the ordinal sequence

You can get the ordinal number of any character by using the function ORD, as in the following example:

```
WRITELN(ORD('A'));
```

This statement displays the ordinal of the character A, which is 65.

In the following program the user enters a character and the program displays the corresponding ordinal number.

```
{ --------------------------- Example 2-4 ------------------------------- }
{ Displaying the Ordinal Number of a Character }
PROGRAM OrdinalNumber(INPUT,OUTPUT);
VAR
    SingleChar :CHAR;
BEGIN
    WRITE('Give me a character, please: ');
    READLN(SingleChar);
    WRITELN('The ordinal number of this character is ', ORD(SingleChar));
    READLN                    {The program will pause until you press Enter}
END.
{ ------------------------------------------------------------------------ }
```

Sample Run:

```
        Give me a character, please: A          → Type A and press Enter
        The ordinal number of this character is 65   → The program response
```

Tip: Notice the use of the last READLN statement. When READLN is used without parentheses, it holds the program until you press Enter. You cannot use READ for this purpose. This type of READLN statement is commonly preceded by a user prompt such as:

```
WRITELN('Press ENTER to continue');
```

The counterpart of ORD is the function CHR, which takes an ordinal number as a parameter and returns the character that corresponds to this number. Look at this example:

```
WRITELN(CHR(66));
```

This statement displays the letter B.

In the following program, the user enters an ordinal number and the program displays the corresponding character.

```
{ --------------------------- Example 2-5 ------------------------------- }
{ Displaying the Character, Knowing its Ordinal Number }
PROGRAM CharDisplay(INPUT,OUTPUT);
VAR
    OrdinalNum :BYTE;
BEGIN
    WRITE('Give me a number between 0 and 255: ');
    READLN(OrdinalNum);
    WRITELN('This corresponds to the character "', CHR(OrdinalNum),'"');
    WRITELN('Press ENTER to continue ...');
    READLN                    {The program will pause until you press Enter}
END.
{ ------------------------------------------------------------------------ }
```

Sample Run:

```
Give me a number between 0 and 255: 66      → Enter the number 66
This corresponds to the character "B"       → The program response
Press ENTER to continue ...
```

Note: Notice the use of the Turbo Pascal type BYTE to store an ordinal number, which is a positive integer between 0 and 255. If you don't have this type in your compiler, you can use the INTEGER type.

The following program demonstrates the use of the functions PRED and SUCC. You enter a character and the program displays the characters preceding and succeeding it.

```
{ ---------------------------- Example 2-6 ---------------------------- }
{ The Predecessor and the Successor to a Character }
PROGRAM CharPredAndSucc(INPUT,OUTPUT);
VAR
   Letter: CHAR;
BEGIN
   WRITE('Please Enter a character: ');
   READLN(Letter);
   WRITELN('The Predecessor to this character is "',PRED(Letter),'"');
   WRITELN('The Successor to this character is "',SUCC(Letter),'"');
   WRITELN('Press ENTER to continue ...');
   READLN
END.
{ -------------------------------------------------------------------- }
```

Sample Run:

```
Please Enter a character: K               → Enter the character K
The Predecessor to this character is "J"  → The program response
The Successor to this character is "L"
Press ENTER to continue ...
```

You can use numbers or any special symbols from your keyboard to test this program. Remember, though, that some machines (mainframes) use a different sequence known as EBCDIC (Extended Binary Coded Decimal Interchange Code).

You may also use the function ORD with the type INTEGER, in which case it returns the sequence of the integer in the set of integers (from –(MAXINT+1) to MAXINT). Thus:

```
ORD(0)=0, ORD(1)=1, ORD(255)=255, and ORD(-22)=-22
```

The functions SUCC and PRED work with integers in the same way, which means:

```
SUCC(1)=2 and PRED(1)=0
```

Some programmers increment their counters with a statement like this:

```
Counter := SUCC(Counter);
```

If you replace the type CHAR with the type INTEGER in the last program (Example 2-6), you can test these relations.

Strings in Standard Pascal

As mentioned earlier, you can represent a string constant using single quotes like this:

```
'This is a string enclosed in single quotes'
```

To include an apostrophe in the string constant, you need two of them:

```
'This is an apostrophe '' included in a string'
```

You can also assign a string to a named constant:

```
CONST
    Name = 'Sally Shuttleworth';
```

After this declaration you can use the named constant Name instead of the string itself, but remember that in the program you cannot assign any value to a named constant. The string variable, however, is not defined in standard Pascal. A string, in standard Pascal, is stored in a PACKED ARRAY OF CHAR which is declared like this:

```
VAR
    Name : PACKED ARRAY[1..15] OF CHAR;
```

This declaration lets you store a string of exactly 15 characters in the variable Name—no more, no less.

Look at the following example, where the variable Message is declared and assigned the string 'Press any key ... '. Extra spaces are padded to the end of the string constant to make it fit into the variable Message, which was declared as a PACKED ARRAY OF CHAR 21 characters long.

```
{ --------------------------- Example 2-7 --------------------------- }
{ Packed Array Of Characters }
PROGRAM PackedArray(OUTPUT);
VAR
   Message :PACKED ARRAY[1..21] OF CHAR;
BEGIN
   Message := 'Press any key ...    ';
   WRITELN(Message)
END.
{ ------------------------------------------------------------------- }
```

Output:

```
Press any key ...
```

2-5 The STRING Type

Actually, you will never need to use the PACKED ARRAY OF CHAR unless you are using one of the old implementations of Pascal on a mainframe computer. In the modern implementations (such as Turbo and UCSD), the type STRING is defined.

Declaration of a String

You can declare a variable of the type STRING, as in this example:

```
VAR
      StudentName : STRING;
```

This declaration lets you store a string of up to a certain size in the variable StudentName. Although the maximum length of the string variable is 255 in Turbo (80 in UCSD), the actual length (also referred to as *dynamic length*) of the string is the number of stored characters. You can declare the string variable and its maximum length in the same statement:

```
VAR
      StudentName : STRING[20];
```

In this case the maximum length of a string stored in the variable StudentName is 20 characters. Look at this program, which reads a name with a maximum length of 20 characters and displays it on the screen.

```
{ --------------------------- Example 2-8 --------------------------- }
{ String Type in Turbo Pascal }
PROGRAM StringDemo(INPUT,OUTPUT);
VAR
   Name :STRING[20];
BEGIN
   WRITE('Please enter a name of 20 characters or less: ');
   READLN(Name);
   WRITELN('The name you entered is ',Name, '. Is that right?')
END.
{ ------------------------------------------------------------------- }
```

Sample Run:

```
      Please enter a name of 20 characters or less: Peter Rigby
      The name you entered is Peter Rigby. Is that right?
```

Note that if you assign a string constant of more than 20 characters to the variable Name, the extra characters will be truncated.

The Length of a String

You can measure the dynamic length of a string using the function LENGTH. If you want, for instance, to measure the length of the string Name in the last program, you may use the expression:

```
LENGTH(Name)
```

If you display the value of this expression, you get the exact number of characters contained in the string variable, including the spaces. If the string variable is empty, the dynamic length is zero. In the following program, you enter a name and the program displays the actual length both before and after the variable assignment.

```
{ --------------------------- Example 2-9 ---------------------------- }
{ Dynamic Length of a String }
PROGRAM StringLen(INPUT,OUTPUT);
VAR
   Name :STRING[20];
BEGIN
   WRITELN('The dynamic length of the string is now ',LENGTH(Name),
                     ' characters');
   WRITE('Please enter a name of 20 characters or less: ');
   READLN(Name);
   WRITELN('The dynamic length of the string is now ',LENGTH(Name),
                     ' characters')
END.
{ ------------------------------------------------------------------ }
```

Sample Run:

```
The dynamic length of the string is now 0 characters
Please enter a name of 20 characters or less: Dale Sanders
The dynamic length of the string is now 12 characters
```

The introduction of the type STRING in Pascal filled a gap and added a powerful tool, especially in the field of text processing. More on string functions and operations later.

2-6 The BOOLEAN Type

The Boolean values (sometimes called logical values) are the two constants TRUE and FALSE.

They are named after the English mathematician George Boole (1815-1864).

In Pascal you can declare a variable of the type BOOLEAN, which may only hold one of the two Boolean constants TRUE or FALSE, as in the following example:

```
VAR
     Result : BOOLEAN;
```

Simple Boolean Expressions

You can assign a Boolean constant to a Boolean variable, such as:

```
Result := TRUE;
```

You may also assign a Boolean expression to a variable such as:

```
Result := A > B;
```

If A, for example, holds the value 22.5 and B holds the value 2.3, then the expression A > B (A is larger than B) is evaluated as TRUE. If A holds 1.8, then the condition is not satisfied and the expression is evaluated as FALSE. You can build Boolean expressions using the *relational operators* shown in Table 2-4.

Table 2-4: Relational operators

Operator	Meaning	Example
>	Greater than	A > B
<	Less than	C < 54
>=	Greater than or equal	x >= 16.8
<=	Less than or equal	A+B <= 255
=	Equal	SQR(B) = 4*A*C
<>	Not equal	CHR(a) <> 'N'

Relational operators are used with any data type: numeric, character, or Boolean. Here are some examples:

Numeric:	y > 66.5	
	Y = A * x + B	
Character:	FirstCharacter = 'B'	
	CHR(x) > 'A'	
Boolean:	TRUE > FALSE	(always TRUE)
	TRUE < FALSE	(always FALSE)

For characters, an expression such as:

```
'A' < 'B'
```

is always TRUE, because the letter A comes before B in the alphabet; in other words, it has a smaller ordinal number. Using the same logic, the following expressions are TRUE:

```
'9' > '1'
'Y' < 'Z'
```

The following program reads from the keyboard the value of two integers, A and B, and displays the value of the Boolean expression A = B.

```
{ --------------------------- Example 2-10 --------------------------- }
{ Boolean Variables }
PROGRAM Compare1(INPUT,OUTPUT);
VAR
   A, B   :INTEGER;
   Result :BOOLEAN;
BEGIN
   WRITE('Please enter two integers: ');
   READLN(A, B);
   Result := (A = B);
            or,
            Result := A = B;
            The parentheses are not necessary.
   WRITELN('The comparison is ', Result)
END.
{ ------------------------------------------------------------------- }
```

Sample Runs:

Run 1:

```
Please enter two integers: 5 5
The comparison is TRUE
```

Run 2:

```
Please enter two integers: 50 55
The comparison is FALSE
```

As mentioned earlier, you may not compare two real values for equality because of
their limited precision. In the following program, the difference between the two real
variables x and y is tested to see whether it is less than a specific small value Difference, in which case they are considered to be equal.

```
{ --------------------------- Example 2-11 --------------------------- }
{ Comparing real values }
PROGRAM Compare2(INPUT,OUTPUT);
CONST
   Difference = 0.0001;
VAR
   x, y   :REAL;
   Result :BOOLEAN;
BEGIN
   WRITE('Please enter two real numbers: ');
   READLN(x, y);
   Result := ABS(x - y) < Difference;
   WRITELN('The difference is ', ABS(x-y):2:6);
   WRITELN('The comparison is ', Result)
END.
{ ------------------------------------------------------------------- }
```

Sample Run:

```
Please enter two real numbers: 4.5 4.50001
The difference is 0.000010
The comparison is TRUE
```

Compound Boolean Expressions

The Boolean expressions which use relational operators are called *simple Boolean expressions* (in other languages they are called *relational expressions*). The *compound Boolean expressions* are those which use the *Boolean operators* (also called the *logical operators*): AND, OR, and NOT.

To understand how a compound Boolean expression works, consider the example:

```
(x = 4) AND (y < 50)
```

This expression is evaluated TRUE if both conditions x = 4 and y < 50 are TRUE.

Now consider the same expression using the operator OR:

```
(x = 4) OR (y < 50)
```

This expression is evaluated as TRUE if any one of the conditions is TRUE. For example, if x contains the value 4, the expression is TRUE regardless of the value of y.

The logical operator NOT is used to reverse the value of a Boolean expression. Suppose that the Boolean variable UnderAge means that Age is less than 18, as in the following statement:

```
UnderAge := Age < 18;
```

The variable UnderAge will contain the value TRUE if Age is less than 18.

Now the expression:

```
NOT(UnderAge)
```

is evaluated TRUE if Age is 18 or above.

Truth Tables

To better understand Boolean expressions, use *truth tables*. If A and B are Boolean variables, you can use a truth table to display the values of a specific Boolean expression, which includes A and B, for all possible values of A and B. For example, the following table shows the values of the expression A AND B for all possible values of A and B:

A	B	A AND B
FALSE	FALSE	FALSE
FALSE	TRUE	FALSE
TRUE	FALSE	FALSE
TRUE	TRUE	TRUE

Similarly, the following table displays the values of the expression A OR B for all possible values of A and B:

A	B	A OR B
FALSE	FALSE	FALSE
FALSE	TRUE	TRUE
TRUE	FALSE	TRUE
TRUE	TRUE	TRUE

The following table displays the values of the expression NOT A for all possible values of A:

A	NOT A
TRUE	FALSE
FALSE	TRUE

Turbo Pascal Logical Operators

Turbo Pascal also contains the logical operator XOR, which is called the *exclusive OR*. It is used as in the following expression:

```
(x = 4) XOR (x = 400)
```

The value of this expression is TRUE if either one of the two conditions (x = 4 or x = 400) is TRUE, but the expression is evaluated as FALSE if both conditions are either TRUE or FALSE. In any implementation of Pascal you can use the operator < > as the exclusive OR. You can write the previous expression as:

```
(x = 4) <> (x = 400)
```

Precedence of Pascal Operators

As with arithmetic expressions, the precedence of operators should be considered when building a Boolean expression (relational or logical). Table 2-5 summarizes the relative precedence of all operators you have used so far.

Table 2-5: Precedence of Pascal operators

Operator	Precedence
NOT	Priority 1 (highest)
* / DIV MOD AND	Priority 2
+ − OR (XOR in Turbo Pascal)	Priority 3
= > < >= <= <>	Priority 4 (lowest)

To understand the effects of precedence, try the Boolean expression:

```
x = 4 OR x = 400
```

Because the OR has a higher precedence level than the equality, this will not compile because it will be interpreted as:

```
x = (4 OR x) = 400
```

which is not a valid expression.

Drill 2-3

Write Boolean expressions to express the following conditions:

1. A is less than 55.5
2. x is equal to y, or x is greater than or equal to z
3. either x=40, or y=80; or both
4. either x=40, or y=80; but not both

Summary

1. In this chapter you learned the four standard data types:
    - INTEGER
    - REAL
    - CHAR
    - BOOLEAN
2. You also learned the additional numeric types of Turbo Pascal:
    I. Integers:
        - SHORTINT
        - BYTE
        - INTEGER
        - WORD

- LONGINT

II. Real numbers
- SINGLE
- REAL
- DOUBLE
- EXTENDED
- COMP

3. You learned the standard arithmetic functions, classified into three groups:

Conversion:
- ROUND
- TRUNC

Trigonometric:
- ARCTAN
- COS
- SIN

Miscellaneous:
- ABS
- EXP
- LN
- SQR
- SQRT

4. You also learned some additional arithmetic functions from Turbo Pascal, such as:
- FRAC
- INT
- RANDOM

5. You can now write mathematical expressions using arithmetic operators and functions.

6. You are now familiar with four functions used to manipulate characters:
- CHR
- ORD
- PRED
- SUCC

7. You learned some of the features of text string variables in standard Pascal, and you know that such variables are defined as PACKED ARRAYS OF CHAR. In extensions such as Turbo Pascal and UCSD Pascal, the type STRING was added to the language along with other features and functions.

You learned the STRING function:

LENGTH

which is used to measure the dynamic length of a string.

8. Using the arithmetic, relational, and Boolean operators, you learned how to build simple and compound Boolean expressions and how to use the type BOOLEAN.

You know as well the Boolean operators:

- NOT
- AND
- OR

and you can express the exclusive OR in two ways:

- using the relational operator < >
- using the Turbo Pascal operator XOR

9. Finally, you had one last tour of Pascal operators and learned about their relative precedence.

Exercises

1. Given three Boolean variables X, Y, and Z, design a truth table to display the values of the following expressions for all possible values of X, Y, and Z:

    a. X AND TRUE

    b. X OR FALSE

    c. NOT (Y AND Z)

    d. X OR NOT Y

    e. X AND Y AND Z

    f. X AND (Y OR Z)

2. Write simple or compound Boolean expressions to express the following:

    a. An uppercase letter corresponds to an ASCII code between 65 and 90

    b. A lowercase letter corresponds to an ASCII code between 97 and 122

    c. A digit corresponds to an ASCII code between 48 and 57

3. Using standard mathematical functions, write Pascal statements to calculate the following:

    a. Square of 12

    b. Square root of 64

    c. Absolute value of –1

    d. Value of e (the base of the natural system of logarithms)

    e. Natural logarithm of e

     f. Sine of 45 degrees

     g. Cosine of 45 degrees

     h. Sine of 30 degrees

     i. Cosine of 60 degrees

     j. Cosine of 180 degrees (PI)

     k. Sine of 180 degrees (PI)

4. Write a Pascal program to convert polar coordinates (r and θ) to Cartesian coordinates (x and y) according to the following definitions:

$$x = r * \cos(\theta)$$
$$y = r * \sin(\theta)$$

The following figure shows the point located at (x, y), represented in both types of coordinates.

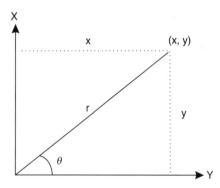

Answers

3. a. 144.00   b. 8.00   c. 1   d. 2.7182818

    e. 1.00   f. 0.707   g. 0.707   h. 0.50

    i. 0.50   j. −1.00   k. 0.00.

Selection Statements

3-1 Making Decisions

So far, each of the programs in this book has been a series of instructions executed sequentially one after the other. In real-life applications, however, you will usually need to change the sequence of execution according to specified conditions. Sometimes you need to use a simple condition like:

If it is cold **then** put your coat on.

In this statement the resultant action is taken if the condition is evaluated as TRUE (the weather is cold). If, however, the weather is fine, the whole statement is skipped.

Some conditions could be multiple, like those in the following conversation:

> Ok then, **if** I come back early from work, I'll see you tonight; **else if** it is too late I'll make it tomorrow; **else if** my brother arrives tomorrow we can get together on Tuesday; **else if** Tuesday is a holiday then let it be Wednesday; **else** I'll call you to arrange for the next meeting!

Actually, your program can easily handle such chained or nested conditions as long as you write the adequate code.

In Pascal there are two *control structures* used to handle conditions and their resultant decisions: the binary choice construct IF-THEN-ELSE, and the multiple choice construct CASE.

3-2 The Simple Decision: IF-THEN

To express a simple condition you can use the IF-THEN statement, as in the following example:

```
IF Age < 18 THEN
    WRITELN('Sorry, this is underage.');
```

The statement starts with the keyword IF, followed by a Boolean expression (the condition to be tested), followed by the keyword THEN, followed by the result to be executed if the condition is TRUE (the WRITELN statement). As you can see, the IF construct is one statement ending with a semicolon. If the value of variable Age is less than 18, the part after the keyword THEN is executed; otherwise, the whole statement is skipped, and the program execution resumes its original flow at the next statement. This type of program control is called *conditional branching*.

The IF-THEN statement takes the general form:

> **IF** condition **THEN**
>   statement;

The construct is written in two lines just for readability, but it is one statement ending with a semicolon, and there is no obligation to leave extra spaces. You only need to separate the keywords (such as IF and THEN) from the rest of the statement by at least one space.

Application: Pascal Credit Card

Take a look at the following program, where a credit card limit is tested for a certain purchase. The program starts with declaration of the constant Limit which represents the credit card limit ($1000), and the variable Amount, whose value will be received from the keyboard. The program displays the message "Your charge is accepted" if the Amount is less than or equal to the Limit. If the condition is FALSE the program will end without response.

```
{ --------------------------- Example 3-1 --------------------------- }
PROGRAM SimpleDecision(INPUT,OUTPUT);
CONST
   Limit = 1000;
VAR
   Amount :REAL;
BEGIN
   WRITE('Please enter the amount:');
   READLN(Amount);
   IF Amount <= Limit THEN
      WRITELN('Your charge is accepted.');          {End of the IF statement}
   WRITELN('Press ENTER to continue..');
   READLN
END.
{ ----------------------------------------------------------------- }
```

A READLN statement is used to pause the screen while displaying the message "Press ENTER to continue." Because this statement is outside the IF statement it will be executed whether the condition is TRUE or FALSE.

Sample Runs:

Run 1:

```
Please enter the amount:200
Your charge is accepted.
Press ENTER to continue..
```

Run 2:

```
Please enter the amount:2000
Press ENTER to continue..
```

You can use two conditional statements to represent the two cases, the TRUE and the FALSE. In the following program another IF statement is added to deal with the other case (the amount is greater than 1000). The message "The amount exceeds your credit limit" is displayed in this case.

```
{ --------------------------- Example 3-2 --------------------------- }
PROGRAM TwoConditions(INPUT,OUTPUT);
CONST
   Limit = 1000;
VAR
```

```
    Amount :REAL;
BEGIN
   WRITE('Please enter the amount:');
   READLN(Amount);
   IF Amount <= Limit THEN
      WRITELN('Your charge is accepted.');
   IF Amount > Limit THEN
      WRITELN('The amount exceeds your credit limit.');
   WRITELN('Thank you for using Pascal credit card.');
   WRITELN('Press ENTER to continue..');
   READLN
END.
{ ----------------------------------------------------------------------- }
```

Sample Runs:

Run 1:

```
Please enter the amount:150
Your charge is accepted.
Thank you for using Pascal credit card.
Press ENTER to continue..
```

Run 2:

```
Please enter the amount:1500
The amount exceeds your credit limit.
Thank you for using Pascal credit card.
Press ENTER to continue..
```

As before, note that the last two lines were displayed in each case, as they do not belong to the conditional statements.

Using BEGIN-END Blocks

If you want to use more than one statement as a result of one condition, you can use the BEGIN-END blocks. You can actually use any number of blocks inside the program main body, using BEGIN and END to mark the territories of each block. A block will be treated as one unit, no matter how many statements it includes. Look at the following example:

```
{ ---------------------------- Example 3-3 ---------------------------- }
PROGRAM UsingBlocks(INPUT,OUTPUT);
CONST
   Limit = 1000;
VAR
   Amount :REAL;
BEGIN
   WRITE('Please enter the amount:');
   READLN(Amount);
   IF Amount <= Limit THEN
```

```
      BEGIN
         WRITELN('Your charge is accepted.');
         WRITELN('Your price plus tax is $',1.05*Amount:0:2)
                  {The semicolon is optional}
      END;
   IF Amount > Limit THEN
      BEGIN
         WRITELN('The amount exceeds your credit limit.');
         WRITELN('The maximum limit is $',Limit)
                  {The semicolon is optional}
      END;
   WRITELN('Thank you for using Pascal credit card.');
   WRITELN('Press ENTER to continue..');
   READLN           {The semicolon is optional}
END.
{ ------------------------------------------------------------------- }
```

In this example more than one statement is executed in either case (TRUE or FALSE). For this reason two blocks were used.

Tip: Notice that in three positions in this program, the statement is not terminated by a semicolon, as the semicolon is optional. The statement in each of these positions is the last one inside a block.

Sample Runs:

Run 1:

```
Please enter the amount:120
Your charge is accepted.
Your price plus tax is $126.00
Thank you for using Pascal credit card.
Press ENTER to continue..
```

Run 2:

```
Please enter the amount:2000
The amount exceeds your credit limit.
The maximum limit is $1000
Thank you for using Pascal credit card.
Press ENTER to continue..
```

If you try the program without the blocks, you will find that only the first statement that follows the keyword THEN belongs to the IF statement, but any other statement belongs to the main program and will be executed regardless of the condition.

> ### Drill 3-1
>
> Write a program to accept from the keyboard a character and test this character to see if it is one of the following:
>
> 1. A number
> 2. A lowercase letter
> 3. An uppercase letter
>
> Display the suitable message in each case.

3-3 The IF-THEN-ELSE Construct

The form you have used so far for the IF statement is actually a simplified version of the complete construct. The complete IF statement includes the two cases that result from testing the condition. It takes the form:

IF condition **THEN**
　　statement
ELSE
　　statement;

Notice here that only one semicolon is used, because the whole construct is treated as one statement. Here is an example:

```
IF AGE < 18 THEN
    WRITELN('Underage.')
ELSE
    WRITELN('Age is OK.');
```

This statement will display the message "Underage" if Age is less than 18. In the other case the message "Age is OK" is displayed.

If you add another statement to either of the two cases, you have to use the BEGIN-END blocks. The new construct will look like this:

```
IF AGE < 18 THEN
    BEGIN
       WRITELN('Underage.');
       WRITELN('Wait another couple of years.')
    END                        {No semicolon is used here}
ELSE
    BEGIN
       WRITELN('Age is OK.');
       WRITELN('You don''t have to wait.')
END;                           {A semicolon is mandatory here}
```

Caution:　At this point the use of semicolons becomes critical and may lead to errors if not done properly. Notice here that the keyword END in the first block is not terminated by a semicolon (as it is not the end of the statement), while in the second block it is terminated by a semicolon, indicating the end of the conditional statement.

Now, back to the Pascal credit card program to enhance it with the complete IF-THEN-ELSE statement.

```
{ --------------------------- Example 3-4 ---------------------------- }
PROGRAM CreditCard(INPUT,OUTPUT);
CONST
   Limit = 1000;
VAR
   Amount :REAL;
BEGIN
   WRITE('Please enter the amount:');
   READLN(Amount);
{ Beginning of the IF construct }
{ --------------------------- }
   IF Amount <= Limit THEN
      BEGIN
         WRITELN('Your charge is accepted.');
         WRITELN('Your price plus tax is $',1.05*Amount:0:2)
      END
   ELSE
      BEGIN
         WRITELN('The amount exceeds your credit limit.');
         WRITELN('The maximum limit is $',Limit)
      END;
{ End of the IF construct }
{ --------------------------- }
   WRITELN('Thank you for using Pascal credit card.');
   WRITELN('Press ENTER to continue..');
   READLN
END.
{ ------------------------------------------------------------------- }
```

Sample Runs:

Run 1:

```
Please enter the amount:1000
Your charge is accepted.
Your price plus tax is $1050.00
Thank you for using Pascal credit card.
Press ENTER to continue..
```

Run 2:

```
Please enter the amount:1001
The amount exceeds your credit limit.
The maximum limit is $1000
Thank you for using Pascal credit card.
Press ENTER to continue..
```

Drill 3-2

Modify the program you wrote in Drill 2-2 to solve a quadratic equation ($Ax^2 + Bx + C$) for both real and imaginary roots.

3-4 The ELSE-IF Ladder

Although the IF-THEN-ELSE statement is intended for binary choice, it can be extended to handle more complicated choices. Look at this new arrangement of the construct, which is sometimes referred to as the ELSE-IF ladder:

IF condition-1 **THEN**
    statement-1
ELSE IF condition-2 **THEN**
    statement-2
ELSE IF condition-3 **THEN**
    statement-3
    ...
ELSE
    statement-*n*;

The conditions in the ladder are evaluated from the top down, and whenever a condition is evaluated as TRUE, the corresponding statement is executed and the rest of the construct is skipped. If no condition has been satisfied, the last ELSE will be brought into action.

Notice that the condition ladder is considered one statement ending with a semicolon, but no semicolons are used inside. If you want to use more than one result-statement, you have to use the BEGIN-END blocks according to the rules mentioned earlier.

Application: A Character Tester

This program starts by asking you to enter a letter, then tests the input character to see if it is a lowercase or uppercase letter. The program can also recognize numbers and deliver an appropriate message, but for any other non-alphabetic character it displays: "Sorry, this is not a letter."

The logic used in the program depends on testing the ASCII code of the input characters using the ORD function. The characters are classified as follows:

- The uppercase letters correspond to the codes from 65 to 90.
- The lowercase letters correspond to the codes from 97 to 122.
- The digits correspond to the codes from 48 to 57.

If you already wrote this program as a solution to Drill 3-1, you will find that the ELSE-IF ladder makes things easier.

```
{ -------------------------- Example 3-5 -------------------------- }
PROGRAM CharsTester(INPUT,OUTPUT);
VAR
   InputChar :CHAR;
BEGIN
   WRITE('Please enter an alphabetic character: ');
   READLN(InputChar);
{ Beginning of the IF construct }
{ --------------------------- }
   IF (ORD(InputChar) > 64) AND (ORD(InputChar) < 91) THEN
      WRITELN('This is an uppercase letter.')
   ELSE IF (ORD(InputChar) > 96) AND (ORD(InputChar) < 123) THEN
      WRITELN('This is a lowercase letter.')
   ELSE IF (ORD(InputChar) > 47) AND (ORD(InputChar) < 58) THEN
      WRITELN('Hey, this is a number!')
   ELSE
      WRITELN('Sorry, this is not a letter.');
{ End of the IF construct }
{ --------------------------- }
   WRITELN('Press ENTER to continue..');
   READLN
END.
{ ------------------------------------------------------------------ }
```

Sample Runs:

Run 1:

```
    Please enter an alphabetic character: a      → Enter a
    This is a lowercase letter.
    Press ENTER to continue..
```

Run 2:

```
    Please enter an alphabetic character: B      → Enter B
    This is an uppercase letter.
    Press ENTER to continue..
```

Run 3:

```
    Please enter an alphabetic character: 5      → Enter 5
    Hey, this is a number!
```

```
         Press ENTER to continue..
```

Run 4:

```
         Please enter an alphabetic character: @        → Enter @
         Sorry, this is not a letter.
         Press ENTER to continue..
```

3-5 Nested Conditions

The statement to be executed upon testing a condition can be of any kind. As a matter of fact, it can be another IF statement nested in the original IF statement.

The IF-THEN-ELSE constructs can be nested inside each other, as in the following form:

IF condition-1 **THEN**
    IF condition-2 **THEN**

        ...

        IF condition-*n* **THEN**
          statement-*n*1
        ELSE
          statement-*n*2

        ...

    ELSE
      statement-2
ELSE
    statement-1;

As you can see, this construct can handle any number of nested conditions, but you have to keep track of each IF and the corresponding ELSE. Let us put the construct into action.

Application: Scores and Grades

This program receives the score of a student and displays the grade according to the following classification:

- Grade A corresponds to scores from 90% to 100%.
- Grade B corresponds to scores from 80% to 89%.
- Grade C corresponds to scores from 70% to 79%.
- Grade D corresponds to scores from 60% to 69%.
- Grade F corresponds to scores less than 60%.

Here is the program:

```
{ --------------------------- Example 3-6 --------------------------- }
PROGRAM ScoresAndGrades1(INPUT,OUTPUT);
VAR
   Score :INTEGER;
BEGIN
   WRITE('Please enter the score: ');
   READLN(Score);
   WRITELN;
{ Beginning of the IF construct }
{ --------------------------- }
   IF Score > 59 THEN
      IF Score > 69 THEN
         IF Score > 79 THEN
            IF Score > 89 THEN
               WRITELN('Excellent. Your grade is ''A''')
            ELSE
               WRITELN('Very good. Your grade is ''B''')
         ELSE
            WRITELN('Good. Your grade is ''C''')
      ELSE
         WRITELN('Passed. Your grade is ''D''')
   ELSE
      WRITELN('Better luck next time. Your grade is ''F''');
{ End of the IF construct }
{ --------------------------- }
   WRITELN('Press ENTER to continue..');
   READLN
END.
{ ------------------------------------------------------------------- }
```

Sample Runs:

Run 1:

```
        Please enter the score: 92          → Enter 92
        Excellent. Your grade is 'A'        → The program response
        Press ENTER to continue..
```

Run 2:

```
        Please enter the score: 70
        Good. Your grade is 'C'
        Press ENTER to continue..
```

Run 3:

```
        Please enter the score: 60
        Passed. Your grade is 'D'
        Press ENTER to continue..
```

Run 4:

```
    Please enter the score: 59
    Better luck next time. Your grade is 'F'
    Press ENTER to continue..
```

As usual, you may cause more than one result statement to be executed upon testing a condition by embedding the statements into a block.

You can use any one of the available variations of the IF-THEN-ELSE construct in your applications. However, some forms are more reliable with one application, and some with others. Look at this program, which processes the same problem of the Scores and Grades application but uses the ELSE-IF ladder. Notice how the program is made easier and more comprehensible to the reader by using the Boolean variables A, B, C, D, F. Note also that illegal numbers are filtered out by the last ELSE.

```
{ --------------------------- Example 3-7 --------------------------- }
PROGRAM ScoresAndGrades2(INPUT,OUTPUT);
VAR
   Score         :INTEGER;
   A, B, C, D, F :BOOLEAN;
BEGIN
   WRITE('Please enter the score: ');
   READLN(Score);
   A := (Score >= 90) AND (Score <= 100);
   B := (Score >= 80) AND (Score < 90);
   C := (Score >= 70) AND (Score < 80);
   D := (Score >= 60) AND (Score < 70);
   F := (Score < 60)  AND (Score >= 0);
   WRITELN;
{ Beginning of the IF construct }
{ --------------------------- }
   IF A THEN
      WRITELN('Excellent. Your grade is ''A''')
   ELSE IF B THEN
      WRITELN('Very good. Your grade is ''B''')
   ELSE IF C THEN
      WRITELN('Good. Your grade is ''C''')
   ELSE IF D THEN
      WRITELN('Passed. Your grade is ''D''')
   ELSE IF F THEN
      WRITELN('Better luck next time. Your grade is ''F''')
   ELSE
      WRITELN('This number is out of range.');
{ End of the IF construct }
{ --------------------------- }
   WRITELN('Press ENTER to continue..');
   READLN
END.
{ ----------------------------------------------------------------- }
```

Tips on the IF-ELSE Puzzles

Nesting the IF constructs inside each other may become confusing (to the programmer), as one may not be able to tell which ELSE belongs to which IF. Look at this simple example:

```
IF X >= 1 THEN
IF y >= 18 THEN
WRITELN('statement#1.')
ELSE
WRITELN('statement#2');
```

The rule is that each ELSE belongs to the last IF in the same block. This means that, in this example, the ELSE belongs to the second IF. Arranging the text with the proper indentation, according to this rule, makes it clearer:

```
IF X >= 1 THEN
    IF y >= 18 THEN
        WRITELN('statement#1.')
    ELSE
        WRITELN('statement#2');
```

If, however, you want to associate ELSE with the first IF, you can use blocks as follows:

```
IF X >= 1 THEN
    BEGIN
        IF Y >= 18 THEN
            WRITELN('statement#1.')
    END
ELSE
    WRITELN('statement#2');
```

Drill 3-3

Write a program to describe the weather according to the following temperature classifications:

Temperature	Classification
greater than 75	hot
50 to 75	cool
35 to 49	cold
less than 35	freezing

3-6 The Multiple Choice: CASE

The CASE construct is used to deal with multiple alternatives, such as the user-menu options. It takes the general form:

CASE expression **OF**
      label-1 : statement-1;
      label-2 : statement-2;

      ...

      label-*n* : statement-*n*;
END

The *case expression*, also called the *selector*, can be of INTEGER, CHAR, or BOOLEAN type (or any *ordinal* type, which will be explained in Chapter 5). According to the value of this expression the control of the program is transferred to one of the *case labels*, and the corresponding statement is executed. The labels actually represent the different possible values of the expression. Look at this example:

Application: A Vending Machine

The coins in the vending machine are sorted according to the weight of each coin, which is assumed to be 35 grams for a quarter, 7 for a dime, and 15 for a nickel.

This logic can be programmed as follows:

```
CASE CoinWeight OF
    35 : Amount := Quarter;
    7  : Amount := Dime;
    15 : Amount := Nickel;
END;
```

The numbers 35, 7, and 15 represent the CoinWeight and are used as labels. Therefore, when the CoinWeight equals 7, for example, the statement:

```
Amount := Dime;
```

is executed. Needless to say, the name Dime is a named constant whose value is 10, and Nickel and Quarter are named constants as well. Look at the complete program:

```
{ ---------------------------- Example 3-8 ---------------------------- }
PROGRAM CaseOfWeights(INPUT,OUTPUT);
CONST
   Quarter = 25;
   Dime = 10;
   Nickel = 5;
VAR
   CoinWeight, Amount :INTEGER;
BEGIN
   WRITE('Please enter the weight: ');
   READLN(CoinWeight);
```

```
    CASE CoinWeight OF
        35 : Amount := Quarter;
        7  : Amount := Dime;
        15 : Amount := Nickel;
    END;
    WRITELN('The amount is ', Amount, ' cents.');
    WRITELN('Press ENTER to continue..');
    READLN
END.
{ ------------------------------------------------------------------- }
```

Sample Run:

```
    Please enter the weight: 35          → Enter 35
    The amount is 25 cents.              → The program response
    Press ENTER to continue..
```

You can use more than one label for the same result statement, which will save a lot of writing as compared to the IF in the same situation.

Application: *Number of Days in a Month*

Consider, for instance, that you want to program a code that reads the number of the month and tells the number of days in that month. The CASE construct will look something like the following:

```
    CASE Month OF
        1,3,5,7,8,10,12    : Days := 31;
        4,6,9,11           : Days := 30;
        2                  : Days := 28;
    END;
```

As you can see, the CASE construct here contains three cases, two of them with more than one label. All months that have 31 days belong to the first case, those that have 30 days belong to the second case, and February is a special case by itself. We assume here that February has 28 days for simplicity, but you can extend the logic to determine if the year is a leap year and assign February a value of 29 or 28 accordingly. You may use a block of statements for one case like this:

```
    CASE Month OF
    1,3,5,7,8,10,12 : Days := 31;
    4,6,9,11        : Days := 30;
    2               : BEGIN
                          WRITE('Enter the year:');
                          READLN(Year);
                          IF YEAR MOD 4 = 0  THEN
                              Days :=29
                          ELSE
                              Days :=28
                      END;
```

Here the case label 2 leads to a block of statements. So, if you enter 2 as the number of the month, the program will ask you to enter the year. The year will be tested and you will get 29 if the year is a leap year and 28 otherwise. Here is the complete program:

```
{ --------------------------- Example 3-9 -------------------------- }
PROGRAM DaysOfMonth1(INPUT,OUTPUT);
VAR
    Days, Month, Year :INTEGER;
BEGIN
    WRITE('Please enter the number of the month: ');
    READLN(Month);
    CASE Month OF
        1,3,5,7,8,10,12 : Days := 31;
        4,6,9,11        : Days := 30;
        2               : BEGIN
                            WRITE('Enter the year:');
                            READLN(Year);
                            IF YEAR MOD 4 = 0  THEN
                                    Days :=29
                            ELSE
                                    Days :=28
                          END;
    END;
    WRITELN('There are ',Days,' days in this month.');
    WRITELN('Press ENTER to continue..');
    READLN
END.
{ -------------------------------------------------------------------- }
```

Sample Runs:

Run 1:

```
Please enter the number of the month: 2
Enter the year: 1987
There are 28 days in this month.
Press ENTER to continue..
```

Run 2:

```
Please enter the number of the month: 2
Enter the year: 1984
There are 29 days in this month.
Press ENTER to continue..
```

Run 3:

```
Please enter the number of the month: 12
There are 31 days in this month.
Press ENTER to continue..
```

In cases like this, using the CASE construct is more efficient than using nested IF-THEN-ELSE constructs or ladders. However, you must have realized that you will sometimes need them both (as in the February case).

Drill 3-4

Write a program that reads the date from the keyboard in the form "mm dd yy" and displays the date as in the following examples:

January 2nd, 1992

October 23rd, 1990

March 5th, 1985

3-7 Unconditional Branching: GOTO

The GOTO statement is used to transfer control of the program from one point to another. It is classified as *unconditional branching*.

Note: Although the GOTO statement is very easy to use, you rarely see it in Pascal programs because it destroys the structure of the program. In some cases, however, it may be useful in escaping from many levels of nesting in one jump.

The syntax of the GOTO statement is as follows:

GOTO label;

The *label* is a positive integer of up to four digits preceding the required statement (in Turbo Pascal the label can be any valid identifier and may begin with a digit).

```
GOTO 1000;
    ...
1000:
    WRITELN('I am a labeled statement.');
    ...
```

When the GOTO is encountered, the program control is transferred to the labeled statement. The label must be declared in the *label section* of the declaration part of the program. The LABEL section starts with the keyword LABEL and comes as the first section in the declaration part in standard Pascal (in Turbo Pascal there is no such obligation). Look at this example:

```
PROGRAM GoToDemo(INPUT,OUTPUT);
LABEL
   1000;
VAR
   InputChar :CHAR;
BEGIN
   WRITE('Please enter a letter (or 0 to quit):');
   READLN(InputChar);
   IF InputChar = '0'  THEN
      GOTO 1000;
   { Other statements may go here... }
1000:
   END.
```

In this example, the value of the input character is tested to see if it is zero, in which case control is transferred to the part following the label 1000, which is the end of the program. If you are using Turbo Pascal, you can use meaningful labels such as Wrapup or Start instead of the numbers.

Infinite Loops

You can use the GOTO statement to build a *closed loop*. For example, if you want to repeat the execution of the Character Tester application you may use the following logic, where the control is always transferred to the label 1000 at the beginning of the program. A condition is used to end the loop (and the program) by examining the input value. If a zero is entered, the control is transferred to the label 2000, ending the program. If you remove this condition from the program, it will be repeated infinitely. The only way to exit the program in this case is to use the control keys Ctrl+Break. This kind of loop is called an *infinite loop*.

```
{ -------------------------- Example 3-10 -------------------------- }
PROGRAM CharsTester2(INPUT,OUTPUT);
LABEL
   1000, 2000;                           { label declaration }
VAR
   InputChar :CHAR;
BEGIN
1000:
   WRITE('Please enter a letter (or 0 to quit): ');
   READLN(InputChar);
{ Beginning of the IF construct }
{ ---------------------------- }
   IF InputChar = '0'  THEN              { a condition to exit }
      GOTO 2000
   ELSE IF (ORD(InputChar) > 64) AND (ORD(InputChar) < 91) THEN
      WRITELN('This is an uppercase letter.')
   ELSE IF (ORD(InputChar) > 96) AND (ORD(InputChar) < 123) THEN
      WRITELN('This is a lowercase letter.')
   ELSE IF (ORD(InputChar) > 47) AND (ORD(InputChar) < 58) THEN
```

```
       WRITELN('Hey, this is a number!')
    ELSE
       WRITELN('Sorry, this is not a letter.');
{ End of the IF construct }
{ ---------------------- }
   GOTO 1000;              { restart the program }
2000:                      { exit the program }
END.
{ ------------------------------------------------------------------- }
```

Sample Run:

```
Please enter a letter (or 0 to quit): W        → Enter W
This is an uppercase letter.
Please enter a letter (or 0 to quit): e        → Enter e
This is a lowercase letter.
Please enter a letter (or 0 to quit): 0        → Enter 0
```

This method, as you can see, is not the best method with which to build loops or control program execution, as it consists of jumps from one point to another. In the next chapter you are introduced to Pascal structured loops.

3-8 Turbo Pascal Additional Features: EXIT, CASE-ELSE

If you entered an illegal value in Example 3-9, such as the number 13 (as the month number), you simply get the message:

```
There are 0 days in this month.
```

In order to handle the invalid data you have to use a suitable IF statement. In Turbo Pascal you can add an ELSE part to the control structure CASE in order to handle data that does not belong to any of the case labels. The CASE structure will then take the form:

> **CASE** expression **OF**
>   label-1 : statement-1;
>   label-2 : statement-2;
>   ...
>   label-n : statement-n;
> **ELSE**
>   statement
> **END**

Another feature of Turbo Pascal is the EXIT statement, which ends the execution of the program at any point. The EXIT statement is classified as an unconditional branching statement. In the following program these two features are illustrated. If you enter any number other than the numbers from 1 to 12, the ELSE part and the EXIT statement will end the program.

```
{ --------------------------- Example 3-11 -------------------------- }
PROGRAM DaysOfMonth2(INPUT,OUTPUT);
LABEL
   Start;
VAR
   Days, Month, Year :INTEGER;
BEGIN
Start:
   WRITE('Please enter the number of the month: ');
   READLN(Month);
   CASE Month OF
      1,3,5,7,8,10,12 : Days := 31;
      4,6,9,11        : Days := 30;
      2               : BEGIN
                           WRITE('Enter the year: ');
                           READLN(Year);
                           IF YEAR MOD 4 = 0   THEN
                              Days :=29
                           ELSE
                              Days :=28
                        END;
   ELSE
      EXIT                          { all other cases }
   END;
      WRITELN('There are ',Days,' days in this month.');
   GOTO Start
END.
{ --------------------------------------------------------------------- }
```

Sample Run:

```
Please enter the number of the month: 1
There are 31 days in this month.
Please enter the number of the month: 4
There are 30 days in this month.
Please enter the number of the month: 13          → Exit the program
```

Summary

In this chapter you learned the branching control structures that help you to handle decisions in your program.

1. You are now familiar with the simple IF-THEN statement used with simple decisions. It takes the form:

> **IF** condition **THEN**
> statement;

2. You also know the complete IF-THEN-ELSE construct that contains the result and the alternative result:

> **IF** condition **THEN**
> statement
> **ELSE**
> statement;

3. You also know how to handle complicated conditions using the ELSE-IF ladder in the form:

> **IF** condition-1 **THEN**
> statement-1
> **ELSE IF** condition-2
> statement-2
> **ELSE IF** condition-3
> statement-3
>
> ...
> **ELSE**
> statement-n;

4. An alternative to the ladder is nesting the IF-THEN-ELSE constructs inside each other in the form:

> **IF** condition-1 **THEN**
> **IF** condition-2 **THEN**
>
> ...
> **IF** condition-n **THEN**
> statement-$n1$
> **ELSE**
> statement-$n2$
>
> ...
> **ELSE**
> statement-2
> **ELSE**
> statement-1;

5. You learned how to use the multiple choice construct CASE, which is ready to handle many cases in the form:

> **CASE** expression **OF**
> label-1 : statement-1;
> label-2 : statement-2;
>
> ...
> label-n : statement-n;
> **END**

6. In Turbo Pascal the CASE construct has more features, as it may contain the ELSE part which handles all the other cases that do not correspond to a label. It takes the form:

> **CASE** expression **OF**
> > label-1 : statement-1;
> > label-2 : statement-2;
> > ...
> > label-*n* : statement-*n*;
> **ELSE**
> > statement
> **END**

You also understand that in any of the above formulas you can replace one statement by a block of statements using the BEGIN-END blocks.

7. You were introduced as well to the unconditional branching statement GOTO which transfers the program control to a labeled statement. It takes the form:

> **GOTO** label;

The label in standard Pascal is a positive integer of up to four digits, while in Turbo Pascal it can be a valid identifier, or it may begin with a number. You also know how to declare a label at the beginning of the declaration part of the program. In Turbo Pascal the LABEL section does not need to be the first section.

8. Finally, you met the Turbo Pascal statement EXIT, which terminates the program at any point.

In the next chapter, you continue the discussion on control structures to learn how to build structured loops.

Exercises

1. What is the output for each of the following WRITELN statements:
   a. WRITELN(300 > 4);
   b. WRITELN((300 < 200) OR (300 > 100));
   c. WRITELN(TRUE OR FALSE);
   d. WRITELN(TRUE AND FALSE);
   e. WRITELN(TRUE OR FALSE AND TRUE);
   f. WRITELN(TRUE OR FALSE AND NOT FALSE);

2. Describe the function of the following case statement:

```
CASE GradePercentage DIV 10 OF
       9, 10:  WRITELN('Distinct');
           8:  WRITELN('Very good');
           7:  WRITELN('Good');
```

```
            5,6:  WRITELN('Passed');
    0,1,2,3,4:  WRITELN('Failed');
END;
```

What is the message displayed when you input each of the following grades?

   a. 84

   b. 63

   c. 52

   d. 33

   e. 99

3. Write an IF statement to read and examine the code numbers of inventory items. The valid numbers are 5, 6, 9, and 0. If the code is valid, the NumberOfItems is incremented by 1, otherwise a proper message is issued.

4. In Example 3-9, the leap year test is a simplified version of the actual logic. It is only useful for the years of one century. The complete logic of the leap year definition is:

■ The year is divisible by 4 AND not divisible by 100

OR

■ The year is divisible by 400.

Write a Pascal program to read the year from the keyboard, check if it is a leap year, and display the result on the screen. You can make use of the following Boolean variables:

```
R4      := Year MOD 4 = 0;
R100    := Year MOD 100 = 0;
R400    := Year MOD 400 = 0;
```

Answers

1. a. TRUE   b. TRUE   c. TRUE   d. FALSE
    e. TRUE   f. TRUE.

2. a. Very good   b. Passed   c. Passed   d. Failed
    e. Distinct.

Chapter 4

Iteration Statements

Chapter Topics:

- **Using the following iteration statements to build loops:**
  FOR
  WHILE-DO
  REPEAT-UNTIL

- **Incrementing and decrementing loop counters using the following FOR loop statements:**
  FOR-TO-DO
  FOR-DOWNTO-DO

- **Nesting loops of different kinds into other constructs, including other loops**

- **Applying different loop constructs to popular applications such as Average, Factorial, Leap Year, Multiplication Table, and Character Graphics**

4-1 Loops

You learned in the previous chapter how to build a repetition loop using the following tools:

■ A branching statement such as GOTO to transfer the control of the program to the starting point repeatedly

■ A condition to terminate the loop as desired

The condition may be used to test the input value and to terminate the loop when a specific value is received. You may also wish to repeat the process in the loop a specific number of times, in which case you need a counter. The condition in this case is used to test the counter with each round of the loop. This type of loop is called a *counted loop*. In the following program these elementary tools are used to display the message "Sorry, say again.." five times.

The algorithm used in the program is as follows:

1. Initialize the counter to zero.
2. Increment the counter by 1.
3. Test the counter to see if it is less than or equal to 5.
4. Display the statement.
5. Go to step 2.

```
{ --------------------------- Example 4-1 --------------------------- }
PROGRAM GoToLoop(OUTPUT);
LABEL
    1000;                                        { label declaration }
VAR
    Kounter :INTEGER;
BEGIN
    Kounter := 0;
1000:
    Kounter := Kounter + 1;
    IF Kounter <= 5 THEN
        BEGIN
            WRITELN('Sorry, say again..');
            GOTO 1000                            { restart }
        END;
    WRITELN;
    WRITELN('Press ENTER to continue..');
    READLN
END.
{ ----------------------------------------------------------------- }
```

In this program the counter is initialized to the value zero before entering the loop, which begins at the label 1000. Inside the loop, the counter is incremented, then tested to see if its value is less than or equal to 5. If so, the WRITELN statement is executed and the loop is repeated using the GOTO statement. If the condition fails (i.e., the counter exceeds 5) the program ends.

Output:

```
Sorry, say again..
Sorry, say again..
Sorry, say again..
Sorry, say again..
Sorry, say again..
Press ENTER to continue..
```

Pascal provides you with ready-made control structures for looping, so you can avoid such messy code. A control structure contains both the branching statement and the condition in one construct.

In this chapter you are introduced to the following constructs:

- The FOR loop
- The WHILE loop
- The REPEAT loop

Each of the three loops has different features that suit different applications.

4-2 The FOR Loop

The FOR loop construct is a counted loop used to repeat a statement or a block of statements a specified number of times. It includes the initialization of the counter, the condition, and the increment.

Look at this example:

```
{ -------------------------- Example 4-2 --------------------------- }
PROGRAM ForLoop(OUTPUT);
VAR
   Kounter :INTEGER;
BEGIN
   FOR Kounter := 1 TO 5 DO
      WRITELN('Sorry, say again..');
   WRITELN;
   WRITELN('Press ENTER to continue..');
   READLN
END.
{ ----------------------------------------------------------------- }
```

This program gives the same results as the previous program does, but is simpler and better organized. The FOR loop does the same work done in the previous program. It assigns the *control variable* Kounter the *initial value* 1, then executes the statement, increments the control variable by one, and repeats the process until the value of the Kounter reaches the *final value* of 5.

The general form of the FOR construct is as follows:

FOR control-variable := expression-1 **TO** expression-2 **DO** statement;

where:

control-variable	is the loop counter,
expression-1	is the initial value, and
expression-2	is the final value.

The control-variable, expression-1, and expression-2 can be of any type except REAL. All three must be of the same type.

Tip: Remember that the FOR construct is one statement ending with a semicolon. If by mistake you add another semicolon, as in the following loop:

```
FOR Kounter := 1 TO 1000 DO;
     WRITELN('Sorry, say again..');
```

do not be surprised if the loop is executed only once, regardless of the final value of the counter. The semicolon after the DO keyword ends the loop at this point.

The value of the control variable may not be modified inside the loop. Look at this assignment statement inside the loop:

```
FOR K := 1 TO 10 DO
    K := 2
...
```

Even if the compiler accepts this statement, it will repeal the effect of the loop counter as it sets it to the value 2 all the time. The same rule applies for the initial value and the final value of the control variable.

As usual, you can include as many statements as you want inside the loop by using the BEGIN-END blocks.

Application: Powers of Two

The number 2 and its powers are very important numbers in the computer field. Some of the numbers, such as 1024 bytes (equivalent to 1 KB) and 65,536 bytes (64 KB), are commonly used. In the following program a FOR loop is used to display the powers of two, using the same logic which was used to calculate the power in Example 2-2. The program output gives the power and the number 2 raised to this power. The initial and final values of the counter are supplied by the user during the execution. Thus, you can determine the range of numbers you would like to examine.

```
{ --------------------------- Example 4-3 --------------------------- }
PROGRAM ForLoop(INPUT, OUTPUT);
VAR
   Base, Power, Start, Final :INTEGER;
BEGIN
   Base := 2;
   WRITE('Enter starting exponent:');
   READLN(Start);
   WRITE('Enter ending exponent:');
   READLN(Final);
   WRITELN;
   WRITELN('Number      Power of two');
   FOR Power := Start TO Final DO
      BEGIN
          WRITE(Power:3);
          WRITELN(EXP(LN(Base)*Power):20:0)
      END;
   WRITELN;
   WRITELN('Press ENTER to continue..');
   READLN
END.
{ ---------------------------------------------------------------------- }
```

Sample Run:

```
Enter starting exponent:1
Enter ending exponent:20

Number      Power of two
   1                   2
   2                   4
   3                   8
   4                  16
   5                  32
   6                  64
   7                 128
   8                 256
   9                 512
  10                1024
  11                2048
  12                4096
  13                8192
  14               16384
  15               32768
  16               65536
  17              131072
  18              262144
  19              524288
```

```
   20              1048576
Press ENTER to continue..
```

Drill 4-1

Write a program to test the leap years in the range from 1990 to 2000. Display on the screen each year and the test result as in the following output:

```
The year 1990 is not a leap year.
The year 1991 is not a leap year.
The year 1992 is a leap year.
The year 1993 is not a leap year.
The year 1994 is not a leap year.
The year 1995 is not a leap year.
The year 1996 is a leap year.
The year 1997 is not a leap year.
The year 1998 is not a leap year.
The year 1999 is not a leap year.
The year 2000 is a leap year.
```

Application: The Average

The following program demonstrates data entry using a loop. It receives from the keyboard a series of numbers and calculates the sum and the average of the numbers. At the beginning of the program you are asked to enter the number of the elements (N), which is used as the final value of the counter. Inside the loop the sum is accumulated in the variable Sum using the statement:

```
Sum := Sum + Number;
```

When the loop exits, the average is calculated from the sum and the number of elements, using the statement:

```
Average := Sum / N;
```

Here is the program.

```
{ ---------------------------- Example 4-4 ---------------------------- }
PROGRAM AverageProg1(INPUT,OUTPUT);
VAR
   Average, Sum, Number :REAL;
   N, Kounter           :INTEGER;
BEGIN
   Sum := 0;
   WRITE('Enter Number of Elements: ');
   READLN(N);
   FOR Kounter := 1 TO N DO
      BEGIN
         WRITE('Enter Element #',Kounter,': ');
```

```
            READLN(Number);
            Sum := Sum + Number          { The semicolon is optional }
         END;
      Average := Sum / N;
      WRITELN;
      WRITELN('Sum of Numbers =     ', Sum:0:2);
      WRITELN('Average of Numbers = ', Average:0:2);
      WRITELN;
      WRITELN('Press ENTER to continue..');
      READLN
END.
{ -------------------------------------------------------------------- }
```

Sample Run:

```
      Enter Number of Elements: 5
      Enter Element #1: 1
      Enter Element #2: 2
      Enter Element #3: 3
      Enter Element #4: 4
      Enter Element #5: 5

      Sum of Numbers     = 15.00
      Average of Numbers = 3.00

      Press ENTER to continue..
```

Notice how the element numbers were displayed inside the loop using the values of the control variable Kounter.

4-3 Stepping Up and Stepping Down

In the previous examples, the FOR loop counter was always incremented. This means that the final value of the counter must be greater than the initial value, or else the loop will never be executed.

You can decrement the counter using an alternative form of the FOR loop, by replacing the keyword TO with the keyword DOWNTO as in the following form:

FOR control-variable := expression-1 **DOWNTO** expression-2 **DO**
statement;

With this formula you can start the counter with the larger value and step down until the final value is reached.

Application: The Factorial

The factorial of a positive integer N is defined as:

$$N! = N * (N-1) * (N-2) \ldots * 3 * 2 * 1$$

Thus the factorial of 4 is 4 * 3 * 2 * 1, and the factorial of 3 is 3 * 2 * 1. You can then express the following relationships for the factorial:

    4! = 4 * 3!
    3! = 3 * 2!
    2! = 2 * 1!
    1! = 1

In general, you can write the following Pascal statement to calculate the factorial using a counter:

```
Factorial := Factorial * Kounter;
```

The variable Kounter can be incremented from 1 to N or decremented from N to 1. The following program uses this logic in a loop with a decremented step.

```
{ --------------------------- Example 4-5 ---------------------------- }
PROGRAM FactorialProg1(INPUT,OUTPUT);
VAR
   Factorial       :REAL;
   Kounter, Number :INTEGER;
BEGIN
   WRITE('Give me a number, and I will tell you the factorial: ');
   READLN(Number);
   Factorial := 1;
   FOR Kounter := Number DOWNTO 1 DO
      Factorial := Factorial * Kounter;
   WRITELN('The factorial of ', Number,' is ', Factorial:0:0);
   WRITELN;
   WRITELN('Press ENTER to continue..');
   READLN
END.
{ -------------------------------------------------------------------- }
```

Notice that the variable Factorial must be initialized to the value 1 before starting the iterative process.

Sample Run:

```
Give me a number, and I will tell you the factorial: 8
The factorial of 8 is 40320

Press ENTER to continue..
```

Tip: Although the factorial of a number is always an integer, using the type REAL (or the Turbo Pascal type LONGINT) for the variable Factorial gives you a large storage size with which to receive the quickly increasing results of factorial calculations. If you use the INTEGER type, the program will start giving you funny results after the factorial of 7!

Drill 4-2

Modify the previous program to test the input value of the number. If the value is zero, the program should exit without going through the loop. You may use a GOTO statement or the Turbo Pascal function EXIT.

4-4 Nested Loops

Like any other statement, the FOR loop statement can be used inside another loop. In this case it is said that the *inner loop* is nested inside the *outer loop*. You can nest as many loops as you wish inside one another, according to your application. The next program displays on your screen the following *array* of numbers.

```
1  2  3  4  5
1  2  3  4  5
1  2  3  4  5
```

The array consists of three rows and five columns. You can control the number of rows and columns by using the counters of two nested loops. As you can see, for each round of the outer loop counter (Row), the inner loop counter (Column) loops five times. The values that appear in the output are the values of the counter Column. Notice that a blank line is displayed after a complete row is done, using the outer loop counter.

```
{---------------------------- Example 4-6 ----------------------------}
PROGRAM NestedLoops(OUTPUT);
VAR
   Row, Column :INTEGER;
BEGIN
   FOR Row := 1 TO 3 DO            { Start of the outer loop }
      BEGIN
         FOR Column := 1 to 5 DO   { Start of the inner loop }
            WRITE(Column, ' ');    { End of the inner loop }
      WRITELN                      { This statement belongs to the outer loop }
      END                          { The end of the outer loop }
END.
{ ------------------------------------------------------------------- }
```

Tip: Notice the two END keywords in the previous program. The first one comes without a semicolon because it is the last statement in the main block (the program main body). Also, the keyword WRITELN, which comes before this END, was not terminated by a semicolon. This is because it is the last statement in the loop block. All of these are options, but you may use the semicolons if you wish. If you add another statement at the end of the program (to suspend the screen, for instance), the situation will change.

Drill 4-3

Modify the last program to draw the fifty stars of the American flag, as shown:

```
* * * * * * * * * *
* * * * * * * * * *
* * * * * * * * * *
* * * * * * * * * *
* * * * * * * * * *
```

4-5 The WHILE Loop

The WHILE loop construct contains the necessary condition to terminate the loop, but unlike the FOR loop, no counter is included. It takes the general form:

WHILE condition **DO**
        statement;

This form simply says: "Execute the following statement as long as the condition is TRUE."

When the loop is entered, the condition (a Boolean expression) is evaluated. If it is TRUE, the statement that follows the keyword DO is executed. The loop will be repeated, and the statement will be reexecuted until the condition becomes FALSE. In your program, you must include the necessary logic to make the condition FALSE at the right time. You may use a counter with this loop, but you need to increment or decrement the counter yourself.

The following program demonstrates the same algorithm of calculating the average of a set of numbers entered from the keyboard but uses the WHILE loop. The condition is used here to test the value of a counter Kounter against the maximum number of elements N. When this maximum is reached the loop exits.

```
{ --------------------------- Example 4-7 --------------------------- }
PROGRAM AverageProg2(INPUT,OUTPUT);
```

```
VAR
    Average, Sum, Number  :REAL;
    Kounter, N            :INTEGER;
BEGIN
    Sum := 0;
    Kounter := 1;
    WRITE('Enter Number of Elements: ');
    READLN(N);
    WHILE Kounter <= N DO
        BEGIN
            WRITE('Enter Element #',Kounter,': ');
            READLN(Number);
            Sum := Sum + Number;
            Kounter := Kounter + 1
        END;
    Average := Sum / N;
    WRITELN;
    WRITELN('Sum of Numbers =      ', Sum:0:2);
    WRITELN('Average of Numbers = ', Average:0:2);
    WRITELN;
    WRITELN('Press ENTER to continue..');
    READLN
END.
{ ------------------------------------------------------------------- }
```

Notice that the counter is initialized at the beginning of the program and incremented inside the loop. The initial value is used for the first round in the loop (Kounter := 1), because the incrementing takes place after the process. This is one way to do it, but other arrangements are used in the next few programs. Notice also that when you want to include more than one statement in the WHILE loop, you must use the BEGIN-END blocks.

Sample Run:

```
Enter Number of Elements: 3
Enter Element #1: 1
Enter Element #2: 2
Enter Element #3: 3

Sum of Numbers    = 6.00
Average of Numbers = 2.00

Press ENTER to continue..
```

If you do not want to enter the number of elements beforehand, you can count them inside the loop. In this case you need a cue to end the loop, like entering a negative number. Look at this modified version of the program, where the input number is tested with every round to see if it is –1.

```
{ ------------------------- Example 4-8 -------------------------- }
PROGRAM AverageProg3(INPUT,OUTPUT);
VAR
    Average, Sum, Number :REAL;
    Kounter              :INTEGER;
BEGIN
    Sum := 0;
    Average := 0;
    Number := 0;
    Kounter := 0;
    WHILE Number <> -1 DO
        BEGIN
            Kounter := Kounter + 1;
            Sum := Sum + Number;
            WRITE('Enter element #',Kounter,' (or -1 to end): ');
            READLN(Number)
        END;
    IF Kounter > 1 THEN
        Average := Sum / (Kounter - 1);
    WRITELN;
    WRITELN('Sum of Numbers     = ', Sum:0:2);
    WRITELN('Average of Numbers = ', Average:0:2);
    WRITELN;
    WRITELN('Press ENTER to continue..');
    READLN
END.
{ --------------------------------------------------------------- }
```

Sample Run:

```
Enter element #1 (or -1 to end): 1
Enter element #2 (or -1 to end): 2
Enter element #3 (or -1 to end): 3
Enter element #4 (or -1 to end): -1

Sum of Numbers     = 6.00
Average of Numbers = 2.00

Press ENTER to continue..
```

Notice the following points in this program:

■ The input statement comes at the end of the loop block so that the input value can be tested before any processing.

■ The average is calculated by dividing the sum by the value of the counter decremented by one. This is to counteract the extra round which took place when Number was –1.

■ The average is calculated only if the variable Kounter is not equal to 1. This is to avoid the divide by zero error, in case you want to exit the program without entering any data. In such a case you would get the following response:

```
Enter element #1 (or -1 to end): -1
Sum of Numbers     = 0.00
Average of Numbers = 0.00

Press ENTER to continue..
```

Drill 4-4

Use the WHILE loop construct to write a program to display a multiplication table as in the following example:

```
1 * X = Y
2 * X = Y
3 * X = Y
4 * X = Y
5 * X = Y
6 * X = Y
7 * X = Y
8 * X = Y
9 * X = Y
...
```

The value of X is received from the keyboard and the value Y is the multiplication result.

4-6 The REPEAT Loop

This loop is used to execute a group of statements until a specified condition is met. It takes the form:

REPEAT
>statement-1;
>statement-2;
>...
>statement-n;
UNTIL condition;

As you can see in the form, this loop is ready to execute more than one statement without using the BEGIN-END blocks. Another difference between the WHILE loop and the REPEAT loop is that the REPEAT loop is executed at least once, regardless of the condition, because it starts each round by executing the statements and ends by testing the condition. In some applications this feature is necessary.

Look at the factorial algorithm using a REPEAT loop:

```
     ...
        Factorial := 1;
        Kounter := Number;
     REPEAT
        Factorial := Factorial * Kounter;
        Kounter := Kounter - 1;
     UNTIL Kounter = 0;
```

When Kounter reaches zero (which means that the value 1 was already used up), no other rounds are needed, and the loop is terminated. You may also use the stepping-up algorithm, like this:

```
     ...
     Factorial := 1;
     Kounter := 1;
     REPEAT
        Factorial := Factorial * Kounter;
        Kounter := Kounter + 1;
     UNTIL Kounter = Number + 1;
```

In this case the loop is terminated when the value of Kounter reaches Number+1, which means that the value of Number was already used up.

In the following program this REPEAT loop is nested in a WHILE loop. The program will be repeatedly executed until you enter 0 to terminate it.

```
{ --------------------------- Example 4-9 --------------------------- }
PROGRAM FactorialProg2(INPUT,OUTPUT);
VAR
   Factorial        :REAL;
   Kounter, Number :INTEGER;
BEGIN
   WRITE('Give me a number (or 0 to exit): ');
   READLN(Number);
   WHILE Number <> 0 DO                      { Start of the WHILE loop }
      BEGIN
         Factorial := 1;
         Kounter    := 1;
         REPEAT                              { Start of the REPEAT loop }
            Factorial := Factorial * Kounter;
            Kounter    := Kounter + 1;
      UNTIL Kounter = Number + 1;            { End of the REPEAT loop }
      WRITELN('The factorial of ', Number,' is ', Factorial:0:0);
      WRITE('Give me a number (or 0 to exit): ');
      READLN(Number)
   END;                                      { End of the WHILE loop }
   WRITELN('I am out of here!')
END.
{ ------------------------------------------------------------------- }
```

Notice here that two similar input statements are used, one before the WHILE loop and one inside it. The first one is used to initialize the variable Kounter before entering the loop, in order to be ready for testing within the loop.

Sample Run:

```
Give me a number (or 0 to exit): 3
The factorial of 3 is 6
Give me a number (or 0 to exit): 5
The factorial of 5 is 120
Give me a number (or 0 to exit): 0
I am out of here!
```

Drill 4-5

Rewrite the last program using an inner FOR loop and an outer WHILE loop.

Application: Prime Numbers

A prime number is an integer greater than 1, whose only positive divisor is 1 and itself. For example, the prime numbers in the range from 1 to 20 are 2, 3, 5, 7, 11, 13, 17, and 19. The numbers 4, 6, 8, 9, 10, 12, 14, 15, 16, 18, and 20 are not prime numbers because they are multiples of other numbers. The following program displays the prime numbers between 1 and a maximum number N, which is read from the keyboard at run time. The algorithm used in the program is as follows:

1. Start with the first prime number 2, and go through all the numbers from 2 to N.
2. Check if the current number is a multiple of any smaller number. The number A is a multiple of another number B if the remainder of integer division (A MOD B) is zero.
3. Exclude the numbers that are multiple of other numbers.
4. Display the remaining numbers, which are all prime numbers.

```
{ -------------------------- Example 4-10 -------------------------- }
PROGRAM PrimaryNumbers(INPUT,OUTPUT);
{ This program reads the number N and displays the prime numbers in the }
{ range from 1 to N. }
LABEL
     100;
VAR
   I, J :INTEGER;   {Loop counters}
   N    :INTEGER;   {The maximum limit of the numbers range}
BEGIN
   WRITE('Please enter the maximum number in the range: ');
   READLN(N);
   WRITELN('Prime numbers between ', 1, ' and ', N, ' are:');
   FOR I := 2 TO N DO
```

```
        BEGIN
          FOR J := 2 TO I-1 DO
              BEGIN
                 IF (I MOD J) = 0 THEN
                     GOTO 100;
              END;  {End of J Loop}
              WRITELN(I);
100:      END; {End of I Loop}
    WRITELN('Press ENTER to continue...');
    READLN
END.
{ ---------------------------------------------------------------------- }
```

Sample Run:

```
    Please enter the maximum number in the range: 10
    Prime numbers between 1 and 10 are:
    2
    3
    5
    7
    Press ENTER to continue...
```

Because you don't have enough Pascal tools yet, you have to use a GOTO statement in this program. However, in the next chapter, when you learn how to use arrays, the prime numbers will be revisited with a stronger algorithm.

Summary

In this chapter you were introduced to three control structures used to build loops. These structures are:

- The FOR loop
- The WHILE loop
- The REPEAT loop

1. The FOR loop is used to repeat a statement or a block of statements a specified number of times. The loop takes the general form:

    FOR control-variable := expression-1 **TO** expression-2 **DO** statement;

    where:

control-variable	is the loop counter,
expression-1	is the initial value, and
expression-2	is the final value.

2. An alternate form of the FOR loop is used to decrement the counter:

> **FOR** control-variable := expression-1
>   **DOWNTO** expression-2 **DO**
> statement;

3. The WHILE loop is used to execute a statement or a block of statements as long as a specified condition is TRUE. The construct takes the general form:

> **WHILE** condition **DO**
> statement;

4. With both the FOR and the WHILE loops you can use multiple statements by including them in a BEGIN-END block.

5. The REPEAT loop is used to execute a group of statements until the specified condition fails. It takes the general form:

> **REPEAT**
> statement-1;
> statement-2;
> ...
> statement-n;
> **UNTIL** condition;

6. You understand now that the main difference between the REPEAT loop and the other two is that the statements inside the REPEAT loop are executed at least once regardless of the condition.

7. You understand also that the REPEAT loop can handle many statements without using BEGIN-END blocks.

8. Finally, you learned in this chapter that loop constructs may be nested inside other constructs (including other loops).

Exercises

1. Determine whether or not each of the following statements is true or false:
   a. The body of the WHILE loop is executed at least once.
   b. The body of the REPEAT loop is executed at least once.
   c. The body of the REPEAT loop, when it contains more that one statement, doesn't have to be included between BEGIN and END.
   d. The body of the WHILE loop, when it contains more that one statement, doesn't have to be included between BEGIN and END.

2. Determine whether or not the following statement is valid. If valid, how many times should it be executed?

```
FOR I := 4 DIV 2 TO 8 DIV 2 DO
    WRITELN('Hello..');
```

3. Describe the expected output from the following loop:

```
FOR I := 1 TO 2 DO
    FOR J := 1 TO 2 DO
        FOR K := 1 TO 2 DO
            WRITELN(I,J,K);
```

How many times will the WRITELN statement be executed if you add a fourth loop?

How many times will the WRITELN statement be executed if you add an nth loop?

4. What is the expected output from the following code?

```
FOR I := 1 TO 6 DO
    BEGIN
        FOR J := 1 TO I DO
            WRITE('*');
        WRITELN;
    END;
FOR I := 6 DOWNTO 1 DO
    BEGIN
        FOR J := I DOWNTO 1 DO
            WRITE('*');
        WRITELN;
    END;
```

5. Write a program to print the even numbers from 1 to 30.

Answers

1. a. False, b. True, c. True, d. False
2. Valid. The loop is repeated three times.
3. The number of repetitions is 2^n, where n is the number of FOR loops.
4. The program displays the figure as shown on the right:
5. You may use the following code segment, which represents the main algorithm in the program:

```
FOR I := 1 TO 30 DO
    IF (I MOD 2) = 0 THEN
        WRITELN(I);
```

```
*
**
***
****
*****
******
******
*****
****
***
**
*
```

Chapter 5

Structured and User-defined Types

Chapter Topics:

- An overview of standard Pascal types
- Features of the ordinal data types
- Subranges
- Enumerations
- Single-dimensional and multidimensional arrays
- The TYPE section in Pascal program
- User-defined types

5-1 Classification of Data Types in Pascal

Before you begin using the advanced features of the language, it is best to get an overview of the data architecture in Pascal. Standard data types consist of the following main categories:

Standard types:

- Simple types (also known as scalar types)
- Structured types
- Pointer types

The data types explained so far are called simple data types, as opposed to *structured* data types. Each datum of a simple data type is one single element, while in structured types (such as arrays) a datum may contain a collection of items. *Pointers* are special types used to build structures such as *linked lists* and *trees*.

Simple types are divided into two main categories, ordinal and real types:

Simple types:

- Ordinal types:
    - Predefined: INTEGER, CHAR, and BOOLEAN
    - User-defined: enumerations and subranges
- Real type: REAL

The structured data types are divided into the following categories:

Structured types:

- Arrays
- Records
- Sets
- Files:
    - Predefined: TEXT files
    - User-defined: non-TEXT files

In this chapter, you will cover the user-defined simple types (*enumerations* and *subranges*) and *arrays*. *Sets* and *records* are introduced in Chapter 8 and expanded on in Chapter 10. The *file* type and its applications are explained in Chapter 9. Pointers are discussed in Chapters 11 and 12 along with linked lists and trees.

5-2 Ordinal Data Types

Simple types fall into two main categories, ordinal and real types. The ordinal types include the INTEGER, CHAR, and BOOLEAN types. An ordinal type is distinguished by data values that form a series of discrete elements such that every element has a discrete predecessor (except the first element) and successor (except the last element). Integers are like that, as they form a set of distinct numbers ranging from $-(MAXINT+1)$ to $+MAXINT$. The element 4, for example, is preceded by 3 and followed by 5. The type CHAR includes a set of characters ordered sequentially according to their ordinal numbers. The type BOOLEAN contains the set TRUE and FALSE. The value FALSE has the ordinal number 0 while TRUE has the ordinal number 1.

Real numbers, on the other hand, are not discrete. For example, between the number 0 and 1 there exists an infinite number of fractions. Between any two real numbers, then, there is another real number.

Enumerations

It is sometimes useful in a program to define days of the week as integers in order to make the program code more readable. In this case, you need to either assign each day a number or declare each a named constant as in:

```
CONST
    Monday = 0;
    Tuesday = 1;
    Wednesday = 2;
    Thursday = 3;
    Friday = 4;
    Saturday = 5;
    Sunday = 6;
```

After these declarations you can refer to any of these days by its name:

```
IF Today = Sunday THEN
    WRITELN('Sorry, we are closed on Sundays..');
```

In this statement an integer variable Today is tested to check if it is Sunday; in other words, if it contains the value 6. Using such declarations will take a lot of programming effort, though, especially when you have a large number of constants (such as the names of the months).

The *enumerated* type gives you a shortcut to doing the same thing. Look at the following declaration:

```
VAR
    Day :(Monday, Tuesday, Wednesday, Thursday, Friday, Saturday, Sunday);
```

In this declaration, the identifiers representing the months are listed in an ordered series and separated by commas. Thus, Monday is internally coded as 0 and Sunday is coded as 6. Other days are represented by numbers between 0 and 6 according to their sequence in the enumeration. It is, however, illegal to read or write these values directly as you do with simple types (using WRITELN and READLN statements). With enumerations you may use any of the following operations:

1. You may assign any one of the enumeration elements to the variable Day like this:

```
Day := Friday;
```

but it is illegal to assign an explicit number to the variable Day, such as Day := 1. This feature assures that the enumeration will only be assigned valid data.

2. You can obtain and use the values associated with the enumeration elements using the ORD function. For example:

```
WRITELN(ORD(Monday));          gives the value 0
WRITELN(ORD(Tuesday));         gives the value 1
```

3. You may also use the functions PRED and SUCC to obtain the predecessor and the successor of a specified element:

```
WRITELN(PRED(Friday));         gives the value 3
WRITELN(SUCC(Monday));         gives the value 1
```

4. You can compare values of the enumerated type using the Boolean operators (simple or compound), like this:

```
IF (Day = Saturday) OR (Day = Sunday) THEN
WRITELN('This is a weekend day.');
```

Again, you cannot use the explicit values in comparisons such as IF Day = 2. This results in an error.

In the following program a FOR loop uses the enumeration Month to display the corresponding integer values from 0 to 11.

```
{ --------------------------- Example 5-1 --------------------------- }
PROGRAM Enumeration1(OUTPUT);
VAR
   Month :(Jan, Feb, Mar, Apr, May, Jun, Jul, Aug, Sep, Oct, Nov, Dec);
BEGIN
   WRITELN;
   FOR Month := Jan TO Dec DO
      WRITE(ORD(Month),' ')
END.
{ ------------------------------------------------------------------- }
```

Output:

```
0 1 2 3 4 5 6 7 8 9 10 11
```

Notice that the values corresponding to the twelve months range from 0 to 11. If you would like to see the values range from 1 to 12 as the months in the calendar do, you can use the expression ORD(month)+1 instead of the expression ORD(month).

The enumerated type is an ordinal data type and is classified as a user-defined type.

Subranges

The subrange, another user-defined ordinal type, helps to eliminate out-of-range data. For example, instead of using the INTEGER type to represent the month numbers, you can declare the variable Month as a subrange like this:

```
VAR
   Month : 1..12;
```

As such, any value outside the range 1 to 12 will be considered an error either in compilation or at run time. In other words, you cannot, after this declaration, write a statement like this in your program :

```
Month := 13;   ---> illegal statement
```

Also, if a user responds to an input statement by entering an out-of-range number, the program will issue the proper error message, though with some compilers you have to set a switch to make the compiler detect out-of-range errors.

The type used to represent month values in this example is INTEGER. It is called the *base type* of the subrange. You may use any ordinal type as the base type. For example, you can declare the uppercase letters as a subrange using the base type CHAR as follows:

```
VAR
    Uppercase : 'A'..'Z'
```

In this case, only the uppercase letters will be permitted as data for the subrange Uppercase.

The following example demonstrates the use of a subrange to represent months, followed by a CASE statement to classify months as seasons. The program prompts you to enter the month number, and displays the season to which this month belongs.

```
{ --------------------------- Example 5-2 --------------------------- }
PROGRAM Subrange1(INPUT,OUTPUT);
VAR
    MonthNumber :1..12;
BEGIN
    WRITE('Please enter the number of the month: ');
    READLN(MonthNumber);
    CASE MonthNumber OF
        12, 1 ,2  :WRITELN('This is wintertime.');
         3, 4, 5  :WRITELN('This is springtime.');
         6, 7, 8  :WRITELN('This is summertime.');
         9, 10, 11 :WRITELN('This is autumn.')
    END
END.
{ ------------------------------------------------------------------- }
```

The following are two sample runs. The second one gave a runtime error message because the number 14 was entered as a month number.

Sample Runs:

Run 1:

```
Please enter the number of the month: 2
This is wintertime.
```

Run 2:

```
Please enter the number of the month: 14
Runtime error 201 at 0000:00BE.
```

The subrange, in general, can be a subset of any previously defined sequence (of the ordinal type). So, if the enumeration Day has already been defined in your program, you may then define a subrange like this:

```
VAR
    WorkingDay : Monday..Friday;
```

This is valid because the words Monday and Friday are already known to the compiler.

Restrictions on Using Enumerations and Subranges

- The first element in a subrange must be less than the last one.
- Though a subrange can be a subset of an enumeration, an enumeration cannot use elements from another enumeration.
- The enumeration elements cannot be used as identifiers for other variables. It is the same as declaring the same variable identifier twice in one program.

Drill 5-1

Write a declaration to define the following subranges:

A.   The uppercase letters

B.   The lowercase letters

C.   The decimal digits

Accept values that correspond to each subrange and display them preceded by the proper message. The output may look something like this:

```
Lowercase letter   : r
Uppercase letter   : T
Digit              : 5
```

5-3 The TYPE Section

The enumerations and subranges are usually associated with the TYPE statement, which is used to declare new user-defined types or to rename predefined types. The TYPE statement comes in the TYPE section of the declaration part. It takes the form:

TYPE
      type-name = type-definition;

where type-name is the type identifier, and type-definition is a predefined type or new type definition.

Renaming Types

It is possible to rename any data type, even the simple types such as INTEGER, as in this example:

```
TYPE
    Day = INTEGER;
```

In this declaration the type INTEGER is given a new name (Day). Thus, in the VAR section, you can declare some other variables of the type Day like this:

```
VAR
    Holiday, Yesterday, Tomorrow : Day;
```

The type Day is actually the type INTEGER, but given another name (a synonym). In your program, you may use either one of the two names (INTEGER or Day) because the type INTEGER is still recognized by the compiler. This is not, however, the proper use of the TYPE statement. It is meant to be used for naming types such as enumerations and subranges.

Naming User-Defined Types

Instead of declaring enumerations and subranges in the VAR section, it would be better to declare them as types. Look at these declarations:

```
TYPE
    Day = (Monday,Tuesday,Wednesday,Thursday,Friday,Saturday,Sunday);
    WorkingDay = Monday..Friday;
```

Here, two new types are declared: the enumerated type Day and the subrange WorkingDay. Notice that the subrange is defined as a subset of the enumeration Day. Needless to say, the enumeration declaration must come first in this case.

You can use these new types in the VAR section to declare variables in the same way you use the predefined types of the language. Thus:

```
VAR
    Today, Yesterday, Tomorrow, Holiday :Day;
    DayOff :WorkingDay;
```

The use of the TYPE statement saves you the effort of writing long declarations for the enumeration variables Today, Yesterday, Tomorrow, and Holiday. They are all simply of the type Day.

Now in your program you may write assignment statements like the following:

```
Holiday := Friday;
DayOff  := Tuesday;
```

```
Tomorrow := Sunday;
```

In order to see the values contained in your variables, use an output statement such as:

```
WRITELN(ORD(Holiday), ', ',ORD(DayOff),', ', ORD(Tomorrow));
```

In this case, the statement will give you the values 4, 1, and 6 respectively.

In standard Pascal the TYPE section should come in the following sequence relative to the other sections:

> LABEL section
> CONST section
> TYPE section
> VAR section

In Turbo Pascal, as mentioned before, the order is not important, but the TYPE section should still precede the VAR section because it contains the definitions of the user-defined types.

Drill 5-2

Which of the following declarations are valid if they all come in one program?

```
TYPE
{1}      Football       = (Saints, Cowboys);
{2}      Games          = (Football, Baseball, Basketball)
{3}      Week           = (Mon, Tue, Wed, Thu, Fri, Sat, Sun);
{4}      Weekend        = Sat..Sun;
{5}      Compiler       = (C, Pascal, Fortran, Ada, Basic);
VAR
{6}      WholeWeek      :Week;
{7}      WorkingDay     :(Mon, Tue, Wed, Fri);
{8}      Weekday        :Mon..Fri;
{9}      SW             :(Compiler, OperatingSystem, ApplicationProgram);
{10}     DpTools        :(Hardware, Software, PeopleWare);
{11}     DpTool         :(HW, SW, PW);
{12}     C              :(TurboC, QuickC);
{13}     Margin         : -10..+10;
```

5-4 Arrays

If you would like to represent the names of the players on a football team using only simple data types, you would need to use one variable for each player's name. In such a case, you would need too many variables, such as:

```
FirstPlayer
SecondPlayer
ThirdPlayer
...
```

This is not a good idea. Now imagine the case if you were dealing with a class of one hundred students. It would be almost impossible to use one hundred variables to store names.

The practical way to store this kind of data is to use the array data structure, which is useful for storing a collection of related data items. In the case of the football team you would need to declare only one *subscripted* variable, and you would represent your data like this:

```
Player[1]
Player[2]
Player[3]
...
```

The name of the variable is Player, and the number between the brackets is called the *subscript* or *index*. Changing the index gives you a new memory location in which to store a new name. This type of data structure is called a *one-dimensional array*. It is useful to represent data such as names of a group of people, scores of one student in several classes, or any similar set of related items (see Table 5-1).

Table 5-1: Example of a one-dimensional array

Player[1]	Player[2]	Player[3]	Player[4]	Player[5]	...
Able	Baker	Charlie	John	Sam	...

In Chapter 2 you met a special type of one-dimensional array (the PACKED ARRAY OF CHAR), which is used to store a string of text in standard Pascal, and you already know that each element (character) in this array is referred to by a number (index).

In other applications you may need a *two-dimensional array*, which is capable of handling more complicated structures. For example, suppose that you want to store the scores of a group of students in different classes, as represented in Table 5-2.

Each element in this table is related to a row (the student number) and a column (the class number); these are the two dimensions of the array. The data item itself is a real number.

Table 5-2: Example of a two-dimensional array

	Class # (second index)				
	1	2	3	4	5
Student # **(first index)**					
1	55.5	60.9	66.5	80.3	70.5
2	89.1	77.6	99.9	88.7	50.3
3	40.5	67.4	90.5	45.1	66.9
...	...	...	...	...	...
100	68.8	87.2	90.4	60.1	60.4

To represent the data in this table your variables will look something like this:

```
StudentScore[3][4]
```

This variable represents the score of student #3 in class #4; in other words, the number at the intersection of row #3 and column #4. You may assign a numeric value which represents a score to this variable, thus:

```
StudentScore[3][4] := 45.1;
```

Compare now the following assignment statements to the values in the table:

```
StudentScore[1][1] := 55.5;    {the score of student #1 in class #1}
StudentScore[1][2] := 60.9;    {the score of student #1 in class #2}
StudentScore[3][5] := 66.9;    {the score of student #3 in class #5}
StudentScore[100][2] := 87.2; {the score of student #100 in class #2}
```

Arrays are classified as structured data types (as opposed to the simple [or *unstructured*] types you have used thus far). There are many other structured data types in Pascal which are useful for different applications.

As a matter of fact, the quality of a program is mainly measured by two criteria:

■ The structural efficiency of the program; that is, how readable, easy to debug, and prone to errors it is

■ The use of the most efficient data structures applicable, to save time and enable the program to manipulate data in the most efficient way

Note: An array variable may be called either a subscripted variable or an *indexed* variable. The array elements referred to by the array variables are also called array *components*. In mathematics, a one-dimensional array is called a *vector*, while a two-dimensional array is called a *matrix*. You may come across these names in mathematical applications.

5-5 One-Dimensional Arrays

A one-dimensional array is declared using the following form:

VAR
array-name : **ARRAY**[index-range] **OF** element-type;

If you want, for example, to declare an array to store test scores of ten students as real numbers, you can declare your array like this:

VAR
Score : **ARRAY**[1..10] **OF REAL;**

This array (named Score) can hold up to ten real numbers. The index range [1..10] indicates that the indexes of the array elements start from 1 and end at 10. The index range, which is a subrange (of integers in this example), can be of any ordinal type, but the array elements can be of any data type. The above declaration, then, reserves a sequence of ten memory locations in which to store ten REAL values of ten array elements.

Application: Scores of One Student

In the following program the array Score is used to store the scores of one student in six different classes. The scores are entered from the keyboard, then the sum and average of the scores are displayed.

```
{ --------------------------- Example 5-3 --------------------------- }
PROGRAM Scores1(INPUT,OUTPUT);
CONST
   NumberOfClasses = 6;
VAR
   Score :ARRAY[1..NumberOfClasses] OF REAL;
   Average, SumOfScores :REAL;
   Index                :INTEGER;
BEGIN
{ Read the scores array }
{ -------------------- }
   FOR Index := 1 TO NumberOfClasses DO
      BEGIN
         WRITE('Enter score for class #', Index,': ');
         READLN(Score[Index])
      END;
{ Calculate the sum }
{ ---------------- }
   SumOfScores := 0;
   FOR Index := 1 TO NumberOfClasses DO
      SumOfScores := SumOfScores + Score[Index];
{ Calculate the average }
{ -------------------- }
```

```
    Average := SumOfScores / NumberOfClasses;
{ Display Results }
{ -------------- }
   WRITELN;
   WRITELN('Sum of scores = ', SumOfScores:0:2);
   WRITELN('Average of scores = ', Average:0:2);
   WRITELN;
   WRITELN('Press ENTER to continue..');
   READLN
END.
{ ------------------------------------------------------------------- }
```

Sample Run:

```
    Enter score for class #1: 90
    Enter score for class #2: 80
    Enter score for class #3: 85
    Enter score for class #4: 75
    Enter score for class #5: 89
    Enter score for class #6: 91

    Sum of scores = 510.00
    Average of scores = 85.00

    Press ENTER to continue..
```

The following points in this program are worthy of your attention:

1. The size of the array is declared as a constant (NumberOfClasses).

2. The index-range of the array is declared using the previously defined constant NumberOfClasses as follows:

```
    Score :ARRAY[1..NumberOfClasses] OF REAL;
```

This is the same as:

```
    Score :ARRAY[1..6] OF REAL;
```

The first declaration, however, is much better, because if you would like to process a different number of classes, you just change the value of the constant NumberOfClasses without modifying the program main body.

3. Notice that after the program reads the scores, they are stored in the array elements and are available in memory. This means that the sum can be processed later in the program. When you calculated the sum and the average of some numbers before (Example 4-4), you had to accumulate the values during data entry in one variable Sum. Now, you have six variables.

4. The index of the array is used as a counter in the FOR loops, both for reading data and calculating the sum. Actually, the index of the array is very useful for displaying results, especially if you like to display the results in table form.

Application: Displaying Tabulated Results

The following program deals with the same problem but displays the results in a tabulated form.

```
{ --------------------------- Example 5-4 --------------------------- }
PROGRAM Scores2(INPUT,OUTPUT);
CONST
   NumberOfClasses = 6;
   Tab = CHR(9);
VAR
   Score :ARRAY[1..NumberOfClasses] OF REAL;
   Average, SumOfScores :REAL;
   Index                :INTEGER;
BEGIN
{ Read the scores array }
{ ------------------ }
   FOR Index := 1 TO NumberOfClasses DO
      BEGIN
         WRITE('Enter score for class #', Index,': ');
         READLN(Score[Index])
      END;
{ Calculate the sum }
{ --------------- }
   SumOfScores := 0;
   FOR Index := 1 TO NumberOfClasses DO
      SumOfScores := SumOfScores + Score[Index];
{ Calculate the average }
{ ------------------ }
   Average := SumOfScores / NumberOfClasses;
{ Display Results }
{ ------------- }
   WRITELN;
   WRITELN(Tab,'CLASS #');
   WRITE('      ');                  { 6 spaces }
   FOR Index := 1 TO NumberOfClasses DO
      WRITE(Index:7);
   WRITELN;
   WRITE(Tab);
   FOR Index := 1 TO NumberOfClasses DO
      WRITE('-------');
   WRITELN;
   WRITE('SCORES  ');
   FOR Index := 1 TO NumberOfClasses DO
      WRITE(Score[Index]:7:2);
   WRITELN;
   WRITE(Tab);
   FOR Index := 1 TO NumberOfClasses DO
      WRITE('-------');
   WRITELN;
```

```
    WRITELN(Tab,'Sum of scores = ', SumOfScores:0:2);
    WRITELN(Tab,'Average of scores = ', Average:0:2);
    WRITELN;
    WRITELN('Press ENTER to continue..');
    READLN
END.
{ ------------------------------------------------------------------- }
```

Sample Run:

```
    Enter score for class #1: 90.5
    Enter score for class #2: 80.5
    Enter score for class #3: 86.2
    Enter score for class #4: 90.3
    Enter score for class #5: 74.8
    Enter score for class #6: 98.5


            CLASS #
              1     2     3     4     5     6
            -----------------------------------------
    SCORES    90.50 80.50 86.20 90.30 74.80 98.50
            -----------------------------------------
            Sum of scores = 520.80
            Average of scores = 86.80
    Press ENTER to continue..
```

In this program extensive use of loops has been made to display the dashed lines, the class numbers, and the scores; this makes the program more generic. For example, the dashed line could be displayed using the statement:

```
    WRITELN('          ----------------------------------------');
```

This is useful only for six classes, but the following statements:

```
    WRITE(Tab);
    FOR Index := 1 TO NumberOfClasses DO
        WRITE('-------');
```

are useful for any number of classes, because a seven-dash segment is displayed for each class. Thus, if you had only four classes, the output would look like this:

```
            CLASS #
              1     2     3     4
            ----------------------------
    SCORES    80.00 90.00 85.00 75.00
            ----------------------------
            Sum of scores = 330.00
            Average of scores = 82.50
```

Notice that the number of dashes is equal to the field width specified in the output format of Score and Index:

```
    WRITE(Index:7);
```

```
WRITE(Score[Index]:7:2);
```

Note also the use of the constant Tab for proper indentation of the output. The control character CHR(9) is used as a value of this constant (See the horizontal tab HT in the Control Characters table in Appendix A). You can also design your own tab by using a literal constant to specify the number of required spaces, for example:

```
Tab = '        ';
```

A weak point of this program is that we have to repeat the same lines of code every time we want to draw a line. Such repetitive tasks can instead be programmed separately as *procedures* and called whenever wanted. This is discussed later in the book.

Drill 5-3

Write a Pascal program to read and store the test scores of five students, then display the output as shown below:

```
Student #          Score
-------------------------
    1              90.00
    2              88.00
    3              91.00
    4              78.00
    5              75.00
-------------------------
Average score = 84.40
```

Application: Prime Numbers—Version 2

In Chapter 4, you wrote the prime numbers program using a GOTO statement, which is not a good programming technique. In this version, you can make use of arrays to store a group of numbers and build a Boolean sieve to filter out all the numbers except the prime ones.

```
{ ------------------------- Example 5-5 ----------------------------- }
PROGRAM PrimeNumbers2(INPUT,OUTPUT);
{This algorithm extracts the prime numbers from a set of integers from 1}
{to NumberOfElements. It starts with an array of TRUE Boolean elements.}
{Then it excludes all the multiples and sets their status to FALSE.}
{Finally, it prints the TRUE elements, which are the prime numbers.}
CONST
    Size = 200;   {The maximum size of the array}
VAR
    Flags         :ARRAY[1..Size] OF BOOLEAN;
    Prime         :INTEGER; {Prime number temporary variable}
    NotPrime      :INTEGER; {Counter for excluded numbers}
    PrimeCount    :INTEGER; {Counter of prime numbers}
```

```
        I                       :INTEGER; {General loop counter}
        NumberOfElements        :INTEGER; {Actual number of elements}
BEGIN
{Read number of elements}
        WRITE('Please enter the number of elements: ');
        READLN(NumberOfElements);
{Initialize variables}
        Prime := 2;                     { First prime }
        NotPrime := Prime * 2;          { First excluded multiple }
        PrimeCount := 0;                { Number of primes }
        I := 1;                         { Array counter }
{Set all the array elements to TRUE}
        WHILE I <= NumberOfElements DO
            BEGIN
                Flags[I] := TRUE;
                I := I +1;
            END;
{The actual algorithm loop}
        WRITELN('Prime numbers from 1 to ', NumberOfElements, ' :');
        WHILE Prime <= NumberOfElements DO
            BEGIN
                {Select only the TRUE elements}
                IF Flags[Prime] = TRUE THEN
                    BEGIN
                        {Start with the first multiple}
                        NotPrime := Prime*2;
                        WHILE NotPrime <= NumberOfElements DO
                            BEGIN
                                {Exclude multiples}
                                Flags[NotPrime] := FALSE;
                                NotPrime := NotPrime + Prime;
                            END;
                        {After the WHILE loop, all the primes are TRUE}
                        PrimeCount := PrimeCount +1;
                        WRITELN(Prime);
                    END;
                {Increment the WHILE counter}
                Prime := Prime + 1;
            END;
        WRITELN('Number of primes = ', PrimeCount);
        WRITELN('Press ENTER to continue..');
        READLN
END.
{ -------------------------------------------------------------------- }
```

Sample Runs:

Run 1:

```
        Please enter the number of elements: 19
        Prime numbers from 1 to 19:
```

```
2
3
5
7
11
13
17
19
Number of primes = 8
Press ENTER to continue...
```

Run 2:

```
Please enter the number of elements: 5
Prime numbers from 1 to 5:
2
3
5
Number of primes = 3
Press ENTER to continue...
```

Declaration of Arrays in the Type Section

It is preferable that array declarations be associated with the TYPE statement, as in this example:

TYPE
AnArray = **ARRAY**[1..6] **OF INTEGER;**
VAR
MyArray :AnArray;

In this case you can declare more than one array of the type AnArray in the VAR section:

VAR
YourArray, MyArray :AnArray;

It is also possible to use a previously declared subrange as an index range for an array, like this:

TYPE
MyRange = 1..6;
AnArray = **ARRAY**[MyRange] **OF INTEGER;**
VAR
MyArray :AnArray;

Although we have started our arrays from the index 1, there is no obligation to do so. The index range can be any valid subrange, but you must always remember not to exceed the defined index range.

Application: *Sorting an Array*

If you would like to sort some numbers (or names), the best way is to store them in an array, then use one of the sorting algorithms. A simple way (but not the most efficient) to sort numbers in an ascending order is known as the *bubble sort*. The algorithm is as follows:

1. Compare the first element to the second one. If the first element is greater, swap them.

2. Repeat the comparison between the first element and each of the rest of the array elements. If it is greater than any element, swap them.

3. By the end of these comparisons the first element will be the smallest in the array.

4. Repeat the previous steps for the second element, the third, and so on until the next-to-last element.

After this process is completed, the array will be sorted in an ascending order. This algorithm is demonstrated in the following program. The comparisons need two nested loops. The outer loop (index I) starts from the first element (I=1) and ends before the last element (I=ArraySize–1). The inner loop (index J) starts one step after the start of the outer loop (J=I+1) and goes all the way to the last element (J=ArraySize).

```pascal
{ --------------------------- Example 5-6 --------------------------- }
PROGRAM Sorting(INPUT,OUTPUT);
CONST
   ArraySize = 6;
TYPE
   Range = 1..ArraySize;
   NumbersArray = ARRAY[Range] OF INTEGER;
VAR
   Numbers    :NumbersArray;
   I, J , Pot :INTEGER;
BEGIN
{ Read the array }
{ -------------- }
   FOR I := 1 TO ArraySize DO
      BEGIN
         WRITE('Enter element #', I,': ');
         READLN(Numbers[I])
      END;
{ Sort the array }
{ -------------- }
   FOR I := 1 TO ArraySize-1 DO            { outer loop }
      BEGIN                                { optional block }
         FOR J := I+1 TO ArraySize DO      { inner loop }
            BEGIN
               IF Numbers[I] > Numbers[J] THEN
                  BEGIN                     { swap contents }
                     Pot := Numbers[J];
```

```
                        Numbers[J] := Numbers[I];
                        Numbers[I] := Pot
                 END
          END                                    { end of inner loop }
      END;                                        { end of outer loop }
{ Display Results }
{ --------------- }
   WRITELN;
   WRITELN('The sorted array is:');
   FOR I := 1 TO ArraySize DO
      WRITELN(Numbers[I]);
   WRITELN('Press ENTER to continue..');
   READLN
END.
{ ----------------------------------------------------------------------- }
```

Sample Run:

```
Enter element #1: 6
Enter element #2: 33
Enter element #3: 4
Enter element #4: 2
Enter element #5: 55
Enter element #6: 9

The sorted array is:
2
4
6
9
33
55
Press ENTER to continue..
```

Swapping the contents of two elements is done by using a third variable (Pot) to hold the contents of one variable temporarily, thus:

```
Pot := Numbers[J];
Numbers[J] := Numbers[I];
Numbers[I] := Pot
```

This process is similar to swapping the contents of two cups, one of which contains coffee and the other tea; all you need is an empty cup (Pot).

To have the array sorted in descending order, simply reverse the greater than process to less than.

In order to sort arrays of different sizes, you can read the number of elements during the execution of the program. To do that, declare a maximum size for the array, for example 100, and the actual size, which must be less than the maximum size. You can then read the actual size by using either one of the following ways:

1. Set a counter that is incremented each time you enter an element from the keyboard. When you finish entering all the array elements, this counter will contain the number of elements.

2. Read the number of elements from the keyboard and use it as a limit for the FOR loop that reads the array elements. The sorting program will be revisited and enhanced in Chapter 12.

Drill 5-4

Modify your program from Drill 5-3 to display the best score and the number of the highest scoring student in the class. The output should look like this:

```
     Student #           Score
     ----------------------------
         1               70.00
         2               88.00
         3               67.00
         4               90.00
         5               86.00
     ----------------------------
     Average score = 80.20
     The best score = 90.00
     The best of the class is student #4
```

You may use the following algorithm to obtain the highest number in the array of scores:

1. Store the score of the first student in a variable such as BestScore, and the index of that student in a variable BestOfClass.

2. Starting from the second element in the array of scores, and continuing all the way to the end, repeat the following comparison:

3. If any number is greater than BestScore, store it in BestScore and store its index in BestOfClass.

4. By the end of the loop, the variable BestScore will contain the highest score, and the corresponding student number will be stored in BestOfClass.

5-6 Multidimensional Arrays

To declare a two-dimensional array, use the form:

VAR
array-name : **ARRAY**[index-range-1, index-range-2] **OF** element-type;

You may also declare it in the type section as follows:

TYPE
> type-name = **ARRAY**[index-range-1, index-range-2] **OF** element-type;

where index-range-1 and index-range-2 are the ranges of the first and second dimensions.

Look at this declaration:

```
TYPE
    Score = ARRAY[1..100, 1..6] OF INTEGER;
```

This statement declares an array Score, which can store the scores of 100 students in six different classes; generally speaking, it can store up to 600 integers. As you can see, each dimension is represented by a subrange.

You can also declare a multidimensional array of any number of dimensions using the general form:

TYPE
> type-name = **ARRAY**[index-range-1, index-range-2,
> ..., index-range-n] **OF** element-type;

In most applications, however, you will not need more than two dimensions.

Application: Scores of Students

The following program is used to read the scores of a number of students in different classes as represented in Table 5-2. For simplicity of demonstration, only four students and three classes will be considered; you can, however, modify the number of students or classes by simply changing the values of the two constants NumberOfClasses and NumberOfStudents.

```
{ -------------------------- Example 5-7 -------------------------- }
PROGRAM Scores3(INPUT,OUTPUT);
{ using two-dimensional array }
CONST
    NumberOfClasses = 3;            { Change this number for more classes }
    NumberOfStudents = 4;           { Change this number for more students }
    Tab = '       ';                { 7 spaces }
    Dash = '-';
    NumberOfDashes = 23;
TYPE
    ScoreArray = ARRAY[1..NumberOfStudents, 1..NumberOfClasses] OF REAL;
    AverageArray = ARRAY[1..NumberOfStudents] OF REAL;
VAR
    Score                                   :ScoreArray;
    Average                                 :AverageArray;
    SumOfScores                             :REAL;
    StudentCount, ScoreCount, DashCount     :INTEGER;
BEGIN
{ Read the scores array }
```

```
{ -------------------- }
    FOR StudentCount := 1 TO NumberOfStudents DO
        BEGIN
            WRITELN;
            WRITELN('Scores of student #', StudentCount,': ');
            FOR ScoreCount := 1 TO NumberOfClasses DO
                BEGIN
                    WRITE('Enter score for class #', ScoreCount,': ');
                    READLN(Score[StudentCount, ScoreCount])
                END;
        END;
{ Calculate the average for each student }
{ ------------------------------------- }
    FOR StudentCount := 1 TO NumberOfStudents DO
        BEGIN
            SumOfScores := 0;  { Initialize for each student }
            FOR ScoreCount := 1 TO NumberOfClasses DO
                SumOfScores := SumOfScores + Score[StudentCount, ScoreCount];
            Average[StudentCount] := SumOfScores/NumberOfClasses
        END;
{ Display results }
{ --------------- }
    WRITELN;
    WRITELN(Tab, 'Student #', Tab, 'Average');
    WRITE(Tab);
    FOR DashCount := 1 TO NumberOfDashes DO
        WRITE(Dash);
    WRITELN;
    FOR StudentCount := 1 TO NumberOfStudents DO
        WRITELN(Tab, StudentCount:3, Tab, Average[StudentCount]:12:2);
    WRITE(Tab);
    FOR DashCount := 1 TO NumberOfDashes DO
        WRITE(Dash);
    WRITELN;
    WRITELN('Press ENTER to continue..');
    READLN
END.
{ ---------------------------------------------------------------------- }
```

Sample Run:

```
    Scores of student #1:

    Enter score for class #1: 90
    Enter score for class #2: 89
    Enter score for class #3: 93

    Scores of student #2:

    Enter score for class #1: 80
    Enter score for class #2: 70
```

```
Enter score for class #3: 60

Scores of student #3:

Enter score for class #1: 77
Enter score for class #2: 78
Enter score for class #3: 90

Scores of student #4:

Enter score for class #1: 91
Enter score for class #2: 94
Enter score for class #3: 95

          Student #        Average
          ----------------------
             1              90.67
             2              70.00
             3              81.67
             4              93.33
          ----------------------
Press ENTER to continue..
```

Notice the following in this program:

1. Two types of arrays were declared in the TYPE section, a two-dimensional array ScoreArray and a one-dimensional array AverageArray. These type identifiers are used in the VAR section to declare the two arrays Score and Average. The first array is used to store the scores of the four students in three classes, while the second is used to hold the averages of the four students (which are, of course, only four values).

2. Data are read through two loops, using the index StudentCount as a counter of students in the outer loop and ScoreCount as a counter of scores in the inner loop. Each value read from the keyboard is assigned to the general array variable:

    ```
    Score[StudentCount, ScoreCount]
    ```

    The exact location of the array element is determined by the two indexes StudentCount and ScoreCount.

3. The average of scores is calculated for each student and stored in the array variable:

    ```
    Average[StudentCount]
    ```

    The index StudentCount indicates which student has each average.

4. Notice the initialization of the variable SumOfScores before the average calculation. This is a very important step because if it is not done, the average of the previous student will remain in the variable and be added to the new average.

Array Initialization

If you are assigning values to only some of the elements of an uninitialized array, do not expect that the rest of the elements will contain zeros. In such applications you have to initialize the whole array using a loop like this:

```
FOR I := 1 TO N DO
    MyArray[I] := 0;
```

You need another loop if the array is two-dimensional:

```
FOR I := 1 TO N DO
    FOR J := 1 TO M DO
        MyArray[I,J] := 0;
```

In the last example, we assigned values to each element of the array, so there was no need for initialization.

Drill 5-5

Modify the last program to display the students' names in descending order according to their scores, as in this example:

```
Student name        Average
-------------------------
Porter, Thomas      84.00
Dalton, Jack        83.33
Dixon, Jane         83.33
Bobbin, Dale        66.67
-------------------------
```

Summary

In this chapter you have had an overview of all Pascal data types.

1. You know that types are either predefined or user-defined. You also know that data types are either simple or structured.

2. You now know that simple data types are classified as either real or ordinal types. Of the ordinal types, you learned how to use the user-defined types, enumerations, and subranges.

3. You learned how to use the TYPE statement to declare a new type or rename a predefined type. It takes the general form:

TYPE
type-name = type-definition;

In standard Pascal the relative sequence of the TYPE section among the other sections in the declaration part is as follows:

LABEL section
CONST section
TYPE section
VAR section

4. You learned about the array as a predefined structured data type that may be declared either in the TYPE section or VAR section. You also learned how to declare and use both one- and two-dimensional arrays. The general form to declare an array of any number of dimensions (in the TYPE section) is:

TYPE
type-name = **ARRAY**[index-range-1, index-range-2,
        ..., index-range-n] **OF** element-type;

Exercises

1. Determine whether or not the following TYPE section declarations are valid:

```
TYPE
      {a}  Size  = 1..100 DIV 2;
      {b}  Size1 = 1..200;
      {c}  Size2 = 1..100/2;
      {d}  Color = (Red, Green, Blue);
      {e}  int   = INTEGER;
```

2. Using the correct declarations in question #1, determine whether or not the following VAR section declarations are valid:

```
VAR
{a} MyArray     :ARRAY[Size] OF INTEGER;
{b} HisArray    :ARRAY[1..Size] OF INTEGER;
{c} YourArray   :ARRAY[Color] OF int;
{d} HerArray    :ARRAY[1..Color] OF INTEGER;
{e} Score       :ARRAY[1..5, Size] of REAL;
{f} I           :int;
{g} Colors      :(Red, Green, Blue);
{h} ColorsComp  :(Cyan, Magenta, Yellow);
{i} Subrange1   :1..12 DIV 2;
{j} Subrange2   :1..7;
```

3. Using the correct declarations in questions #1 and #2, determine whether or not the following statements are valid:

```
{a} FOR I := 1 TO 5 DO
        BEGIN
            MyArray[I]:= I;
            WRITE(MyArray[I]);
        END;
    WRITELN;
```

```
{b} FOR I := 0 TO 2 DO
        WRITE(YourArray[color]);
{c} FOR I:= Red TO Blue DO
        WRITE(YourArray[I]);
{d} ColorsComp := Yellow;
{e} ColorsComp := Cyan + 1;
{f} WRITELN(ORD(Cyan), ' ', ORD(Yellow));
{g} WRITELN(Cyan);
```

4. If you have the following declaration in your program:

```
VAR
        Day :(Mon, Tue, Wed, Thu, Fri, Sat, Sun);
```

determine whether or not the following CASE statement is valid:

```
CASE Day OF
        Mon..Fri:
                WRITELN('Working Day.');
        Sat..Sun:
                WRITELN('Weekend Day.');
        END;
```

Answers

1. The only invalid declaration is c.

2. Invalid declarations are b, d, and g.

3. Invalid statements are b, c, e, and g.

4. Valid—the case selector can be of any ordinal type.

Chapter 6

Working with Text

Chapter Topics:

- **Understanding the standard input and output files: the keyboard and the screen**
- **Using the input and output statements with numbers, strings, characters, and mixed types of data**
- **Reading and manipulating text files using the Boolean functions: EOLN and EOF**
- **Sorting strings**
- **The string functions: LENGTH, CONCAT, COPY, and POS**
- **The string procedures: INSERT and DELETE**

6-1 Standard Input and Output Files

In this chapter, you learn to use characters and strings to manipulate text data, paying special attention to input and output of characters and strings using the keyboard and the screen. These devices are treated as files; they are referred to as the standard INPUT file (the keyboard), and the standard OUTPUT file (the screen).

6-2 Tips on Output Statements

If you would like to display many lines of text, or display numeric results on separate lines, you can use as many WRITELN statements as the number of required lines. Another way to do this (one requiring less effort) is to use the ASCII control codes 13 (carriage return) and 10 (line feed) whenever a new line is required. You can then use one WRITE or WRITELN statement to print all of the results. With most microcomputer systems the carriage return/line feed pair is interpreted as the *end-of-line mark*. In the following example the control character CHR(10) is declared as a named constant LF (a common abbreviation for Line Feed), and the control character CHR(13) as CR (a common abbreviation for Carriage Return). The combination of the two characters CR and LF gives the same effect as pressing Enter.

```
{ --------------------------- Example 6-1 --------------------------- }
PROGRAM Display1(INPUT,OUTPUT);
CONST
   LF = CHR(10);
   CR = CHR(13);
VAR
   X, Y, Z :INTEGER;
BEGIN
   WRITE('Enter three integers: ');
   READLN(X, Y, Z);
   WRITELN('X=', X, CR, LF, 'Y=', Y, CR, LF, 'Z=', Z)
END.
{ ------------------------------------------------------------------- }
```

Sample Run:

```
Enter three integers: 11 22 33
X=11
Y=22
Z=33
```

If you tried this program using the LF only, you would get the following output:

```
X=11
    Y=22
        Z=33
```

Try it now using the CR only, and you will find that the last result overwrites the first two. The output will be only one line like this:

```
Z=33
```

6-3 Tips on Input Statements

When you use the input statements READ or READLN some pitfalls can occur during successive reads, especially with character input. For this reason it is important to understand how the input statements work with different types of data.

When a READ or a READLN statement is executed, values are stored in the standard INPUT file (the keyboard). The stored values are then read from this file and assigned to the variables specified in the input list. Each time you press the Enter key, an end-of-line mark is written to the INPUT file.

Using READLN for Numeric Input

Assume that your input contains the following numbers:

```
123 45 678          <Enter>
```

You may imagine that the numbers are stored in the INPUT file as in the following figure:

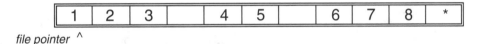

file pointer ^

The end-of-line mark is shown at the last location and is indicated by the asterisk (*). At the first location, there is a little arrow (called the file pointer) pointing to the beginning of the file. Consider now that these values are read by the following statement:

```
READLN(X, Y, Z);
```

After the first integer (123) is read and assigned to the variable X, the pointer moves to the space before the second numeric value (45). The second value is then read and assigned to the variable Y, and the pointer moves to the space before the third value. When the third value is read and assigned to Z, all of the variables will have been assigned values, and the pointer moves past the end-of-line mark, where the work of the READLN statement ends. If you leave more than one space between numeric values, the extra spaces will be ignored and you will still get correct results.

Suppose now that you entered a fourth value by mistake :

```
123 45 678 90        <Enter>
```

The last value (90) will be ignored by the program, as the pointer will move past the end-of-line mark after the three values are read, in order to be ready for a subsequent read.

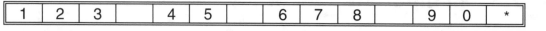

| 1 | 2 | 3 | | 4 | 5 | | 6 | 7 | 8 | | 9 | 0 | * |

file pointer ^

Note: This feature of the READLN statement is inherited from the old days when data were read from *punched cards* (each card represents a line of data). The READLN was used to read only a specific number of items and eject to the next card.

You may also enter your numeric values separated by the Enter key, in which case each numeric value will be followed by the end-of-line mark like this:

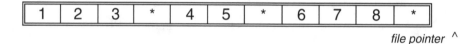

| 1 | 2 | 3 | * | 4 | 5 | * | 6 | 7 | 8 | * |

file pointer ^

As long as the three variables have not yet been assigned values, the end-of-line marks between the values are treated as spaces and are thus ignored. The pointer moves from one end-of-line mark to another until all of the values have been read, then the pointer moves past the end of the next end-of-line mark, ending the READLN statement. Try the following program (which contains two READLN statements) using the values shown in the sample runs.

```
{ --------------------------- Example 6-2 --------------------------- }
PROGRAM ReadLnNumbers(INPUT,OUTPUT);
CONST
    CR = CHR(13);
    LF = CHR(10);
VAR
    A, C , D, E :INTEGER;
    B              :REAL;
BEGIN
    WRITE('Enter A, B, C: ');
{ If you enter more than three values, only the first three will be read }
    READLN(A, B, C);
{ Now a subsequent READLN will start to read values after the end-of-line
  mark, ignoring any leftovers from the previous read }
    WRITE('Enter D, E: ');
    READLN(D, E);
    WRITELN('A=',A,', B=',B:0:2,', C=', C, CR, LF,
            'D=', D,', E= ',E)
END.
{ ----------------------------------------------------------------- }
```

Sample Run:

```
Enter A, B, C: 1 2 3 4 5 6      → Enter these values
Enter D, E: 7 8                 → Enter these values
A=1, B=2.00, C=3                → The program response
D=7, E= 8
```

Notice that the extra values (4, 5, 6) in the first input line were ignored completely and the second read started from the value 7, which follows the end-of-line mark.

Drill 6-1

Try the last program using the following inputs and study the results:

```
1 2                 <Enter>
3 4 5 6             <Enter>
7 8                 <Enter>
```

Using READ for Numeric Input

With the READ statement the reading procedure is different, because after the READ statement is done, the file pointer does not move past the end-of-line mark, and so any subsequent READ will start from where the previous READ left off. Replace the READLN statements in the previous program with READ statements and try the following input:

```
1 2 3 4 5 6 7          <Enter>
```

When you press Enter, the program will not pause at the second input statement because the input file contains sufficient numeric values for five variables. In this case, the program displays the following results:

```
A=1, B=2.00, C=3
D=4, E= 5
```

Drill 6-2

Using the last program with the READ statement, try the following inputs:

1.
```
1 2                 <Enter>
3 4 5 6 7           <Enter>
```
2.
```
1 2 3 4             <Enter>
5 6 7               <Enter>
```

Using READ for Character Input

With character input, the input statements work in a different way. The READ statement reads successive characters from the keyboard file, including the end-of-line mark (which is actually two characters CR and LF), and assigns each character to the next variable in the input list. Consider the following input statement:

```
READ(C1, C2, C3, C4);
```

where C1, C2, C3, and C4 are variables of the type CHAR.

If you enter the four characters that follow:

```
ABCD
```

they will all be read and assigned to the variables, thus:

C1 contains 'A'
C2 contains 'B'
C3 contains 'C'
C4 contains 'D'

Now consider the case of an input like this:

```
A B C D
```

The first four characters (including blank spaces) in this input will be assigned to the four variables and the rest ignored, giving the following result:

C1 contains 'A'
C2 contains ' '   (blank space)
C3 contains 'B'
C4 contains ' '   (blank space)

Run the following program and use the sample run values to see how things work. Notice that the output of the program gives you both the variables' contents and the corresponding ASCII codes, which will help you to recognize any nonprintable character such as the space, the line feed, or the carriage return.

```
{ ---------------------------- Example 6-3 ---------------------------- }
PROGRAM CharRead1(INPUT,OUTPUT);
CONST
   LF = CHR(10);
   CR = CHR(13);
VAR
   C1, C2, C3, C4 :CHAR;
BEGIN
   WRITE('Enter four characters: ');
   READ(C1, C2, C3, C4);
   WRITELN('Your inputs have been assigned to the variables as follows:',
           CR, LF,
               'C1= ', C1, CR, LF,
               'C2= ', C2, CR, LF,
```

```
              'C3= ', C3, CR, LF,
              'C4= ', C4);
   WRITELN('The corresponding ASCII codes are:', CR, LF,
              ORD(C1),' ', ORD(C2),' ', ORD(C3),' ',ORD(C4))
END.
{ ------------------------------------------------------------------- }
```

Sample Runs:

Run 1:

```
Enter four characters: A BCD
Your inputs have been assigned to the variables as follows:
C1= A
C2=          blank space
C3= B
C4= C
The corresponding ASCII codes are:
65 32 66 67
```

The second variable was here assigned the ASCII code 32, which is the code of the blank space.

Run 2:

```
Enter four characters: ABCDEFG
Your inputs are assigned to the variables as follows:
C1= A
C2= B
C3= C
C4= D
The corresponding ASCII codes are:
65 66 67 68
```

In the second case, the first four characters are read and the rest are ignored. If there were a subsequent READ statement in the program, it would start at the letter E.

The end-of-line mark is treated like any other nonnumeric character. For example, if you test the program using these inputs:

```
AB          <Enter>
CD          <Enter>
```

the program will terminate after entering the first two characters and you will get an output like this:

Run 3:

```
C1= A
C2= B
C3=          { CR }
C4=          { LF }
The corresponding ASCII codes are:
```

```
65 66 13 10
```

The third and the fourth characters contain CR and LF respectively, because when you press Enter, you send two characters to the INPUT file, CR and LF. Notice that the CR appears as a blank space (actually, it returns the cursor to the beginning of the line), while the LF advances to a new line.

The same thing will happen if you use two separate READ statements. To see this, replace the READ statement in the program by two READ statements:

```
READ(C1, C2);
READ(C3, C4);
```

When you run the program now, you will notice that if you type the first two characters and press Enter, the program will be terminated and you get the same output as in Run 3.

Also, if you enter more characters than are required, only the first four will be read.

Using READLN for Character Input

If you would like to enter your characters like this:

```
AB          <Enter>
CD          <Enter>
```

you have to get rid of the extra characters remaining in the file (the CR and the LF) by using the READLN statement.

In the following program two READLN statements are used, so you are able to enter two characters (or more) followed by Enter and start the next read with a clean buffer.

```
{ --------------------------- Example 6-4 --------------------------- }
PROGRAM CharReadln3(INPUT,OUTPUT);
CONST
   LF = CHR(10);
   CR = CHR(13);
VAR
   C1, C2, C3, C4 :CHAR;
BEGIN
   WRITE('Enter two characters: ');
   READLN(C1, C2);
   WRITE('Enter two characters: ');
   READLN(C3, C4);
   WRITELN('Your inputs have been assigned to the variables as follows:',
        CR, LF,
             'C1= ', C1, CR, LF,
             'C2= ', C2, CR, LF,
             'C3= ', C3, CR, LF,
             'C4= ', C4);
   WRITELN('The corresponding ASCII codes are:',
        CR, LF, ORD(C1),' ', ORD(C2),' ', ORD(C3),' ',ORD(C4))
```

```
END.
{ ---------------------------------------------------------------------- }
```

Sample Run:

```
Enter two characters: abcd                      <Enter>
Enter two characters: efgh                      <Enter>
Your inputs have been assigned to the variables as follows:
C1= a
C2= b
C3= e
C4= f
The corresponding ASCII codes are:
97 98 101 102
```

Reading Mixed Types

It is legal to use one READ (or READLN) statement for mixed numeric and character data, but this requires extra attention. It is better to use a separate READLN statement for each type, as in the following program. This way is less prone to data entry errors.

```
{ --------------------------- Example 6-5 ---------------------------- }
PROGRAM CharNumRead(INPUT,OUTPUT);
CONST
   LF = CHR(10);
   CR = CHR(13);
VAR
   A, B       :CHAR;
   X, Y       :INTEGER;
BEGIN
   WRITE('Enter two characters: ');
   READLN(A, B);
   WRITE('Enter two integers: ');
   READLN(X, Y);
   WRITELN('Your inputs have been assigned to the variables as follows:',
           CR, LF,
              'A= ', A, CR, LF,
              'B= ', B, CR, LF,
              'X= ', X, CR, LF,
              'Y= ', Y)
END.
{ ---------------------------------------------------------------------- }
```

Sample Runs:

Run 1:

```
Enter two characters: ABCD
Enter two integers: 3 4
Your inputs have been assigned to the variables as follows:
```

```
A= A
B= B
X= 3
Y= 4
```

As you can see in the output, the extra characters (C and D) were skipped after the first READLN. Remember, however, that the rules of character entry still apply; in other words, if you press Enter after the first letter, a CR will be assigned to the variable B. Here is the sample run:

Run 2:

```
Enter two characters: A          <Enter>
B                                <Enter>
Enter two integers: 5 6
Your inputs have been assigned to the variables as follows:
A= A
B=                   B is assigned a CR
X= 5
Y= 6
```

Application: Scrambling Letters

The following example is good practice both for handling characters and building loops. The program asks you to enter four characters, then it displays all of the possible combinations of those characters. If you are a Basic programmer, you would have had to use a lot of GOTOs to achieve these results. In Pascal the program is better structured.

```
{ --------------------------- Example 6-6 --------------------------- }
PROGRAM Scrambling(INPUT,OUTPUT);
TYPE
   ScrambleArray = Array[1..4] OF CHAR;
VAR
   A                :ScrambleArray;
   I1, I2, I3, I4 :INTEGER;
BEGIN
   WRITE('Enter four letters: ');
   READ(A[1], A[2], A[3], A[4]);
   FOR I1 := 1 TO 4 DO
      BEGIN
         FOR I2 := 1 TO 4 DO
            BEGIN
               IF I2 <> I1 THEN
                  FOR I3 := 1 TO 4 DO
                     BEGIN
                        IF I3 <> I1 THEN
                           IF I3 <> I2 THEN
                              BEGIN
                                 I4 := 10 - (I1 + I2 + I3);
```

```
                        WRITELN(A[I1],' ',A[I2],' ',
                               A[I3],' ',A[I4]);
                    END       { End of IF }
                END         { End of I3 loop }
            END      { End of I2 loop }
        END      { End of I1 loop }
END.
{ -------------------------------------------------------------------- }
```

Sample Run:

```
Enter four letters: ABCD
A B C D
A B D C
A C B D
A C D B
A D B C
A D C B
B A C D
B A D C
B C A D
B C D A
B D A C
B D C A
C A B D
C A D B
C B A D
C B D A
C D A B
C D B A
D A B C
D A C B
D B A C
D B C A
D C A B
D C B A
```

An array A of four elements (of the type CHAR) is used to hold the four characters, and three nested loops are used to build the different combinations of the elements. The algorithm is based on choosing four different indexes corresponding to the four different array elements.

Note that all of the BEGIN-END blocks (except the innermost one) are optional and are used only for clarity.

6-4 Reading a Line of Text: EOLN

The EOLN function is a Boolean function used to detect the end of the line during reading of the INPUT file. The function is FALSE until the end-of-line mark is detected, then it becomes TRUE.

This function is useful when you do not know the number of characters to expect.

In order to read a line of text up to (but not including) the end-of-line mark, you can use a loop like this:

```
WHILE NOT EOLN DO
    BEGIN
        READ(Ch);
        ...
    END;
```

The READ statement will continue to read characters until the end-of-line mark is detected, thus terminating the WHILE loop. Notice, however, that the end-of-line mark is still in the buffer and could be read by any subsequent READ statement, so before any subsequent READ you have to clean the buffer with a READLN.

Application: Character Counter

The following program reads a line of text from the keyboard and displays the number of characters in the line. The program will continue to read the characters you type until you press Enter, at which time it displays the result.

```
{ --------------------------- Example 6-7 --------------------------- }
PROGRAM CharCounter1(INPUT,OUTPUT);
VAR
    Ch      :CHAR;
    Counter :INTEGER;
BEGIN
    Counter := 0;
    WHILE NOT EOLN DO
        BEGIN
            READ(Ch);
            Counter := Counter + 1
        END;
    WRITELN;
    WRITELN('Number of characters= ', Counter)
END.
{ ----------------------------------------------------------------- }
```

Drill 6-3

Modify the previous program to count only the alphabetic characters in the text.

6-5 Reading a File of Text: EOF

Another Boolean function, EOF, is used to detect the *end-of-file* mark. The function is FALSE until the end-of-file mark is reached, at which time it becomes TRUE. When using the keyboard for input, the end of file is reached if you press Ctrl+Z (ASCII 26). This function is useful for reading several lines of text (a file). You can use EOF along with EOLN to read and analyze several lines of text as follows:

```
WHILE NOT EOF DO
    BEGIN
        WHILE NOT EOLN DO
            BEGIN
                READ(Ch);
                ...                 { Processing data }
            END;                    { End of line }
        READLN                      { Advance the pointer }
    END;                            { End of file }
```

In this code, the file is read line by line. After a complete line has been read, the EOLN function becomes TRUE and no more characters are read from this line. The READLN statement is then used to advance the pointer to the beginning of the next line. The program ends when the end-of-file mark is detected and the outer loop is terminated. Let us see an example.

Application: Frequency Counter

The following program asks you to enter a letter. Then it starts reading whatever you type from the keyboard. When you press Ctrl+Z the program ends and displays how many times the specified letter was repeated in the file.

```
{ ------------------------- Example 6-8 ----------------------------- }
PROGRAM FreqCounter1(INPUT,OUTPUT);
VAR
    Ch, SpecificChar        :CHAR;
    Counter, FreqCounter    :INTEGER;
BEGIN
    Counter := 0;
    FreqCounter := 0;
    WRITE('Enter the required letter: ');
    READLN(SpecificChar);
    WRITELN('Start typing. Press Ctrl+Z to finish.');
    WHILE NOT EOF DO
        BEGIN
            WHILE NOT EOLN DO
                BEGIN
                    READ(Ch);
                    IF (Ch >= 'A') AND (Ch <= 'Z') OR
                        (Ch >= 'a') AND (Ch <= 'z') THEN
```

```
                    Counter := Counter + 1;
                IF Ch = SpecificChar THEN
                    FreqCounter := FreqCounter + 1;
             END;
          READLN
      END;
   WRITELN('Total number of letters= ', Counter);
   WRITELN('The letter ''', SpecificChar, ''' was repeated ',
           FreqCounter, ' time(s)');
   WRITELN('Frequency of repetition= ', FreqCounter/Counter*100:2:2,'%')
END.
{ ------------------------------------------------------------------- }
```

The specific letter is assigned to the variable SpecificChar and compared to the input letter Ch. If the comparison is TRUE, the FreqCounter is incremented by one. The total number of letters is accumulated in the variable Counter. The frequency of repetition of the letter is calculated by dividing FreqCounter by Counter and multiplying the result by 100.

Sample Run:

```
Enter the required character: a
Start typing. Press Ctrl+Z to finish.
This is a test to count the repetition frequency
of the letter "a" in a keyboard file
^Z

Total number of letters= 67
The letter 'a' was repeated 4 time(s)
Frequency of repetition= 5.97%
```

6-6 String Manipulation

In Chapter 2, you learned how to declare, read, and write variables of the type STRING, which was introduced by the modern Pascal implementations (such as Turbo, UCSD, and Macintosh). You also learned how to use the function LENGTH to count the number of letters in a string. In this section you are introduced to more string features that help in manipulating text.

Tips on String Input/Output

For both input and output, you may either treat a string variable as one unit, or you may treat it as an array whose elements are the characters that make up the string. Look at this simple program, which reads a string variable and displays it character by character, with each character on a separate line (using the LF character).

```
{ --------------------------- Example 6-9 --------------------------- }
PROGRAM String1(INPUT,OUTPUT);
CONST
   LF = CHR(10);
VAR
   Name :STRING[30];
   I    :INTEGER;
BEGIN
   WRITE('Please enter a name: ');
   READLN(Name);
   FOR I := 1 TO LENGTH(Name) DO
      WRITE(Name[I],LF)
END.
{ ------------------------------------------------------------------- }
```

Sample Run:

```
Please enter a name: PASCAL
P
 A
  S
   C
    A
     L
```

Application: Sorting Names

You may build an array of the type STRING to store related items such as names or addresses. In this way, you can sort names in alphabetical order using the same algorithm which you have used before to sort numbers. Each two strings are compared character by character. So, the following expressions are TRUE:

```
'Able' < 'Baker'
'Baker' < 'Charlie'
'Charley' < 'Charlie'
```

All uppercase letters are greater than lowercase letters. Also, the leading and trailing spaces are included in the comparison. The ASCII code of the blank space (32) is less than that of any letter or digit. In the following program an array of four names is read, sorted, and displayed.

```
{ --------------------------- Example 6-10 --------------------------- }
PROGRAM SortStrings(INPUT,OUTPUT);
CONST
   Tab = '            ';
   NumOfElements = 4;
TYPE
   StringArray = ARRAY[1..NumOfElements] OF STRING[30];
```

```
VAR
   Name      :StringArray;
   I, J      :INTEGER;
   Temp      :STRING[30];
BEGIN
{ Read the array elements }
{ ---------------------- }
   FOR I := 1 TO NumOfElements DO
      BEGIN
         WRITE('Please enter name #', I, ': ');
         READLN(Name[I])
      END;
{ Sort names }
{ ---------- }
   FOR I := 1 TO NumOfElements-1 DO
      FOR J := I+1 TO NumOfElements DO
         IF Name[I] > Name[J] THEN
            BEGIN
               Temp := Name[I];
               Name[I] := Name[J];
               Name[J] := Temp
            END;
      { End of inner and outer loops }
{ Display sorted names }
{ -------------------- }
   WRITELN('Serial #    Name');
   WRITELN('----------------------------');
   FOR I := 1 TO NumOfElements DO
      WRITELN(I:2, Tab, Name[I])
END.
{ ---------------------------------------------------------------------- }
```

Sample Run:

```
Please enter name #1: Laurence Smith
Please enter name #2: Clara Bui
Please enter name #3: Brian Welcker
Please enter name #4: Craig Combel

Serial #  Name
------------------------------
   1        Brian Welcker
   2        Clara Bui
   3        Craig Combel
   4        Laurence Smith
```

Drill 6-4

Write a program to scramble three strings. The following is an example of the output for the strings "WHO," "ARE," and "YOU":

```
WHO ARE YOU
WHO YOU ARE
ARE WHO YOU
ARE YOU WHO
YOU WHO ARE
YOU ARE WHO
```

6-7 String Functions and Procedures

When working with text editors, you sometimes need to cut and paste, delete a part from here, and insert a part there. The tools that make these operations possible are included in the modern implementations of Pascal to help the programmer process strings. Some of them are called functions because they return a value which replaces the function call (e.g., LENGTH). Others are called procedures, as they perform specific operations that do not necessarily return a value (e.g., WRITELN). They are all shown in Table 6-1.

In addition to these tools you may find more functions, procedures, or operators in a specific implementation, but here we are concerned only with the most common tools, which are almost standardized.

Table 6-1: String functions and procedures

Form	Use
Functions:	
LENGTH(str)	Returns the number of character in the string str.
CONCAT(str1, str2,...)	Returns the string formed by concatenating str1, str2,...
COPY(str, pos, len)	Returns a substring from the string str, starting at the position pos, with length len.
POS(str1, str2)	Returns the position of the first occurrence of the first character of str1 within str2.If str1 does not occur within str2 it returns zero.
Procedures:	
INSERT(str1, str2, pos)	Inserts the string str1 into the string str2, at the position pos.
DELETE(str, pos, len)	Deletes a substring from a string str starting from position pos with length len.

LENGTH

You can measure the dynamic length of a string using the function LENGTH. If you want, for instance, to measure the length of the string Name in the last program, you may use the expression:

```
LENGTH(Name)
```

If you display the value of this expression, you get the exact number of characters contained in the string variable, including the spaces. If the string variable is empty, the dynamic length is zero.

CONCAT

As an example of using the function CONCAT, you can concatenate the three strings 'John ', 'M.', and 'Smith' and assign the result to a string variable Name, as follows:

```
Name := CONCAT('John ','M. ','Smith');
```

Now the variable Name contains the complete name: John M. Smith. In Turbo Pascal the operator + may also be used to concatenate strings:

```
Name := 'John '+ 'M. '+ 'Smith';
```

The variable Name has the same contents as before.

COPY

Using the function COPY you can do the opposite, i.e., extract a substring from the string Name. The following statement extracts the first name from the string Name and assigns it to the variable FirstName:

```
FirstName := COPY(Name, 1, 4);
```

As you can see, you have to include the starting position of the extracted substring (1 in this case) and the length of the substring (4 in this case).

POS

The function POS returns an integer that indicates the position of the first occurrence of a substring in a string. For example, the statements:

```
Str1 := 'This is a test';
WRITELN(POS('is', Str1));
```

result in displaying the number 3, which is the position of the letter i in This.

INSERT

You can insert the substring that you deleted in the right place again. Use the INSERT procedure to put the last name Smith back in the string:

```
      INSERT('Smith', Name, 9)
```

Now the variable Name contains 'John M. Smith'.

DELETE

To delete the substring 'Smith' from a name string, use the DELETE procedure as follows:

```
      DELETE(Name, 9, 5);
```

Note that the substring 'Smith' starts at the ninth position and contains five characters.

Using a procedure changes the value of the original variable Name, while using a function does not. If you checked the contents of the variable now, it would be 'John M.'

The following program demonstrates the use of string functions. It accepts from you the first, middle, and last name and produces the complete name, including the trailing spaces. Also, the middle name is converted to an initial.

```
{ --------------------------- Example 6-11 --------------------------- }
PROGRAM StringFunctions1(INPUT,OUTPUT);
VAR
   Name                 :STRING[30];
   First, Middle, Last  :STRING[10];
BEGIN
   WRITE('Please enter your first name: ');
   READLN(First);
   First := CONCAT(First, ' ');
   WRITE('Please enter your middle name: ');
   READLN(Middle);
   Middle := COPY(Middle, 1, 1);
   Middle := CONCAT(Middle, '. ');
   WRITE('Please enter your last name: ');
   READLN(Last);
   Name := CONCAT(First, Middle, Last);
   WRITELN;
   WRITELN('Your complete name is: ',Name)
END.
{ ------------------------------------------------------------------ }
```

Sample Run:

```
      Please enter your first name: Sally
      Please enter your middle name: Ann
      Please enter your last name: Abolrous

      Your complete name is: Sally A. Abolrous
```

Drill 6-5

Modify the last program to make it capitalize the first letter of each name if lowercase.

Summary

In this chapter you learned how the input statements READ and READLN work with numeric values and characters. You also learned how to use the end-of-line function EOLN to read a line of text from the keyboard, and the end-of-file function EOF to read a file of text. You also learned some of the important string-processing functions and procedures which are available in the modern implementations of Pascal.

- LENGTH
- CONCAT
- COPY
- POS
- INSERT
- DELETE

Most importantly, through the examples and drills you gained experience in text processing with both strings and individual characters.

Exercises

1. Write a program to read a line of text and display it backwards. The following is a sample run of the required program:

   ```
   Please enter a name: Camelia Solomon
   The reversed name is:
   nomoloS ailemaC
   ```

2. Write a program to read a line of text, or a text file, and reverse the case of each letter. Thus all the uppercase letters are changed to lowercase letters and vice versa. The following is a sample run of the required program:

   ```
   Please enter a name: Mr. John Martin Smith
   The reversed name is:
   mR. jOHN mARTIN sMITH
   ```

3. Write a program to encode a text string such that each character is replaced by its successor. Also write the decoding program that converts to the original text before encoding. The following is a sample run of the required program:

   ```
   Please enter a string: THIS TEXT IS CODED
   The coded string is:
   UIJT!UFYU!JT!DPEFE
   ```

You can enhance the program by encoding the space and the letter Z separately in order to avoid using the non-alphabetic characters in the encoded string. For example, you can encode the letter Z as A. You can also keep the space character unchanged. This is a sample run of the enhanced program:

```
Please enter a string: This is a secret message
The coded string is:
Uijt jt b tfdsfu nfttbhf
```

Answers

1. You may use the following code segment, which represents the main algorithm, in your program:

```
READLN(Name);
WRITELN('The reversed name is:');
FOR I := LENGTH(Name) DOWNTO 1 DO
    WRITE(Name[I])
```

2. You may use the following code segment in your program. It represents the main algorithm to replace each lowercase letter in the string Name by an uppercase letter, and vice versa:

```
FOR I := 1 TO LENGTH(Name) DO
    BEGIN
        UpperCase := (ORD(Name[I]) > 64) AND (ORD(Name[I]) < 91);
        LowerCase := (ORD(Name[I]) > 96) AND (ORD(Name[I]) < 123);
        IF UpperCase THEN
            Name[I] := CHR(ORD(Name[I])+32)
        ELSE IF LowerCase THEN
            Name[I] := CHR(ORD(Name[I])-32);
        WRITE(Name[I])
    END;
```

3. In the following code segment, each character of the string Name is replaced by its successor:

```
FOR I := 1 TO LENGTH(Name) DO
    BEGIN
        Name[I] := SUCC(Name[I]);
        WRITE(Name[I])
    END;
```

Chapter 7

Procedures and Functions

- **An overview of the program architecture: programs and subprograms**
- **Defining and calling procedures and functions**
- **The scope of variables in the program and its subprograms**
- **Using actual and formal parameters**
- **Changing parameter values passed to procedures**
- **Understanding recursion and recursive subprograms**
- **Applications on using subprograms**

7-1 Programs and Subprograms

When you deal with real applications the problems get more complex than those you have met so far, so you usually have to break the main problem down into simpler tasks and program each individually in a *subprogram*. The subprograms are then combined together to build up the complete program. If you can break your application down into the smallest possible modules, you will find that many of them are common problems such as sorting names or numbers. This means that you can write some generic subprograms and use them later in different applications. Another advantage of using subprograms is that you can thus avoid the repetition of several statements to print a header or display a menu; you can program such tasks as subprograms and call them whenever needed. In Pascal you can divide your program into smaller subprograms called procedures and functions. Actually, the Pascal language itself is made up of predefined procedures and functions. When the compiler encounters a WRITELN statement in a program, for example, the predefined procedure WRITELN is invoked to perform the required task.

7-2 Procedures

If divided into procedures, the main body of the Scores program from Chapter 5 might look something like this:

```
BEGIN
    ReadScores;
    GetAverage;
    DisplayResults
END.
```

The main program contains only three *calls*, each of them the name of a procedure which performs a specific task. The procedure ReadScores reads the array of the scores, GetAverage calculates the average score, and DisplayResults displays the results. As you can see, a user-defined procedure is called by its name just like any standard procedure.

Before calling a procedure it must be defined in the *subprogram section*, which is the last section of the declaration part. The following is a complete list of all the sections of the declaration part:

LABEL section
CONST section
TYPE section
VAR section
PROCEDUREs and FUNCTIONs section

7-3 Procedure Definition

A procedure definition is very similar to a program definition in that it consists of a header, a declaration part, and statements. Let us begin with a simple procedure to draw a line 20 characters long.

```
{ -------------------------- Example 7-1 ------------------------- }
PROGRAM Procedures1(OUTPUT);
{ ------------ Beginning of Procedure ------------ }
PROCEDURE DrawLine;
CONST
   Dash = '-';
   LineLength = 20;
VAR
   Counter :INTEGER;
BEGIN
   FOR Counter := 1 TO LineLength DO
      WRITE(Dash);
   WRITELN
END;
{ -------------- End of Procedure -------------- }
{ -------------- Main program ---------------- }
BEGIN
   WRITELN;
   DrawLine;
   WRITELN('** THIS IS A TEST **');
   DrawLine
END.
{ --------------------------------------------------------------- }
```

Output:

```
--------------------
** THIS IS A TEST **
--------------------
```

There are no variables or constants in the main program here, so the declaration part contains only the procedure definition. The definition starts with the procedure header:

```
PROCEDURE DrawLine;
```

The header includes the name of the procedure (DrawLine), which must be a valid identifier. Then comes the declaration part:

```
CONST
   Dash = '-';
   LineLength = 20;
VAR
   Counter :INTEGER;
```

The declaration part of the procedure includes the same sections as that of the main program. In our example, two named constants and a variable were declared. Then come the statements of the procedure which represent the task to be done (drawing a line), enclosed in a block.

```
BEGIN
   FOR Counter := 1 TO LineLength DO
```

```
        WRITE(Dash);
    WRITELN
END;
```

Notice that the END statement in a subprogram is terminated by a semicolon rather than a period. In the main program, the procedure is called twice to draw a line both before and after the displayed text.

Passing Parameters to Procedures

The procedure DrawLine is used to draw a line of a specific length (20), which may not be useful for any other application. In the following program the procedure is modified to draw a line whose length varies according to the length of the displayed text. When you run the program it asks you to enter a sentence, then displays the sentence between two lines of the same length as that sentence. Try the program first and then read the discussion.

```
{ ------------------------- Example 7-2 ------------------------- }
PROGRAM Procedures2(OUTPUT);
VAR
    Len              :INTEGER;
    TestSentence    :STRING;
{ ------------ Beginning of Procedure ------------- }
PROCEDURE DrawLine(LineLength :INTEGER);
CONST
    Dash = '-';
VAR
    Counter :INTEGER;
BEGIN
    FOR Counter := 1 TO LineLength DO
        WRITE(Dash);
    WRITELN
END;
{ --------------- End of Procedure ---------------- }
{ ---------------- Main program ------------------- }
BEGIN
    WRITE('Please enter a sentence: ');
    READLN(TestSentence);
    Len := LENGTH(TestSentence);
    WRITELN;
    DrawLine(Len);
    WRITELN(TestSentence);
    DrawLine(Len)
END.
{ ----------------------------------------------------------------- }
```

Sample Run:

```
    Please enter a sentence: Learn C++ in Three Days
    -------------------------------------
```

```
Learn C++ in Three Days
----------------------------------------
```

Instead of defining the number of dashes as a constant, the length of the sentence is declared in the main program as a variable Len. After the sentence is entered, its length is calculated and passed to the procedure as a *parameter*. The procedure call in this case becomes:

```
DrawLine(Len);
```

The procedure header must also include a receiver parameter:

```
PROCEDURE DrawLine(LineLength :INTEGER);
```

Between the parentheses comes the parameter LineLength, followed by a colon, followed by the type of the parameter (INTEGER).

Actual and Formal Parameters

When the procedure is invoked, the value of the variable Len (from the main program) is passed to the procedure and assigned to the variable LineLength, where it is used in processing. The variable Len is called the *actual parameter*, and the variable LineLength is called the *formal parameter*. After the procedure has been executed, the control is transferred back to the main program, and execution resumes at the next statement following the procedure call. Except during the procedure execution, the value of the formal parameter is undefined.

Note: Functions and procedures can also be passed as parameters, but many implementations forbid this.

A procedure call may contain more than one parameter, like this:

```
Process(A, B, C);
```

The number of actual parameters in the procedure call must be the same as the number of formal parameters, which means that the procedure header may look something like this:

```
PROCEDURE Process(X, Y :INTEGER; Z :REAL);
```

The variables A and B in the calling program must be of the type INTEGER as they correspond to X and Y respectively, while the variable C must be of the type REAL as it corresponds to Z. Note the semicolon that separates the declarations in the procedure header.

In brief, the actual and formal parameters must match in number, type, and position.

Passing Parameters by Value and by Reference

You may use literal values as actual parameters to call the procedure, such as:

```
DrawLine(30);
```

This call results in the drawing of a line 30 characters long.

When a value is used as a parameter, it is said that the parameter is passed *by value*; if the parameter is a variable, it is said to be passed *by reference*.

Drill 7-1

Modify the last program so that you can pass to the procedure the type of line character ("-" or "*", etc.), and have the output displayed in the middle of the line (assume that the line is 80 characters wide). This is a sample run of the required program:

```
Please enter a sentence: Learn C in Three Days
Please enter the line character: *
                        **********************
                        Learn C in Three Days
                        **********************
```

7-4 Returning Values from Procedures: VAR

A procedure may be used to change the value of a variable and pass it back to the calling program. In such a case, the formal parameters must be preceded by the word VAR. Consider the case of a procedure that receives the value of two variables and returns the cube of each. The procedure header might look something like this:

```
PROCEDURE CubeThem(VAR X, Y :REAL);
```

You can only pass parameters to this procedure by reference:

```
CubeThem(A, B);
```

The values of A and B will be passed to the procedure, substituted for X and Y respectively, cubed, and sent back to the calling program. It is illegal in this case to use literal values or expressions as actual parameters.

When formal parameters are preceded by the word VAR they are called *variable parameters*; otherwise they are *value parameters*.

The general form of the procedure header is:

PROCEDURE name;
or
PROCEDURE procedure-name(formal-parameter-list);

The general form of a procedure call is:

    procedure-name;

    or

    procedure-name(actual-parameter-list);

The following program is an example of using both types of formal parameters. It demonstrates the same logic as in Example 2-2 does but uses a procedure to receive the base and the power and send back the result.

```
{ ------------------------- Example 7-3 --------------------------}
PROGRAM VarParms(INPUT,OUTPUT);
VAR
    a, b, c :REAL;
{ ------------- Procedure Definition ------------ }
PROCEDURE PowerOperator(X, Y :REAL; VAR Z:REAL);
BEGIN
    Z := EXP(LN(X)*Y)
END;
{ ---------------- Main Program ---------------- }
BEGIN
   WRITE('Enter the base and the exponent separated by a space: ');
   READLN(a, b);
   PowerOperator(a, b, c);
   WRITELN('The value of ',a:0:2,' raised to the power of ',b:0:2,' is ',c:0:2)
END.
{ ------------------------------------------------------------- }
```

Sample Run:

```
Enter the base and the exponent separated by a space: 2 5
The value of 2.00 raised to the power of 5.00 is 32.00
```

Notice in the procedure that X and Y were declared as value parameters because they only receive values from the calling program, while Z was declared as a variable parameter because it sends back the result.

7-5 Global and Local Variables

Both the formal parameters and the variables declared in a procedure are called *local variables* because they are accessible only within their procedure; in other words, they are invisible to the main program or to any other subprogram. The variables declared in the main program, on the other hand, are called *global variables* because they are accessible from any program unit. In Example 7-2, for example, the variable TestSentence is a global variable and may be accessed from the procedure DrawLine without passing it as a parameter. Any assignment to this variable in the procedure will change its value in the main program. The local variable Counter, however, is not accessible from the main program.

Consider now the case if you declared two variables with the same name (such as X), one in the main program and one in a procedure. The redeclaration of the global variable X in a procedure will create a local variable with the same name and hide the global variable from the procedure. This means you will have two different variables that correspond to two different locations in memory. When the procedure exits, there will be one global variable with the name X. These restrictions help the programmer not to modify the value of a global variable from a subprogram by accident.

The variables in the main program can only be modified from other procedures if they are global (and not redeclared in the procedure) or are passed by reference as variable parameters to the procedure. Accessing global variables from a subprogram is not recommended, as it repeals the modularity of the program. Using parameters is safer, and it also keeps the subprogram independent and useful with different programs.

Application: Sorting Procedure

Go back to Example 5-5, and split it into generic procedures. This program was used to read, sort, and display an array of six elements. What you need to do now is write three procedures that read, sort, and display an array of any size. By passing the array and the number of elements to the procedures, the same results will be achieved as before. The main body of the program will contain only three calls:

```
ReadNumbers(ArraySize, Numbers);
SortNumbers(ArraySize, Numbers);
PrintNumbers(ArraySize, Numbers);
```

In this way, any one of the three procedures can be used in any program. One important point to mention here is that when you pass an array to a procedure or function, it must be declared in the TYPE section. The formal parameters in the procedure header will then look something like this:

```
PROCEDURE ReadNumbers(L: INTEGER; VAR R :NumbersArray);
```

The parameter L corresponds to ArraySize, and the array R corresponds to the array Numbers. As you can see in the parameter declaration it is of the type NumbersArray, which is the same type as the array Numbers. Here is the complete program:

```
{ ------------------------ Example 7-4 ------------------------ }
PROGRAM Sorting(INPUT,OUTPUT);
CONST
   ArraySize = 6;
TYPE
   Range       = 1..ArraySize;
   NumbersArray = ARRAY[Range] OF INTEGER;
VAR
   Numbers :NumbersArray;
{ ---------------- Read procedure ---------------- }
PROCEDURE ReadNumbers(L: INTEGER; VAR R :NumbersArray);
VAR
```

```
        I :INTEGER;
BEGIN
   FOR I := 1 TO L DO
      BEGIN
         WRITE('Enter element #', I,': ');
         READLN(R[I])
      END
END;
{ ---------------- Sort procedure ---------------- }
PROCEDURE SortNumbers(M: INTEGER; VAR S :NumbersArray);
VAR
   I, J, Pot :INTEGER;
BEGIN
   FOR I := 1 TO M-1 DO
      FOR J := I+1 TO M DO
         IF S[I] > S[J] THEN
            BEGIN                           { Swap contents }
               Pot := S[J];
               S[J] := S[I];
               S[I] := Pot
            END
END;
{ ---------------- Print procedure ---------------- }
PROCEDURE PrintNumbers(N: INTEGER; T :NumbersArray);
VAR
   I :INTEGER;
BEGIN
   WRITELN;
   WRITE('The sorted array is: ');
   FOR I := 1 TO N DO
      WRITE(T[I],'  ');
   WRITELN;
END;
{ ---------------- Main Program ------------------ }
BEGIN
   ReadNumbers(ArraySize, Numbers);
   SortNumbers(ArraySize, Numbers);
   PrintNumbers(ArraySize, Numbers);
   WRITELN('Press ENTER to continue..');
   READLN
END.
{ ---------------------------------------------------------------- }
```

Sample Run:

```
     Enter element #1: 44
     Enter element #2: 22
     Enter element #3: 8
     Enter element #4: 1
     Enter element #5: 667
```

```
Enter element #6: 3
The sorted array is: 1  3  8  22  44  667
Press ENTER to continue..
```

Note that the array is passed as a variable parameter to the procedures which are expected to change the value of the array (e.g., ReadNumbers and SortNumbers), but there was no need to do that for the procedure PrintNumbers, which displays the array without returning any value to the main program. In the latter case the array was passed as a value parameter. Notice also the use of local variables in different procedures, which makes each an independent unit. If any of these procedures have to be used with a different type of array, you need only change the type NumbersArray or use the same type name for the new array in the main program. In this example it is possible to use procedures without any parameters at all and process the global variables directly, but in that case you would have to use the same variable names in all of the procedures and the main program, which is a lot of effort and also entails the risk of dealing with global variables.

Tip: Like arrays, enumerated types and subranges must be declared in the TYPE section if they are to be used as formal parameters in a subprogram.

7-6 Functions

A function is a subprogram that returns a value, which is then assigned to the function name in the calling program. Like predefined functions, user-defined functions have one or more parameters. The function definition comes in the subprogram section of the declaration part and includes a header, a declaration part, and statements. Look at this header of a function that returns the average of three numbers:

```
FUNCTION Avg(X, Y, Z :REAL) :REAL;
```

The header is similar to the procedure header except that the type of the return value follows the function header (:REAL). You can call this function using statements like these:

```
D := Avg(A, B, C);
WRITELN(Avg(F, G, H):2:2);
WRITELN(Avg(94, 33.5, 45*1.2):2:2);
```

As you can see, the parameter may be a literal constant, an expression, or a variable.

The function header takes the following form:

FUNCTION function-name(formal-parameter-list) :return-type;

Like procedures, functions are independent subprograms. All parameters, variables, and constants declared within the function body are local to it and are invisible to other program units. In a function subprogram, the function must be assigned a value.

Application: The Fibonacci Sequence

A Fibonacci sequence is the sequence of numbers, 1, 1, 2, 3, 5, 8, 13,..., in which each successive number is equal to the sum of the two preceding numbers (named after the Italian mathematician Leonardo Fibonacci). The following example reads the number of elements and displays the Fibonacci sequence up to this number.

```
{ ------------------------- Example 7-5 ------------------------- }
PROGRAM FibonacciNumbers(INPUT, OUTPUT);
{ Fibonacci sequence example}
CONST
    TAB = CHR(9);
VAR
    I   : INTEGER;   { General loop counter }
    N   : INTEGER;   { Maximum number of elements }
{ --------------------------------------------------------------- }
{ --------------------- FUNCTION Fibonacci --------------------- }
FUNCTION Fibonacci(I: INTEGER): LONGINT;
{ The function returns the Fibonacci numbers according to the argument I }
BEGIN
    IF I <= 1 THEN
        Fibonacci := 1
    ELSE
        Fibonacci := Fibonacci(I-1) + Fibonacci(I-2)
END;
{ --------------------------------------------------------------- }
{ ----------------------- Main Program ----------------------- }
BEGIN
    WRITE('Please enter the maximum number of elements: ');
    READLN(N);
    WRITELN('Number', TAB, 'Fibonacci number');
    I := 0;
    WHILE I < N DO
        BEGIN
            WRITELN(I, TAB, Fibonacci(i));
        I := I + 1;
      END;
    WRITELN;
    WRITELN('Press ENTER to continue..');
    READLN
END.
{ --------------------------------------------------------------- }
```

Sample Run:

```
Please enter the maximum number of elements: 20
Number    Fibonacci number
0         1
1         1
2         2
3         3
4         5
5         8
6         13
7         21
8         34
9         55
10        89
11        144
12        233
13        377
14        610
15        987
16        1597
17        2584
18        4181
19        6765
```

Note: In a function subprogram, the function name cannot be treated like a variable; i.e., it may not be involved in expressions. It may only be assigned a value.

Drill 7-2

Write a function to return the maximum number in a one-dimensional array and include the function in a program. You may use any procedures you wrote before to build the program.

7-7 Tips on the Scope of Variables

The following program frame consists of three program units, procedure Kid1, procedure Kid2, and the main program Parent. According to the rules of variable scope, any variable declared in Parent (global variable) is accessible to both Kid1 and Kid2 unless it is redeclared locally in either of them. On the other hand, any local variable declared in Kid1 is hidden from both Parent and Kid2. The same thing applies for Kid2 variables. If you consider the main program as a parent and the subprograms as kids, it then follows that whatever belongs to the parent belongs to the kids, but the opposite is not valid. In other words, the kids inherit everything from the parent, but each one of them has his own property, which is not inherited by a parent or a sibling.

```
{ ------------------------- Example 7-6 ------------------------ }
PROGRAM Parent;
      { -------------- PROCEDURE KID1 -------------- }
      PROCEDURE Kid1(...);
      ...
      BEGIN
      ...
      END; { -------- END OF PROCEDURE KID1 ---------- }
      { --------------- PROCEDURE KID2 ------------- }
      PROCEDURE Kid2(...);
      ...
      BEGIN
      ...
      END; { -------- END OF PROCEDURE KID2 ---------- }
{ ------------------------ MAIN PROGRAM ------------------------ }
BEGIN
...
END.
{ ------------------------------------------------------------- }
```

Either of the two procedures may be called from the main program. The procedure Kid1 may also be called from Kid2 because it has already been defined, but the procedure Kid2 cannot be called from Kid1 because it has not yet been defined. There is a way to get around this restriction using a *forward declaration* by including the header of Kid2, followed by the keyword FORWARD, at the beginning of the program, like this:

```
PROGRAM Parent;
{ Forward declaration of Kid2 }
    PROCEDURE Kid2(...); FORWARD;
{ Definition of Kid1 }
    PROCEDURE Kid1(...);
        ...
{ Definition of Kid2 }
    PROCEDURE Kid2(...);
        ...
{ Main program }
        ...
```

Now take a look at the new program structure in the following example. The procedure GrandKid is defined inside the procedure Kid, which means that Kid has become the parent of another subprogram. In such a case, any variable in Kid is global in GrandKid, and so are the variables of the Parent (unless any of them is redeclared in GrandKid). The local variables in GrandKid, however, are not accessible to either Kid or Parent.

```
{ ------------------------ Example 7-7 ------------------------ }
PROGRAM Parent;
     { ---------------- PROCEDURE KID ---------------- }
     PROCEDURE Kid(...);
     ...
          { ---------- PROCEDURE GRANDKID ------------ }
          PROCEDURE GrandKid(...);
          BEGIN
          ...
          END; { ------ END OF PROCEDURE GRANDKID ------ }
     BEGIN
     ...
     END; { ---------- END OF PROCEDURE KID ----------- }
{ ------------------------ MAIN PROGRAM ----------------------- }
BEGIN
...
END.
{ ------------------------------------------------------------- }
```

To summarize:

- The scope of a variable is the program unit in which it is declared.

- A global variable is accessible in any program unit unless it is redeclared locally in that unit.

- A local variable is not accessible outside the program unit in which it is declared. It is, however, accessible to any subprogram defined within this program unit unless redeclared inside that sub-subprogram.

- Any subprogram can be called from any program unit as long as its definition (or its forward declaration) preceded the call.

7-8 Recursive Functions and Procedures

A function or procedure may call itself, a property called *recursion*. The factorial function is a good example of recursion. You know (from Chapter 4) that the factorial of a number X can be obtained from the relation:

$$\text{factorial}(X) = X * \text{factorial}(X-1)$$

In other words, to get the factorial of 4 you multiply 4 by the factorial of 3; to get the factorial of 3 you multiply 3 by the factorial of 2, etc. This continues until you reach the value 1.

Here is the program that contains the factorial function.

```
{ ------------------------ Example 7-8 ------------------------ }
PROGRAM FunctionRecursion(INPUT, OUTPUT);
VAR
```

```
    A :INTEGER;
{ ------------- Function Definition ------------- }
FUNCTION Factorial(X :INTEGER) :REAL;
BEGIN
   IF X <= 1 THEN
      Factorial := 1
   ELSE
      Factorial := X * Factorial(X-1);
END;
{ ----------------- End of Function ---------------- }
{ ----------------- Main program ---------------- }
BEGIN
   WRITE('Enter a number: ');
   READLN(A);
   WRITELN('The Factorial of ', A,' = ', Factorial(A):0:0)
END.
{ ------------------------------------------------------------------ }
```

Sample Run:

```
Enter a number: 6
The Factorial of 6 = 720
```

Notice in the function program that in the statement:

```
Factorial := X * Factorial(X-1);
```

the left side contains the name of the function, while in the right side there is a call of the function to calculate the factorial of X–1. This process will continue until the condition terminates the function.

Drill 7-3

Write the factorial subprogram as a procedure and compare it to the factorial function.

Summary

In this chapter you learned about the Pascal program structure.

You know how to divide your program into subprograms, whether functions or procedures. These are important points to remember:

1. A subprogram is declared in the last section of the declaration part and consists of a header, a declaration part, and statements.

The header of a procedure takes the form:

      PROCEDURE name;
      or
      PROCEDURE procedure-name(formal-parameter-list);

The header of a function takes the form:

      FUNCTION function-name(formal-parameter-list) :return-type;

2. A procedure is called by its name exactly like a statement.

When parameters are used in a procedure call, they must match the parameters in the procedure header. Procedure parameters are either value or variable parameters. A variable parameter is used when it is required to have the procedure change the value of the parameter.

3. A function is usually called as part of an expression; it returns a single value that replaces the name of the function in that expression.

4. You now know that each variable has a scope, and you learned the rules that control the scope and the relationship between global and local variables.

Exercises

1. True or false:

  a. The scope of a variable is the program unit in which it is declared.

  b. A global variable is accessible in any program unit unless it is redeclared locally in that unit.

  c. A local variable is not accessible outside the program unit in which it is declared. It is, however, accessible to any subprogram defined within this program unit unless redeclared inside that sub-subprogram.

  d. Any subprogram can be called from any program unit as long as its definition, or its forward declaration, precedes the call.

2. True or false:

  a. A function must have one or more parameters.

  b. A procedure may have one or more parameters.

  c. A function always returns a value.

  d. A procedure cannot return a value.

  e. In a procedure definition, the formal parameters must be preceded by the keyword VAR.

  f. Unlike a value parameter, a variable parameter is preceded by the keyword VAR.

  g. The function name can be assigned a value.

  h. The function name can be involved in expressions.

  i. Arrays, enumerations, and subranges must be declared in the TYPE section if they are to be used as formal parameters in a subprogram.

3. Write a procedure definition that takes three integer parameters x, y, and z. The parameter x is changed by the procedure and returned back to the caller. Also write the procedure call.

4. Write the Prime Numbers procedure (see the Prime Numbers program, Example 5-5, in Chapter 5).

5. Write a function to calculate and return the average of three real numbers.

Answers

1. All true.

2. d, e, and h are false.

3. PROCEDURE MyProcedure(VAR X:REAL; Y, Z:REAL);

4. Following is the Prime Numbers procedure:

```
{ ---------------------------------------------------------------- }
PROCEDURE DisplayPrimes(N: INTEGER);
CONST
    Size = 200;    {The maximum size of the array}
VAR
    Flags          :ARRAY[1..Size] OF BOOLEAN;
    Prime          :INTEGER; {Prime number temporary variable}
    NotPrime       :INTEGER; {Counter for excluded numbers}
    PrimeCount     :INTEGER; {Counter of prime numbers}
    I              :INTEGER; {General loop counter}
BEGIN
{Initialize variables}
    Prime := 2;              { First prime }
    NotPrime := Prime * 2;   { First excluded multiple }
    PrimeCount := 0;         { Number of primes }
    I := 1;                  { Array counter }
    {Set all the array elements to TRUE}
    WHILE I <= NumberOfElements DO
        BEGIN
            Flags[I] := TRUE;
            I := I +1;
        END;
    {The actual algorithm loop}
    WRITELN('Prime numbers from 1 to ', NumberOfElements, ' :');
    WHILE Prime <= NumberOfElements DO
        BEGIN
            {Select only the TRUE elements}
            IF Flags[Prime] = TRUE THEN
                BEGIN
                    {Start with the first multiple}
                    NotPrime := Prime*2;
                    WHILE NotPrime <= NumberOfElements DO
                        BEGIN
```

```
                              {Exclude multiples}
                              Flags[NotPrime] := FALSE;
                              NotPrime := NotPrime + Prime;
                    END;
                  {After the WHILE loop, all the primes are TRUE}
                  PrimeCount := PrimeCount +1;
                  WRITELN(Prime);
              END;
            {Increment the WHILE counter}
            Prime := Prime + 1;
        END;
    WRITELN('Number of primes = ', PrimeCount);
    WRITELN('Press ENTER to continue..');
    READLN
END;
{ -------------------------------------------------------------------- }
```

5. Following is the code of the average function and the main program:

```
PROGRAM MyFunctions(INPUT, OUTPUT);
VAR
   A, B, C :REAL;
{ -------------------------------------------------------------------- }
FUNCTION Avg(X, Y, Z :REAL) :REAL;
BEGIN
   AVG := (X + Y + Z) / 3
END;
{ -------------------------------------------------------------------- }
BEGIN
   WRITE('Enter three numbers: ');
   READLN(A, B, C);
   WRITELN('The average is= ', Avg(A, B, C):0:2)
END.
```

Chapter 8

Sets and Records

8-1 The SET Data Type

The set is a structured data type that may include ordered or unordered elements. The set elements are referred to as *members*. You can express a set literal constant by listing its elements between brackets separated by commas, for example:

```
['a'..'z']              (The set of lowercase letters)
['A'..'Z', 'a'..'z']    (The set of all letters)
[0..9]                  (The set of digits)
[1,3,5,7]               (The set of odd numbers between 1 and 7)
```

Unlike arrays, the order of elements in a set is not important. For example, the set:

```
[1,3,5,7]
```

is the same as the set:

```
[1,7,5,3]
```

This leads to another difference between sets and arrays. In arrays you can access any element by its position in the array, but with sets you cannot access individual elements. You can only test a data item to see if it is a member of the set using the IN operator. For example, if you would like to test a character to see if it is an uppercase letter, you may use the following condition:

```
IF Character IN ['A'..'Z']  THEN ...
```

This statement speaks for itself; it is almost plain English. It says: "if the character is in the set of uppercase letters then...." It is equivalent to, but simpler than, the conditional statement:

```
IF (Character >= 'A') AND (Character <= 'Z') THEN ...
```

If the elements of a set form a continuous subrange, you may use the two periods (..); for example, the set:

```
[1,2,3,4,6,8]
```

can be written as:

```
[1..4,6,8]
```

The elements of a set can be of any ordinal type, but all of the elements must be of the same type, which is called the *base type*.

8-2 Declaration and Assignment: SET OF

To declare set variables use the keywords SET OF, as in the following example where two sets of the base type CHAR are declared:

```
VAR
        LowerCase, UpperCase :SET OF CHAR;
```

After this declaration you can assign the variables LowerCase and UpperCase set constants of the base type CHAR, for example:

```
LowerCase := ['a'..'z'];
UpperCase := ['A'..'Z'];
```

You may then test a variable of the type CHAR for *membership* in these sets using expressions like:

```
IF Character IN LowerCase THEN ...
IF Character IN UpperCase THEN ...
```

Note that the expression IN LowerCase is equivalent to the expression IN ['a'..'z'], and the expression IN UpperCase is equivalent to the expression IN ['A'..'Z'].

As with other structured types, it is preferable to declare sets in the TYPE section; you can then use this type in the VAR section to declare variables. The declaration takes the general form:

> type-identifier = SET OF base-type;

Declaration Examples

The following are examples of set declarations in the TYPE and the VAR sections:

```
TYPE
    Days = (Monday,Tuesday,Wednesday,Thursday,Friday,Saturday,Sunday);
    Languages = (C,CPP,Pascal,Fortran,Basic,Cobol,Assembly);
    Digits = SET OF 0..9;
    Lowercase = SET OF 'a'..'z';
    Uppercase = SET OF 'A'..'Z';
    DaySet = SET OF Days;
    LanguageSet = SET OF Languages;
    CharacterSet = SET OF CHAR;
VAR
    WholeWeek, WorkingDays, WeekEnd        :DaySet;
    OddNum, EvenNum, Numbers               :Digits;
    Small                                  :Lowercase;
    Capital                                :Uppercase;
    ProgCodes, HLL, LLL, MLL               :LanguageSet;
    Alphabet                               :CharacterSet;
```

In the preceding declarations, variables such as WeekEnd, WorkingDays, and WholeWeek are all sets of the base type Days. Any of these set variables may be assigned one or more elements of the enumeration Days, such as:

```
    WeekEnd := [Saturday,Sunday];
    WorkingDays := [Monday..Friday];
    WholeWeek := [Monday..Sunday];
```

The last statement is equivalent to the statement:

```
WholeWeek := [Monday,Tuesday,Wednesday,Thursday,Friday,Saturday,Sunday];
```

The value of a set variable is undefined until it is assigned a value. When you assign a set constant to a set variable, their base types must be *compatible*, i.e., they must be of the same type, subranges of the same type, or one of them must be a subrange of the other. Here are more assignments:

```
    OddNum := [1,3,5,7,9];
    EvenNum := [2,4,6,8];
    ProgCodes := [C..Assembly];
    LLL := [Assembly];
```

The *empty set* is a set with no members and is denoted by the constant [ ]. You may assign this constant to any set variable of any base type, for example:

```
OddNum := [];
```

8-3 Rules of Using Sets

The following are the main rules and restrictions that control the use of sets:

1. All the set members must be of the same base type.

2. There is usually a limit on the maximum number of elements of a set. This limit varies with different Pascal implementations; in Turbo Pascal, for example, it is 255. The declaration SET OF INTEGER is not allowed because the range of integers exceeds this maximum number, but you can get around that by using subranges such as SET OF 0..99.

   In some implementations, the declaration SET OF CHAR is not allowed either, in which case a subrange of the type CHAR might be used.

3. You may assign a set to another set:

   ```
   NewSet := OldSet;
   ```

   In this case, NewSet is an exact copy of OldSet.

4. You may declare an array of sets, as in:

   ```
   DaysArray = ARRAY[1..10] OF DaySet;
   ```

   where DaySet is a previously declared set type.

5. You cannot read or write a set using the input/output statements, but there are some programming techniques using set operations (explained in the next section) that may be used.

6. Sets can be passed as parameters of subprograms, in which case they must be declared as types.

8-4 Set Operators and Expressions

In addition to the membership operator IN, which is specific to sets, other Pascal operators may be used in set operations. However, when used with sets, many operators have different meanings, and some have different names.

The arithmetic operators +, –, and * perform special operations on sets of compatible types. These operations are shown in the following table along with the corresponding operator:

Table 8-1: Set operations

Operation	Operator
Union	+
Intersection	*
Difference	–

To demonstrate these operations, consider the two sets, A and B, shown in the following figure. Each set is represented by a circle. (This representation is known as a Venn diagram.)

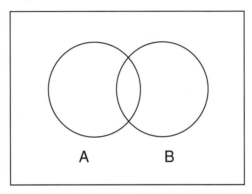

Union: +

The union of the two sets A and B is a set whose elements are in either A or B, or in both, as shown in the following figure. The operator + is used to perform this operation.

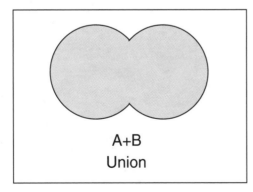

For example, if Small is the set of lowercase letters and Capital is the set of uppercase letters, the union of these two sets is the Alphabet set, that is:

```
Alphabet := Small + Capital;
```

The set Alphabet will thus contain both the lowercase and the uppercase letters.

Intersection: *

The intersection of the two sets, A and B, is a set whose members are the elements common to both sets, as shown in the following figure. The operator * is used to perform this operation.

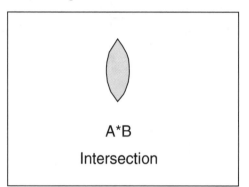

A*B

Intersection

For example, the statement:

```
MLL := [C,CPP,Cobol] * [Basic,Fortran,C,CPP]
```

results in the set MLL, which contains both C and CPP.

Difference: –

The difference A–B is a set whose members are in A but not in B, as shown in the following figure. The operator – is used to perform this operation.

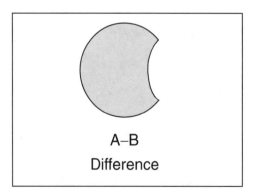

A–B

Difference

For example, the statement (see the preceding declarations):

```
HLL := ProgCodes - [Assembly];
```

results in the set HLL, which contains all the elements of the set ProgCodes except Assembly.

It is obvious that the difference B–A is a set whose members are in B but not in A.

Tips on Using Set Operators

■ You can make use of the union operation to construct a new set (read a set) by reading one element at a time and adding it to the set, for example:

```
Read(NewElement);
Set1 := Set1 + [NewElement];
```

■ You can also make use of the difference operation to display the elements of a set. This is done by testing the membership of a variable of the same base type as that of the set. If the element is a set member, it is displayed, subtracted from the set, and replaced by its successor. This continues until the set is empty.

Drill 8-1

Evaluate the following expressions:

(See the answers in the file DRL8-1.TXT on the companion CD. The program DRL8-1.PAS is also provided to help you test the results.)

```
1. ['A','B','C','D'] + ['E','F']
2. ['A','B','C','D'] + ['B','C','E','F']
3. [1,3,7] + []
4. ['A','D','F'] * ['O','F']
5. [1,2,3,4] * [5,6,7]
6. [1,2,3,4] - [5,6,7]
7. [5,6,7] - []
8. [Able, Baker, Charlie] - [Able, Charlie]
```

Relational Operators

The relational operators =, >=, <=, and <> can be used with sets of compatible types.

The meanings of the set relational operators are indicated in Table 8-2 by comparing two sets, A and B. The table contains TRUE expressions as examples of each operation.

The operators > and < are not mentioned in the table as they may not be used with sets.

Table 8-2: Set relational operators

Expression	Meaning	Example
A = B	Both A and B contain the same elements	[1,0] = [1,0]
A <> B	A and B do not contain the same elements	[1,0] <> [1,4]
A >= B	All elements of B are in A	[1,2,3,4] >= [1,2]
		[1,2,3] >= [1,2,3]
A <= B	All elements of A are in B	[] <= [1,2,3]
		[1,2,3] <= [1,2,3]

In order to test the relational expressions, use a Boolean variable to store the expression, then print the variable to see if it is TRUE or FALSE. For example:

```
VAR
    H :BOOLEAN;
...
BEGIN
    H:= [Able, Baker, Charlie] - [Able, Charlie] = [Baker];
    WRITELN('H = ',H);
...
```

The output of this code is:

```
H = TRUE
```

You can also check to see if a specific member belongs to the resulting set. For example, you can test the preceding expression to see if Able, Baker, or Charlie are in the resulting set. Only Baker's test will be TRUE.

Drill 8-2

Write a program to test the expressions in Table 8-2.

Note: Remember that the membership operator IN is used to test the membership of one element. In order to determine whether a set A is a subset of B, in other words, all the elements of A are in B, use the relational operators <= or >=. That is:

```
A <= B
-or-
B >= A
```

Precedence of Pascal Operators

After introducing the set operators, all Pascal operators are now complete. The relative precedence of Pascal operators is shown in Table 8-3. Notice that the set operators (+, –, *) use the same symbols as the arithmetic operators. Also, the relational operators are used with either simple data types or sets.

Table 8-3: Precedence of Pascal operators

Operator	Precedence
NOT	Priority 1 (highest)
* / DIV MOD AND	Priority 2
+ – OR (XOR in Turbo Pascal)	Priority 3
= > < >= <= <> IN	Priority 4 (lowest)

You may combine relational expressions using the Boolean operators AND, OR, and NOT, but you must watch the precedence of operators, for example:

```
IF (Ch IN Small) AND (Ch IN Capital) THEN ...
```

The parentheses are necessary in this expression because the IN operator has a lower precedence than the AND operator.

Application: Text Analyzer

In the following program, the printable characters are divided into the following sets:

■ Lowercase letters
■ Uppercase letters
■ Alphabetic characters (which is the union of the above two sets)
■ Digits
■ Punctuation characters
■ Other characters

The program reads a text file from the keyboard, character by character, and tests each character to see if it is a member in any one of these sets. The program is straightforward and contains four parts: declarations of sets, initialization of counters, testing memberships of characters, and displaying results.

```
{ ------------------------- Example 8-1 ------------------------- }
PROGRAM TextAnalyzer(INPUT,OUTPUT);
TYPE
   LowerCase  = SET OF 'a'..'z';
   UpperCase  = SET OF 'A'..'Z';
   Digits     = SET OF '0'..'9';
   Characters = SET OF CHAR;
VAR
```

```
          Capital                            :UpperCase;
          Small                              :LowerCase;
          Numerals                           :Digits;
          Alphabet, Punctuation, Others      :Characters;
          A, C, S, N, P, O, Counter          :INTEGER;
          Ch                                 :CHAR;
BEGIN
   Counter := 0;     { counter of all characters }
   A := 0;           { counter of alphabetic characters }
   C := 0;           { counter of capital letters }
   S := 0;           { counter of small letters }
   N := 0;           { counter of numeric characters }
   P := 0;           { counter of punctuation characters }
   O := 0;           { counter of other characters }
   Small       := ['a'..'z'];
   Capital     := ['A'..'Z'];
   Alphabet    := Small + Capital;
   Numerals    := ['0'..'9'];
   Punctuation := [',',';','-','''','.','!','?',')','(','"',':','_'];
   WRITELN('Start typing your text file. To terminate press Ctrl+Z:');
   WHILE NOT EOF DO
      BEGIN
         WHILE NOT EOLN DO
            BEGIN
               READ(Ch);
               Counter := Counter + 1;
               IF Ch IN Alphabet THEN
                  BEGIN
                     A := A + 1;
                     IF Ch IN Small THEN
                        S := S + 1
                     ELSE IF Ch IN Capital THEN
                        C := C + 1
                  END
               ELSE IF Ch IN Numerals THEN
                  N := N + 1
               ELSE IF Ch IN Punctuation THEN
                  P := P + 1
               ELSE
                  O := O + 1
            END;
         READLN
      END;
   WRITELN('Total number of characters      = ', Counter);
   WRITELN('Number of alphabetic characters    = ', A);
   WRITELN(' .Number of lowercase letters: ', S);
   WRITELN(' .Number of uppercase letters: ', C);
   WRITELN('Number of numeric characters    = ', N);
   WRITELN('Number of punctuation characters = ', P);
   WRITELN('Number of other characters      = ', O)
```

```
END.
{ ---------------------------------------------------------------- }
```

Sample Run:

```
Start typing your text file. To terminate press Ctrl+Z:
The standard set operators are:
        1. Union (+).
        2. Intersection (*).
        3. Difference (-).
^Z                                            → Press Ctrl+Z to end the text
Total number of characters       = 85
Number of alphabetic characters  = 53
 .Number of lowercase letters: 49
 .Number of uppercase letters: 4
Number of numeric characters     = 3
Number of punctuation characters = 14
Number of other characters       = 15
```

Sets are useful for testing conditions. One common use of sets is to precede a CASE statement in order to filter out the unwanted data, which do not belong to any case.

8-5 Records

A *record*, another structured type in Pascal, is a collection of related data items, which may be of different types. Each item in the record is called a *field*. Take a look at this record, which is used to store information about each employee in a company:

	Employee Record	
Field #	*Information*	*Possible Data Type*
1.	Name	STRING
2.	Address	STRING
3.	Phone number	STRING/INTEGER
4.	Hourly rate	REAL
5.	Marital status	CHAR/Enumeration

Unlike arrays (which contain elements of the same type), records may contain fields of any data type, including the type RECORD itself.

Record Declaration

The declaration of a record takes the form:

type-identifier = **RECORD**

field-list

END;

The field list contains the name and type of each field as in this declaration of the record EmployeeRecord.

```
TYPE
EmployeeRecord =    RECORD
                        Name            :STRING[25];
                        Address         :STRING[40];
                        Phone           :STRING[12];
                        Rate            :REAL;
                        MaritalStatus   :CHAR;
                    END;
```

Note: If your Pascal implementation does not support the STRING type, you may replace the STRING variables by INTEGER or CHAR variables, in which case you need to replace the variable Name with another variable like ID, etc.

A record declaration must be terminated by the keyword END.

In the VAR section, the record is then declared as a variable of the type EmployeeRecord:

```
VAR
        EmployeeRec :EmployeeRecord;
```

As with other structured and user-defined data types, you can declare a record in the VAR section directly, but you now know the advantages of declaring data structures as types.

Accessing Record Fields

Each field in a record can be accessed using both the record identifier and the field identifier separated by a period. For example, you can assign values to the fields with statements like:

```
EmployeeRec.Name := 'Charles A. Dixon';
EmployeeRec.Rate := 22.5;
```

You can do the same thing with input and output operations:

```
WRITELN('Employee Name: ', EmployeeRec.Name);
```

This type of compound variable is called a *fielded variable*. Actually, the scope of the field identifier (such as Name) is the record in which it was declared, and it may be used elsewhere in the program as the name of another variable if desired.

In the following example, the record EmployeeRec is filled and then displayed.

```
{------------------------- Example 8-2 -------------------------}
PROGRAM RecordExample1(OUTPUT);
```

```
TYPE
   EmployeeRecord = RECORD
                           Name            :STRING[25];
                           Address         :STRING[40];
                           Phone           :STRING[12];
                           Rate            :REAL;
                           MaritalStatus   :CHAR;
                   END;
VAR
   EmployeeRec :EmployeeRecord;
BEGIN
{ Assign values to the fielded variables }
   EmployeeRec.Name := 'Diane J. Bedford';
   EmployeeRec.Address := '20 Carmen Avenue, New Orleans, LA 70112';
   EmployeeRec.Phone := '504-666-5043';
   EmployeeRec.Rate := 28.5;
   EmployeeRec.MaritalStatus := 'S';
{ Display record information }
   WRITELN('Employee Name:   ', EmployeeRec.Name);
   WRITELN('Address:         ', EmployeeRec.Address);
   WRITELN('Telephone #:     ', EmployeeRec.Phone);
   WRITELN('Hourly Rate:    $', EmployeeRec.Rate:0:2);
   WRITELN('Marital Status:  ', EmployeeRec.MaritalStatus)
END.
{ ------------------------------------------------------------- }
```

Output:

```
Employee Name:    Diane J. Bedford
Address:          20 Carmen Avenue, New Orleans, LA 70112
Telephone #:      504-666-5043
Hourly Rate:      $28.50
Marital Status:   S
```

8-6 The WITH Statement

The WITH statement enables you to access record fields without using the fielded variables. Look at this block of assignments using the WITH statement:

```
WITH EmployeeRec DO
   BEGIN
      Name := 'Charles A. Dixon';
      Address := '202 Greenwood, Gretna, LA 70088';
      Phone := '504-666-7574';
      Rate := 22.5;
      MaritalStatus := 'M'
   END;
```

The effect of using the WITH statement is to attach each field name to the record name. If one of the variables inside the block is not a field identifier, it will not be modified by the WITH statement.

If WITH is followed by only one statement, there is of course no need for the BEGIN-END block.

You can use the WITH statement to call a procedure to process the fields of a record, for example:

```
WITH EmployeeRec DO
    DisplayResults(Name, Rate);
```

This statement is equivalent to:

```
DisplayResults(EmployeeRec.Name, EmployeeRec.Rate);
```

The WITH statement takes the general form:

>**WITH** record-identifier **DO**
>statement;

The following example demonstrates the same logic as that used in Example 8-2, but the program is divided into three subprograms: GetData, DisplayInfo, and DrawLine (which you wrote before). The output of this program is displayed in the proper format, using a header for the record.

```
{------------------------- Example 8-3 -------------------------}
PROGRAM RecordExample2(OUTPUT);
TYPE
   EmployeeRecord = RECORD
                          Name           :STRING[25];
                          Address        :STRING[40];
                          Phone          :STRING[12];
                          Rate           :REAL;
                          MaritalStatus  :CHAR;
              END;
VAR
   EmployeeRec    :EmployeeRecord;
{ ------------ Procedure Drawline ------------ }
PROCEDURE DrawLine(LineLength, TabLength :INTEGER);
CONST
   Dash = '-';
VAR
   Counter :INTEGER;
BEGIN
   FOR Counter := 1 TO TabLength DO
      WRITE(' ');
   FOR Counter := 1 TO LineLength DO
      WRITE(Dash);
   WRITELN
END;
```

```
{ ------------- Procedure GetData ------------- }
PROCEDURE GetData(VAR Employee :EmployeeRecord);
{ Assign values to fields }
BEGIN
   WITH Employee DO
      BEGIN
      Name := 'Diane J. Bedford';
      Address := '20 Carmen Avenue, New Orleans, LA 70112';
      Phone := '504-666-5043';
      Rate := 28.5;
      MaritalStatus := 'S'
      END
END;
{ ------- Procedure DisplayInfo -------- }
PROCEDURE DisplayInfo(Employee :EmployeeRecord);
{ Display record information }
CONST
   Header ='Record of ';
VAR
   Len, Tab, Counter  :INTEGER;
   HeaderText, Status :STRING;
BEGIN
   WITH Employee DO
      BEGIN
         HeaderText := CONCAT(Header, Name);
         Len := LENGTH(HeaderText);
         Tab := (80- Len) DIV 2;
         DrawLine(Len, Tab);
         FOR Counter := 1 TO Tab DO
            WRITE(' ');
         WRITELN(HeaderText);
         DrawLine(Len, Tab);
         WRITELN('Address:          ', Address);
         WRITELN('Telephone #:     ', Phone);
         WRITELN('Hourly Rate:     $', Rate:0:2);
         IF MaritalStatus = 'M' THEN
            Status := 'Married'
         ELSE
            Status := 'Single';
         WRITELN('Marital Status:  ', Status)
      END
END;
{ ---------------------- Main Program ---------------------- }
BEGIN
   GetData(EmployeeRec);
   DisplayInfo(EmployeeRec)
END.
{ -------------------------------------------------------------- }
```

Output:

```
                              ----------------------------
                              Record of Diane J. Bedford
                              ----------------------------
        Address:         20 Carmen Avenue, New Orleans, LA 70112
        Telephone #:     504-666-5043
        Hourly Rate:     $28.50
        Marital Status:  Single
```

The points which are worthy of your attention in the program are the use of the WITH statement and the passing of the record as a parameter to the subprograms. Notice also that the record is passed once as a variable parameter (using VAR), when it was to return values of the fields, and once as a value parameter, when it was only a receiver.

The actual value of such a program comes when it reads the employee information from a data file, which will be discussed shortly.

8-7 Nesting Records

In Example 8-2 you may split the field address information into street address, city, state, and zip code. This means that the address field becomes a record nested in the EmployeeRecord. The new record will look as follows:

```
TYPE
    AddressRecord = RECORD
                        Street    :STRING[18];
                        City      :STRING[15];
                        State     :STRING[2];
                        Zip       :String[5];
                    END;
    EmployeeRecord = RECORD
                        Name           :STRING[25];
                        AddressRec     :AddressRecord;
                        Phone          :STRING[12];
                        Rate           :REAL;
                        MaritalStatus  :CHAR;
                    END;
VAR
    EmployeeRec    :EmployeeRecord;
```

In this declaration, you have two record types: AddressRecord and EmployeeRecord. The field AddressRec in the employee record is of the type AddressRecord which was defined before. To deal with any fielded variables in the AddressRec you have to attach both names of the two records EmployeeRec (which is the grandparent) and AddressRec (which is the parent). Here are some sample assignments:

```
        EmployeeRec.AddressRec.Street := '15 Darell Street';
        EmployeeRec.AddressRec.Zip := '60108';
```

When you display any of these fields you use the same method:

```
        WRITELN(EmployeeRec.AddressRec.Street);
        WRITELN(EmployeeRec.AddressRec.City);
```

Here is the complete program:

```
{ ------------------------- Example 8-4 ----------------------- }
PROGRAM NestedRecord(OUTPUT);
TYPE
   AddressRecord   = RECORD
                            Street    :STRING[18];
                            City      :STRING[15];
                            State     :STRING[2];
                            Zip       :String[5];
                     END;
   EmployeeRecord = RECORD
                            Name            :STRING[25];
                            AddressRec      :AddressRecord;
                            Phone           :STRING[12];
                            Rate            :REAL;
                            MaritalStatus   :CHAR;
                     END;
VAR
   EmployeeRec    :EmployeeRecord;
BEGIN
   EmployeeRec.Name := 'Jean L. Krauss';
   EmployeeRec.AddressRec.Street := '15 Darell Street';
   EmployeeRec.AddressRec.City := 'Bloomingdale';
   EmployeeRec.AddressRec.State := 'IL';
   EmployeeRec.AddressRec.Zip := '60108';
   EmployeeRec.Phone := '312-987-5432';
   EmployeeRec.Rate := 27.5;
   EmployeeRec.MaritalStatus := 'M';
   WRITELN('Employee Name:    ', EmployeeRec.Name);
   WRITELN('Address:          ', EmployeeRec.AddressRec.Street);
   WRITELN('                  ', EmployeeRec.AddressRec.City);
   WRITE('                  ', EmployeeRec.AddressRec.State);
   WRITELN('                  ', EmployeeRec.AddressRec.Zip);
   WRITELN('Telephone #:      ', EmployeeRec.Phone);
   WRITELN('Hourly Rate:      $', EmployeeRec.Rate:0:2);
   WRITELN('Marital Status:   ', EmployeeRec.MaritalStatus)
END.
{ ------------------------------------------------------------ }
```

Output:

```
Employee Name:     Jean L. Krauss
Address:           15 Darell Street
                   Bloomingdale
                   IL 60108
Telephone #:       312-987-5432
Hourly Rate:       $27.50
Marital Status:    M
```

If you would like to use the WITH statement with such a nested record you need two nested WITH blocks, thus:

```
WITH EmployeeRec DO
    WITH AddressRec DO
        BEGIN
        Name := 'Tammy M. Ockman';
        Street := '344 Temple Dr.';
        ...
        END;
```

If any field identifier belongs to the AddressRec, it will be modified by both AddressRec and EmployeeRec, but if it belongs to the EmployeeRec directly, it will be modified by EmployeeRec only. If it is a regular variable, it will not be modified at all.

Drill 8-3

Write the complete program that initializes and displays the employee record using the WITH statement with the nested address record shown above.

Summary

In this chapter you have met two structured data types, the set and the record, and are now familiar with their features.

1. You now know how to declare a set of a specific base type using the form:

    type-identifier = **SET OF** base-type;

2. You also know the standard set operators (union (+), intersection (*), and difference (–)) and the set relational operators (= >= <= <>), and learned how to use these operators to process sets.

3. You are familiar with restrictions on sets, as well as their main uses in programming.

4. You declare record types using the form

RECORD
    field-list
END;

5. You can access fields using either fielded variables or the WITH statement, which takes the form:

WITH record-identifier **DO**
    statement;

Exercises

1. Determine whether each of the following statements is true or false:

    a. For sets to be passed as parameters, they must be declared in the TYPE section.

    b. You can read and write sets by using input/output statements.

    c. You can declare an array whose elements are sets.

    d. The main difference between arrays and sets is that sets may contain unordered items (members).

    e. The main difference between arrays and records is that records may contain items (fields) of different data types.

    f. A record can contain fields of any data type except the type RECORD.

    g. Elements of sets and arrays can be accessed by their relative position in the set or the array.

2. Given the following declarations and assignments:

```
{Declarations:}
   V1, V2              :SET OF CHAR;
   A, B, C, D, E, F    :BOOLEAN;
{Assignments:}
   V1 := ['A', 'B'];
   V2 := ['C', 'D', 'E'];
```

evaluate the following expressions:

```
A := V1*V2 <= V1;
B := V1*V2 <= V2;
C := V1+V2 >= V1;
D := V1+V2 >= V2;
E := V1-V2 <= V1+V2;
F := V1-V2 >= V1+V2;
```

3. Given the following declarations and assignments:

```
{Declarations:}
    S1, S2, S3, S4      :SET OF 1..99;
    A, B, C, D, E, F, G :BOOLEAN;
{Assignments:}
    S1 := [2,4,6,8];
    S2 := [1,3,5,7,9];
    S3 := [1..9,11,13];
    S4 := [2..8,10,12];
```

evaluate the following expressions:

a. S1 + S2

b. S1 * S2

c. S1 – S2

d. S4 – S1

e. S1 + S2 * S3

f. (S1 + S2) * S3

g. S2 + [5]

4. Write a record declaration using the appropriate data types for each of the following items:

- Inventory item, which includes Name, Shelf #, Stock #, Available Amount, and Price.

- Employee, which includes Name, ID, Network Domain, E-mail Alias, and Office #.

- Employee, which contains the same fields as in the previous Employee record, in addition to the Address record. The Address record should contain: Street Address, City, State, and Zip Code.

- Newly born baby, which includes Name, Family Name, Father's Name, Mother's Name, Weight, Place of Birth, and Date of Birth.

Answers

1.
a. True	b. False	c. True	d. True
e. True	f. False	g. False.	

2.
a. True	b. True	c. True	d. True
e. True	f. False.		

3.
a. [1..9]	b. [ ]	c. S1;	d. [3,5,7,10,12]
e. S1 + S2	f. S1 + S2	g. S2;	

Chapter 9

Data Files

Chapter Topics:

- **The FILE data type**
- **TEXT files**
- **Non-TEXT files**
- **Reading, displaying, and processing data files**
- **Creating data files and storing them on the hard disk**
- **Appending and updating data files**
- **Miscellaneous applications**

9-1 The FILE Type

In the previous chapters you have used different data structures in which to store data items and you know how to organize your data for optimum processing efficiency. If you do not store data to the disk, however, every data item you entered into a program will evaporate when the program exits. Using disks to store your data in files will enable you to save your data permanently and retrieve them later for either reviewing or further processing.

171

A FILE (which is a structured type) is generally defined as a collection of related items stored on disk or any other external storage medium and arranged in sequence as shown in the following figure.

item-1	item-2	item-3	item-4	...	EOF

A file item (also called a file component or file element) may be of any simple or structured type except the type FILE.

Files may be accessed to perform either one of the following operations:

- Reading from a file (input)
- Writing to a file (output)

Files can be organized as either *sequential* access files or *random (direct)* access files. In the first method no item in the file can be reached unless all the preceding items are read. One example of a sequential access file is a purchase list which has to be read from the top down to access a specific item. The random access file is organized like a set of post office boxes, which are identified by numbers and accessed directly without the need to go through them all.

While standard Pascal allows only sequential access files, many implementations of Pascal (including Turbo and UCSD) provide random access files as well. The files discussed in this chapter are all sequential access files.

9-2 TEXT Files

Standard Pascal provides two types of files, TEXT files and non-TEXT files (also called *binary* or *typed* files).

A TEXT file is the simpler file structure as its elements are all characters (of the type CHAR). You have already used the standard INPUT file (the keyboard) and the standard OUTPUT file (the screen), which are classified as TEXT files. A TEXT file consists of successive lines of characters separated by end-of-line marks and ends with the end-of-file mark, as in this example:

> This is a text file. (**EOLN**)
> Each line is composed of successive characters. (**EOLN**)
> Lines are separated by end-of-line marks. (**EOLN**)
> The file is terminated by an end-of-file mark. (**EOLN**)
> (**EOF**)

The file on the disk looks exactly the same as the file you type onto the screen from the keyboard. The characters in a TEXT file are stored in the ASCII format (or EBCDIC in some systems), which means that if the file contains a number like 1234 it will be stored in four bytes, each byte representing the ASCII code of a digit. This is not the case if the number is treated as an INTEGER, in which case it is stored in the internal binary format (0000010011010010) in two bytes.

9-3 Reading TEXT Files

In Chapter 8 you used the program Example 8-1 to read a TEXT file from the keyboard character by character and categorize each character in the file. In this section, the same logic will be used to read and analyze a previously stored text file on the disk. You need to make a few changes in Example 8-1 to make it read a disk file. As we discuss these changes, you will learn the protocols necessary to retrieve information from a TEXT file.

The File Variable

In order to use a disk TEXT file, you have to declare a *file variable* of the type TEXT. If you choose a name like DiskFile for this purpose, the declaration will be:

```
VAR
    DiskFile :TEXT;
```

File Parameters

To use a file in standard Pascal, you must include the file variable (DiskFile in our example) among the other file parameters in the program header (this is not necessary in other implementations).

```
PROGRAM TextAnalyzer2(OUTPUT, DiskFile);
```

Here, the parameter INPUT is not needed as long as no data are to be read from the keyboard. The parameter OUTPUT, however, is necessary for displaying the output.

Opening a File for Input: RESET

To read a text file, it must be *opened* using the standard procedure RESET as follows:

```
RESET(DiskFile);
```

The parameter of the procedure is the file variable.

In Turbo Pascal another procedure, ASSIGN, must also be used to link the actual data file on the disk to the file variable. If the text file to be read is the file C:\CONFIG.SYS (which already exists in the root directory of the hard disk C:), then the following statement must be used before opening the file:

```
ASSIGN(DiskFile, 'C:\CONFIG.SYS');
```

You may replace the file CONFIG.SYS with any other existing file, or you can write a new text file with any text editor (such as EDIT or EDLIN). In any case, if the file is not in the current directory or on the current disk, you have to include the complete PATHNAME of the file as shown in the statement above (for more details on PATHNAME refer to your DOS manual).

Because Turbo Pascal was used to compile the programs in this book, the following two statements were used to open the file:

```
ASSIGN(DiskFile, 'CONFIG.SYS');
RESET(DiskFile);
```

Now the file CONFIG.SYS is ready for input, and the file pointer is pointing to the first item (character) in the file.

Some implementations (such as UCSD) link the file variable and the file name with the RESET procedure, thus making the ASSIGN procedure unnecessary:

```
RESET(file-variable, file-name);
```

Closing the File: CLOSE

The last step after you are finished with reading or writing to a disk file is to close it using the CLOSE procedure, or else data will be lost. This procedure is neither available nor necessary in standard Pascal, where punched cards and magnetic tape files were used.

To close a file, the procedure CLOSE is used as in:

```
CLOSE(DiskFile);
```

Some versions use more parameters for the CLOSE procedure. For example, in UCSD the file must be closed after writing to it using the form:

```
CLOSE(file-variable, action);
```

where action is replaced by either the keyword LOCK if the file will be retained, or PURGE if the file will be deleted.

To summarize, these are the general formulas for preparing a text file for input:

■ Program header:

PROGRAM Program-name(file-list);
(The file-list is optional in most versions.)

- File variable declaration:

  file-variable :**TEXT**;
- Linking file variable to file name (Turbo only):

  ASSIGN(file-variable, file-name);
- Opening a file for input:

  RESET(file-variable);
- Closing a file (for versions other than standard Pascal):

  CLOSE(file-variable);
  CLOSE(file-variable, action); (UCSD)

File Input Procedures: READ, READLN

The input/output statements you have used before are actually special cases of the general form. The complete form of the READLN (or READ) procedure is:

READLN(file-variable, input-list);
READ(file-variable, input-list);

If no file-variable is used, the form is reduced to the one you have been using:

READLN(input-list);

This is the same as using the name of the standard INPUT file:

READLN(INPUT, input-list);

Now, in our example we are going to use the file-variable DiskFile. The input statement will be:

```
READ(DiskFile,Ch);
```

where Ch is the character variable to be read.

The EOF and EOLN Functions

The general form of the EOLN function includes the file variable as follows:

EOLN(file-variable)

If the file-variable and parentheses are omitted, the standard INPUT file (the keyboard) is assumed.

The same thing goes for the EOF function:

EOF(file-variable)

Note: In this chapter, you will use a number of text files as you go through the examples and drills. Some examples create data files, while other examples read them. Therefore, it is best to go through the examples in sequence. However, if you would like to jump to any of the examples randomly, make sure the required text files exist in the current directory. For your convenience, we put all the data files in the examples' directories, in addition to a fresh copy of all the data files in the directory \TextFiles on the companion CD. In case you accidentally overwrite one of the files, you can copy it from this directory. When you run the examples, make sure the example and the data files it uses are all in the current directory.

Application: Disk-File Text Analyzer

Now that you have all the tools for reading a file you can examine the following program, which will give you a complete report on the file CONFIG.SYS, provided on the companion CD in the same directory as the program. If you want to read the CONFIG.SYS file from the root directory of your hard disk, replace the statement:

```
ASSIGN(DiskFile, 'CONFIG.SYS')
```

with the statement:

```
ASSIGN(DiskFile, 'C:\CONFIG.SYS')
```

Do not expect to get the same result as the one obtained from this sample run, because different computers may have different configuration files.

Following the program, the CONFIG.SYS file is listed to check the validity of the report.

```
{ -------------------------- Example 9-1 ------------------------- }
PROGRAM TextAnalyzer2(OUTPUT,DiskFile);
{ Reading from a disk text file one character at a time }
TYPE
   LowerCase  = SET OF 'a'..'z';
   UpperCase  = SET OF 'A'..'Z';
   Digits     = SET OF '0'..'9';
   Characters = SET OF CHAR;
VAR
   DiskFile                      :TEXT;      { declare a text file variable }
   Capital                       :UpperCase;
   Small                         :LowerCase;
   Numerals                      :Digits;
   Alphabet, Punctuation, Others :Characters;
   A, C, S, N, P, O, Counter     :INTEGER;
   Ch                            :CHAR;
BEGIN
{ Link the file variable to the file 'CONFIG.SYS' in the current directory }
```

```
        ASSIGN(DiskFile, 'CONFIG.SYS');
{ Open the file for input }
    RESET(DiskFile);
{ The program logic }
    Counter := 0;      { counter of all characters }
    A := 0;            { counter of alphabetic characters }
    C := 0;            { counter of capital letters }
    S := 0;            { counter of small letters }
    N := 0;            { counter of numeric characters }
    P := 0;            { counter of punctuation characters }
    O := 0;            { counter of other characters }
    Small := ['a'..'z'];
    Capital := ['A'..'Z'];
    Alphabet := Small + Capital;
    Numerals := ['0'..'9'];
    Punctuation := [',',';','-','''','.','!','?',')','(','"',':','_'];
{ Check for the end of the disk file }
    WHILE NOT EOF(DiskFile) DO
        BEGIN
{ Check for the end of line in the disk file }
        WHILE NOT EOLN(DiskFile) DO
            BEGIN
{ Read one character from the disk file }
                READ(DiskFile,Ch);
                Counter := Counter + 1;
                IF Ch IN Alphabet THEN
                    BEGIN
                        A := A + 1;
                        IF Ch IN Small THEN
                            S := S + 1
                        ELSE IF Ch IN Capital THEN
                            C := C + 1
                    END
                ELSE IF Ch IN Numerals THEN
                    N := N + 1
                ELSE IF Ch IN Punctuation THEN
                    P := P + 1
                ELSE
                    O := O + 1
            END;
{ Advance the pointer to the next line }
        READLN(DiskFile)
        END;
{ End of the file is reached }
{ Close the file }
    CLOSE(DiskFile);
{ Display the report }
    WRITELN;
    WRITELN('Total number of characters        = ', Counter);
    WRITELN('Number of alphabetic characters   = ', A);
```

```
    WRITELN(' .Number of lowercase letters: ', S);
    WRITELN(' .Number of uppercase letters: ', C);
    WRITELN('Number of numeric characters     = ', N);
    WRITELN('Number of punctuation characters = ', P);
    WRITELN('Number of other characters       = ', O);
    WRITELN('Press ENTER to continue..');
    READLN
END.
{ ----------------------------------------------------------------- }
```

Listing of the file CONFIG.SYS:

```
    DEVICE=C:\SCSI\ASPI2DOS.SYS /D /Z /P140
    DEVICE=C:\SCSI\ASPICD.SYS /D:ASPICD0
    device=C:\WINDOWS\himem.sys
    [common]
    DEVICE=C:\CDROM\AOATAPI.SYS /D:IDECD000
```

Output:

```
    Total number of characters       = 149
    Number of alphabetic characters  = 107
      .Number of lowercase letters: 20
      .Number of uppercase letters: 87
    Number of numeric characters     = 8
    Number of punctuation characters = 10
    Number of other characters       = 24
    Press ENTER to continue..
```

9-4 Displaying TEXT Files

You can display the contents of any text file by using the same logic as in the previous program, but adding a WRITE statement after each read:

```
    READLN(DiskFile,Ch);
    WRITE(Ch);
```

You also need to advance one line on the screen using a WRITELN statement whenever the EOLN is detected, or else the separate lines will be joined together.

Here is the program, which reads the same file (CONFIG.SYS). The name of the file is declared as a constant, and you may replace it with any file name. It is also possible to use the program source file itself (its name is 9-02.PAS on the companion CD), in which case the program reads itself.

```
{ ------------------------- Example 9-2 ------------------------- }
PROGRAM ReadTextFile(INPUT,OUTPUT,DiskFile);
{ Reading a text file stored on the disk }
CONST
{ You may replace the following constant by any existing file name }
```

```
        FileName = 'C:\CONFIG.SYS';
VAR
   DiskFile :TEXT;
   Ch       :CHAR;
BEGIN
   ASSIGN(DiskFile, FileName);
   RESET(DiskFile);
   WHILE NOT EOF(DiskFile) DO
      BEGIN
         WHILE NOT EOLN(DiskFile) DO
            BEGIN
{ Read and display one character from the text file }
               READ(DiskFile,Ch);
               WRITE(Ch)
            END;
{ Advance the pointer to the next line }
        READLN(DiskFile);
{ Advance one line on the screen }
        WRITELN
     END;
   CLOSE(DiskFile);
   WRITELN('Press ENTER to continue..');
   READLN
END.
{ ---------------------------------------------------------------- }
```

Output:

The output may look something like this:

```
DEVICE=C:\SCSI\ASPI2DOS.SYS /D /Z /P140
DEVICE=C:\SCSI\ASPICD.SYS /D:ASPICD0
device=C:\WINDOWS\himem.sys
[common]
DEVICE=C:\CDROM\AOATAPI.SYS /D:IDECD000
Press ENTER to continue..
```

Reading a TEXT File as a Set of Strings

If your version of Pascal supports the STRING type, you may read a TEXT file one line at a time.

The following program deals with the file as if it is made of strings rather than characters. Each string has a maximum length of 80 characters, which is the expected line length. After each line is read the file pointer moves to the next line. If any line contains less than 80 characters, the dynamic length of the string will be set to the actual number of characters in the line. If, on the other hand, a line contains more than 80 characters, the rest are ignored. When you run the program it asks you to enter the name of the file to be displayed, so this program acts like the DOS command TYPE.

```
{ -------------------------- Example 9-3 ------------------------ }
PROGRAM DisplayTextFile(OUTPUT,MyFile);
{ Reading a text file stored on the disk one line at a time }
VAR
   MyFile             :TEXT;
   OneLine, FileName  :STRING[80];
BEGIN
   WRITE('Please enter the file name to be displayed: ');
   READLN(FileName);
   WRITELN;
   WRITELN('The contents of the file ',FileName,' are: ');
   ASSIGN(MyFile, FileName);
   RESET(MyFile);
{ Check for the end of the text file }
   WHILE NOT EOF(MyFile) DO
      BEGIN
{ Read and display the text file one line at a time }
         READLN(MyFile,OneLine);
         WRITELN(OneLine);
      END;
   CLOSE(MyFile);
   WRITELN('Press ENTER to continue..');
   READLN
END.
{ ---------------------------------------------------------------- }
```

If the file does not exist or its name is written incorrectly, the program gives an error message like this:

```
Please enter the file name to be displayed: CNFIG.SYS
The contents of the file CNFIG.SYS are:
Runtime error 002 at 0000:00F2.
```

Notice that a READLN statement was used to read each string. If you used a READ statement you would still have to use another READLN to skip over the end-of-line mark at the end of each line and move the file pointer to the beginning of the next line. This is because when you use the READ statement, it will read the string characters until the end-of-line mark (or a CR) is detected, then stop. It also does not move the pointer.

In this program you may check the EOLN after each read as you did when you read characters, but you do not need to.

Reading Multiple Strings

It is possible to read more than one string with only one READLN (or READ), but this is sometimes iffy. To understand the possible pitfalls, take a look at this example which reads three strings, each of them declared as STRING[5], from a text file named TEST.TXT. This file contains the following line:

This is a test text file.

```
{ ----------------------- Example 9-4 -------------------------- }
PROGRAM ReadMultipleStrings1(OUTPUT,F);
VAR
    F                :TEXT;
    Str1,Str2,Str3 :STRING[5];
BEGIN
    ASSIGN(F,'test.txt');
    RESET(F);
    READLN(F,Str1,Str2,Str3);
    WRITELN('Str1= ', Str1);
    WRITELN('Str2= ', Str2);
    WRITELN('Str3= ', Str3);
    CLOSE(F);
    WRITELN('Press ENTER to continue..');
    READLN
END.
{ ------------------------------------------------------------- }
```

Output:

```
Str1= This
Str2= is a
Str3= test
```

As you can see in the output, each string variable is assigned five characters (including the blank spaces). Now replace the declaration of the string variables with the following:

```
Str1,Str2,Str3  :STRING;
```

If you run the program using this declaration, the length of each string will default to the maximum length supported by the language, and you will get the result:

```
Str1= This is a test text file.
Str2=
Str3=
```

What happened here was, the first variable was assigned the whole line (up to the end-of-line mark) and nothing was left for the other two. In short, you can only read multiple strings safely if you know the length of each one.

9-5 Creating a File: REWRITE

To create a file you have to open the file to receive output. The procedure REWRITE (which is the counterpart of RESET) is used for this purpose. It takes the form:

REWRITE(file-variable);

In Turbo Pascal you have to link the file variable to the actual file name on the disk using ASSIGN as you did with input.

Some implementations (such as UCSD) instead use a modified formula of the procedure REWRITE, where both the file variable and the file name are used:

REWRITE(file-variable, file-name);   { UCSD }

The rules of inventing a file name (which is the actual name of the disk file) depend on the operating system. In DOS the name can be made of up to eight characters and an optional extension of up to three characters (such as EMPLOYEE.DAT). After this statement an empty file is open and ready for writing.

Note: If you open an existing file for output, the data in this file will be lost and overwritten by the new data.

The Output Procedures: WRITE, WRITELN

To write one or more items to a file use the general form of the WRITELN (or WRITE) procedure:

WRITELN(file-variable, output-list);
or
WRITE(file-variable, output-list);

If the file variable is omitted from these formulas, the standard OUTPUT file (the screen) is assumed and the form is reduced to the one you have been using:

WRITELN(output-list);

which is equivalent to:

WRITELN(OUTPUT, output-list);

After you are finished writing to a disk file you must close it with the CLOSE procedure as mentioned before.

In the following example, a file HELLO.TXT is created, then the constant Hello Pascal is written to this file.

```
{ ------------------------- Example 9-5 ------------------------- }
PROGRAM CreateFile(F);
CONST
   TestSentence = 'Hello Pascal';
VAR
   F :TEXT;
BEGIN
   ASSIGN(F, 'HELLO.TXT');   { Turbo only }
   REWRITE(F);               { open the file for output }
```

```
    WRITELN(F, TestSentence);
    CLOSE(F)
END.
{ ------------------------------------------------------------ }
```

When this program is executed a new file, HELLO.TXT, is added to your current directory. In order to be sure that the file was written properly, you can display it using either the DOS command TYPE or Example 9-3 (which replaces it). In either case you will see the two words Hello Pascal on the screen.

As mentioned earlier, a text file can be created and written to with any text editor, but the importance of creating a file with a Pascal program comes when the information in the new file is based on data processed from other files.

Drill 9-1

Write a program to accept from the keyboard the name and/or ID number and the hours worked per month for each employee and write the data to a file called TIMSHEET.TXT. The program should process the data for any number of employees.

Application: Employee File

In Chapter 8 you created an employee record to contain information about the name, address, wages, etc., of each employee. In the following program, you are going to write the employee record information to a disk file EMPFILE.TXT using the nested record structure. Take a look at the program first:

```
{ -------------------------- Example 9-6 ------------------------- }
PROGRAM CreateEmpFile(INPUT,OUTPUT,F);
TYPE
   AddressRecord   = RECORD
                        Street     :STRING[18];
                        City       :STRING[15];
                        State      :STRING[2];
                        Zip        :String[5];
                     END;
   EmployeeRecord = RECORD
                        ID            :INTEGER;
                        Name          :STRING[20];
                        AddressRec    :AddressRecord;
                        Phone         :STRING[12];
                        Rate          :REAL;
                        MaritalStatus :CHAR;
                     END;
VAR
   F           :TEXT;          { The file variable }
```

```
        EmployeeRec :EmployeeRecord;
BEGIN
    ASSIGN(F, 'EMPFILE.TXT');
        REWRITE(F);
        WITH EmployeeRec DO
            WITH AddressRec DO
                BEGIN
                    WRITE('Please enter Employee ID: ');   READLN(ID);
                    WRITE('Employee Name: ');              READLN(Name);
                    WRITE('Address: Street: ');            READLN(Street);
                    WRITE('           City: ');            READLN(City);
                    WRITE('          State: ');            READLN(State);
                    WRITE('       Zip code: ');            READLN(Zip);
                    WRITE('Phone Number: ');               READLN(Phone);
                    WRITE('Hourly Rate: ');                READLN(Rate);
                    WRITE('Marital Status (S/M): ');        READLN(MaritalStatus);
{ Store the information to the file }
                    WRITELN(F, ID);
                    WRITELN(F, Name);
                    WRITELN(F, Street);
                    WRITELN(F, City);
                    WRITELN(F, State);
                    WRITELN(F, Zip);
                    WRITELN(F, Phone);
                    WRITELN(F, Rate:0:2);
                    WRITELN(F, MaritalStatus)
                END;
        CLOSE(F)
END.
{ ------------------------------------------------------------------- }
```

Sample Run:

```
    Please enter Employee ID: 122
    Employee Name: Tammy M. Ockman
    Address: Street: 322 Temple Dr.
               City: New Orleans
              State: LA
           Zip code: 70112
    Phone Number: 504-285-3434
    Hourly Rate: 22.45
    Marital Status (S/M): S
```

The following is a display of the file contents:

```
    122
    Tammy M. Ockman
    322 Temple Dr.
    New Orleans
    LA
    70112
    504-285-3434
```

```
22.45
S
```

Notice that a numeric field ID has been added to the record, which is otherwise as before (in Chapter 8). Again, if your compiler does not support the STRING type (which is not likely), you can use the numeric and character fields only.

The resulting file contains as many lines as the number of fields in the record. Actually, you can write all of the fields in one line if you so wish by replacing the WRITELNs by WRITEs.

Drill 9-2

Modify the last program so that it can store more than one employee record. You may wish to rebuild it as a procedure which can be called for each data entry of one employee.

Application: Payroll

The file you have just created contains a good deal of information about employees and can be used for more than one purpose. You can use some or all of the information in this file to create different reports or other data files. In the following application, the file EMPFILE.TXT is read but only three fields from each record are used: ID, Name, and HourlyRate. The program first displays an employee's information on the screen, then the user is prompted to enter HoursWorked for this employee. The Wages are then calculated by multiplying HourlyRate and HoursWorked. After processing each record the ID, Name, and Wages are stored in a new file PAYFILE.TXT. The new file is used to produce a payroll report for this pay period.

The program consists of three procedures:

■ GetInfo to read one record of the file EMPFILE.TXT and display only the selected fields. Notice that you have to read all of the record fields even if you do not need them all.

■ CalcWages to carry out the calculations.

■ FilePayRoll to write the record PayRec to the file PAYFILE.TXT.

```
{ ------------------------ Example 9-7 ------------------------ }
PROGRAM PayRoll(INPUT,OUTPUT,MasterFile,PayFile);
{ This program reads the file EMPFILE.TXT, calculates the wages, and
stores the information to the file PAYFILE.TXT }
TYPE
   AddressRecord   = RECORD
                        Street   :STRING[18];
                        City     :STRING[15];
                        State    :STRING[2];
```

```
                        Zip        :String[5];
              END;
   EmployeeRecord = RECORD
                    ID                  :INTEGER;
                    Name                :STRING[20];
                    AddressRec          :AddressRecord;
                    Phone               :STRING[12];
                    Rate                :REAL;
                    MaritalStatus       :CHAR;
              END;
   PayRecord = RECORD
                ID        :INTEGER;
                Name      :STRING[20];
                Wages     :REAL;
             END;
VAR
   MasterFile, PayFile   :TEXT;
   EmployeeRec           :EmployeeRecord;
   PayRec                :PayRecord;
   HoursWorked, Wages    :REAL;


{ -------------- Procedure GetInfo --------------- }
{ This procedure reads the employee file EMPFILE.TXT
  and displays the ID, Name, and Hourly Rate.         }
PROCEDURE GetInfo(VAR F:TEXT);
BEGIN
     WITH EmployeeRec DO
        WITH AddressRec DO
          BEGIN
             READLN(F,ID);              WRITELN('ID: ',ID);
             READLN(F,Name);        WRITELN('Name: ',Name);
             READLN(F,Street);
             READLN(F,City);
             READLN(F,State);
             READLN(F,Zip);
             READLN(F,Phone);
             READLN(F,Rate);        WRITELN('Hourly rate: $', Rate:0:2);
             READLN(F,MaritalStatus);
          END;
END;


{ ------------- Procedure CalcWages -------------- }
{ This procedure is used to calculate wages.
  The result is returned to the main program }
PROCEDURE CalcWages(HoursWorked:REAL; VAR Wages:REAL);
BEGIN
     WITH EmployeeRec DO
        Wages := Hoursworked * Rate;
     Wages := ROUND(100 * Wages) / 100   { rounding cents }
END;
```

```
{ -------------- Procedure FilePayRoll ------------- }
{ This procedure is used to write one record to
   the output file PAYFILE.TXT                         }
PROCEDURE FilePayRoll(VAR P :TEXT; Wages :REAL);
BEGIN
     WITH EmployeeRec DO
        BEGIN
           PayRec.ID    := ID;
           PayRec.Name  := Name;
           Payrec.Wages := Wages
        END;
     WITH PayRec DO
        WRITELN(P, ID:3, Name:20, Wages:10:2)
END;


{ ----------------- Main Program ---------------- }
BEGIN
   ASSIGN(MasterFile, 'EMPFILE.TXT');    RESET(MasterFile);
   ASSIGN(Payfile, 'PAYFILE.TXT');       REWRITE(PayFile);
   WHILE NOT EOF(MasterFile) DO
      BEGIN
         GetInfo(MasterFile);
         WRITE('Please enter hours worked for this pay period: ');
         READLN(HoursWorked);
         CalcWages(HoursWorked, Wages);
         FilePayRoll(PayFile, Wages)
      END;
   CLOSE(MasterFile);
   CLOSE(PayFile)
END.
{ ---------------------------------------------------------------- }
```

Sample Run:

Assume that the file EMPFILE.TXT contains three records. The program will use these records as follows:

```
ID: 122                                               → Information from file
Name: Tammy M. Ockman                                 → Information from file
Hourly rate: $22.45                                   → Information from file
Please enter hours worked for this pay period: 160    → Entered by user
ID: 123
Name: Tara S. Strahan
Hourly rate: $15.24
Please enter hours worked for this pay period: 160
ID: 125
Name: John G. Trainer
Hourly rate: $28.55
Please enter hours worked for this pay period: 140.5
```

The program creates the file PAYFILE.TXT containing the following records:

```
122     Tammy M. Ockman    3592.00
123     Tara S. Strahan    2438.40
125     John G. Trainer    4011.28
```

■ When file variables (such as MasterFile and PayFile) are passed to subprograms, they must be passed as variable parameters (using VAR). The type TEXT is used with such parameters:

```
PROCEDURE FilePayRoll(VAR P :TEXT; Wages :REAL);
```

■ Some identifiers (such as Name and ID) are used in both EmployeeRec and PayRec. This does not cause any problem because they are all fielded variables; remember that the scope of a fielded variable is limited to its own record. Also, the identifier Wages was declared both as a global variable and as a fielded variable (in the record PayRec) and was also used as a local variable in the procedure FilePayroll.

■ Take a look at these assignment statements in the procedure FilePayRoll:

```
WITH EmployeeRec DO
     BEGIN
          PayRec.ID := ID;
          PayRec.Name := Name;
          PayRec.Wages := Wages
```

The first two statements copy the values of the fields ID and Name from EmployeeRec to the corresponding fields in PayRec. The WITH statement modifies only the variables which belong to the record EmployeeRec (ID and Name). A variable such as PayRec.ID is not affected by the WITH statement because it is explicitly modified by PayRec. In the last statement, no variables at all are affected by the WITH statement.

Drill 9-3

Add a procedure to the last program to display a Payroll Summary report as shown:

```
-------- PayRoll Summary ----------
ID --------- Name -------- Salary
122      Tammy M. Ockman    $3592.00
123      Tara S. Strahan    $2438.40
125      John G. Trainer    $4011.28
------------------------------------
```

The program may also be modified in such a way as to read the HoursWorked from the file TIMSHEET.TXT which you created in Drill 9-1.

9-6 Files of Other Types: FILE OF

The TEXT file is a special predefined type of file, but as mentioned earlier the general definition of a file allows the file components to be of any type other than the type FILE. You can declare a file of any predefined or user-defined type using the form:

type-identifier = **FILE OF** component-type;

The component type can be a simple type (like INTEGER), a structured type (like an array), or a user-defined type (like a record).

The following is an example of a file declaration whose components are records (a simplified form of EmployeeRecord is used to make the program shorter):

```
TYPE
    EmployeeRecord = RECORD
                         ID   :INTEGER;
                         Name :STRING[20];
                         Rate :REAL;
                     END;
    EmpFileRec = FILE OF EmployeeRecord;
VAR
    F           :EmpFileRec;       { The file variable }
    EmployeeRec :EmployeeRecord;   { The record variable }
```

The main properties of non-TEXT files are:

■ Data are represented in the internal binary format, which means that you cannot display the contents of a file using the DOS command TYPE. This also speeds up the transfer of data to and from the file.

■ The main advantage of non-TEXT files comes when using structured types such as arrays or records, because then you do not need to read or write the record field by field. For example, after the previous declarations you may read or write the whole record using these statements:

```
READ(F, EmployeeRec);
WRITE(F, EmployeeRec);
```

■ Because non-TEXT files are not made up of lines as TEXT files are, the procedures READLN and WRITELN may not be used with these files.

Application: Payroll System

This is the same payroll program but in a better shape. The program is divided into two separate modules (programs). The first module (Example 9-8) reads the employees' records from the keyboard and stores them in a non-TEXT file EMPFILE.BIN. In the second module (Example 9-9) the HoursWorked are entered from the keyboard and wages are calculated and written to the file PAYFILE.TXT, which is a TEXT file.

The first program may be used only once to create the employee file, but the second program is used every pay period to create the PayFile.

The First Module:

```
{ --------------------------- Example 9-8 ------------------------- }
PROGRAM EmpPayInfo(INPUT,OUTPUT,F);
{ This program is used to create a user-defined file "EMPFILE.BIN"
  whose components are records. }
TYPE
   EmployeeRecord = RECORD
                         ID     :INTEGER;
                         Name   :STRING[20];
                         Rate   :REAL;
                      END;
   EmpFileRec = FILE OF EmployeeRecord;
VAR
   F            :EmpFileRec;          { The file variable }
   EmployeeRec :EmployeeRecord;
{ ------------ Procedure WriteRecord ------------ }
PROCEDURE WriteRecord;
BEGIN
{ Store one record in the file }
   WRITE(F, EmployeeRec)
END;
{ ------------ Procedure GetData ------------ }
PROCEDURE getdata;
VAR
   Counter :INTEGER;
BEGIN
   Counter := 0;
   WITH EmployeeRec DO
      BEGIN
         WRITE('Please enter Employee ID (or 0 to end):'); READLN(ID);
         WHILE ID <> 0 DO
            BEGIN
               Counter := Counter + 1;
               WRITE('Employee Name: ');  READLN(Name);
               WRITE('Hourly Rate: ');    READLN(Rate);
               WriteRecord;
               WRITE('Please enter Employee ID (or 0 to end):'); READLN(ID)
               END
         END;
   WRITELN(Counter, ' Employee records have been filed.')
END;
{ -------------- Main Program -------------- }
{ Main Program }
BEGIN
   ASSIGN(F, 'EMPFILE.BIN');   REWRITE(F);
   GetData;
```

```
        CLOSE(F);
        WRITELN('Press ENTER to continue..');
        READLN
END.
{ ----------------------------------------------------------------- }
```

The second module (PayRoll2) is made up of four procedures:

■ GetInfo to read a record from the file EMPFILE.BIN.

■ CalcWages to carry out the calculations.

■ FilePayRoll to write a record to the file PAYFILE.TXT.

■ ReadPayRoll to read the file PAYFILE.TXT and display the payroll at the end of the process.

The Second Module:

```
{ ------------------------- Example 9-9 ------------------------- }
PROGRAM PayRoll2(INPUT,OUTPUT,MasterFile,PayFile);
{ This program reads the file EMPFILE.BIN one record at a time,
  then calculates wages and stores the output in the text file
  PAYFILE.TXT }
TYPE
   EmployeeRecord = RECORD
                         ID   :INTEGER;
                         Name :STRING[20];
                         Rate :REAL;
                    END;
   PayRecord = RECORD
                    ID    :INTEGER;
                    Name  :STRING[20];
                    Wages :REAL;
               END;
   EmployeeFile = FILE OF EmployeeRecord;
VAR
   MasterFile          :EmployeeFile;
   PayFile             :TEXT;
   EmployeeRec         :EmployeeRecord;
   PayRec              :PayRecord;
   HoursWorked, Wages  :REAL;
{ --------------- Procedure GetInfo --------------- }
{ This Procedure reads and displays a record from
the file EMPFILE.BIN                               }
PROCEDURE GetInfo(VAR F :EmployeeFile);
BEGIN
     READ(F,EmployeeRec);
     WITH EmployeeRec DO
        BEGIN
           WRITELN('ID: ',ID);
           WRITELN('Name: ',Name);
           WRITELN('Hourly rate: $', Rate:0:2);
```

```
            END;
    END;
    { -------------- Procedure CalcWages -------------- }
    PROCEDURE CalcWages(HoursWorked :REAL; VAR Wages :REAL);
    BEGIN
          WITH EmployeeRec DO
          Wages := Hoursworked * Rate;
          Wages := ROUND(100 * Wages) / 100    { rounding cents }
    END;
    { ------------- Procedure FilePayRoll ------------- }
    { This procedure writes a record to PAYFILE.TXT     }
    PROCEDURE FilePayRoll(VAR P :TEXT; Wages :REAL);
    BEGIN
          WITH EmployeeRec DO
             BEGIN
                PayRec.ID := ID;
                PayRec.Name := Name;
                Payrec.Wages := Wages
             END;
          WITH PayRec DO
             BEGIN
                WRITELN(P, ID);
                WRITELN(P, Name);
                WRITELN(P, Wages);
             end;
    END;
    { -------------- Procedure ReadPayRoll -------------- }
    { This procedure reads and displays PAYFILE.TXT        }
    PROCEDURE ReadPayRoll(VAR P:TEXT);
    VAR
       I :INTEGER;
    BEGIN
       WITH PayRec DO
          BEGIN
             READLN(P, ID);
             READLN(P, Name);
             READLN(P, Wages);
             WRITE(ID:3,' ');
             WRITE(Name);
    { Fill the rest of the 20 places with blanks }
             FOR I := 1 TO 20-LENGTH(Name) DO
                 WRITE(' ');
             WRITELN(' $',Wages:0:2)
          END;
    END;
    { ------------------ Main Program --------------------- }
    BEGIN
       ASSIGN(MasterFile, 'EMPFILE.BIN');    RESET(MasterFile);
       ASSIGN(Payfile, 'PAYFILE.TXT');        REWRITE(PayFile);
       WHILE NOT EOF(MasterFile) DO
```

```
      BEGIN
         GetInfo(MasterFile);
         WRITE('Please enter hours worked for this pay period: ');
         READLN(HoursWorked);
         CalcWages(HoursWorked, Wages);
         FilePayRoll(PayFile, Wages)
      END;
   CLOSE(MasterFile);
   CLOSE(PayFile);
   RESET(PayFile);
   WRITELN('---------- PayRoll Summary ----------- ');
   WRITELN('ID # ------- Name -------- Salary');
   WHILE NOT EOF(PayFile) DO
      ReadPayroll(PayFile);
   WRITELN('------------------------------ ');
   CLOSE(PayFile);
   WRITELN('Press ENTER to continue..');
   READLN
END.
{ ----------------------------------------------------------------- }
```

Appending a File

If you would like to add the information for a new employee to the file EMPFILE.BIN, you cannot run Example 9-8 again because it will erase the whole file. There is another way to do this.

Adding data to an existing file is called *appending*, as the new data are written to the end of a sequential file. In some implementations (including Turbo) the file can be opened for appending using the procedure APPEND, which takes the form:

APPEND(file-variable);

While the REWRITE procedure positions the file pointer at the beginning of the file, APPEND positions the file pointer at the end of the file, so any new data will be written there. If your implementation does not have the procedure APPEND you need to use the following technique to add new items to the file:

■ Open the file EMPFILE.BIN for reading using RESET.

■ Open a scratch file (e.g., NEWFILE.TMP) for writing using REWRITE.

■ Copy each item from EMPFILE.BIN to NEWFILE.TMP, then accept the new data from the keyboard and write them to NEWFILE.TMP.

■ Open NEWFILE.TMP for reading and EMPFILE.BIN for writing, then copy the contents of NEWFILE.TMP back to EMPFILE.BIN.

■ Erase the scratch file NEWFILE.TMP.

In standard Pascal, if the file variable is not included in the program header, the file is considered a temporary file and will be erased right after the program execution. You get the same result in UCSD if you close the file using the keyword PURGE.

In Turbo you can erase a file after closing it by using the procedure ERASE, which takes the form:

ERASE(file-variable);

If the information in the file needs to be changed (as in the case of a salary increase for employees), you can use a similar algorithm to update a sequential file as demonstrated later in the following chapters.

Drill 9-4

Write a program that puts all the file tools you have learned together in one menu, using the payroll application. The menu should contain the following options:

■ Display the employee file.

■ Display an employee record.

■ Add a new employee.

The following Menu procedure may be used in this program:

```
{ --------------- Procedure Menu ----------------- }
PROCEDURE Menu;
VAR
    Option :INTEGER;
BEGIN
    WRITELN(Header);
    WRITELN;
    WRITELN('1. Display employee file.');
    WRITELN('2. Display an employee record.');
    WRITELN('3. Add a new employee.');
    WRITELN('4. Exit.');
    WRITELN(Separator);
    WRITE('Make a choice and press a number: ');
    READLN(Option);
    CASE Option OF
        1 : Readit(DbFile);
        2 : ReadRec(DbFile, EmployeeRec);
        3 : AddRec(NewFile, DbFile, EmployeeRec);
        4 : Exit
    END;
    Menu
END;
```

> ### *Drill 9-4 (Cont.)*
>
> As you can see in the Menu procedure, the options 1 to 3 correspond to the procedures you have to design. For the fourth option you may use the Turbo Pascal procedure (EXIT), a GOTO, or any suitable statement in your compiler that lets you exit from the repeated menu. Notice also that in this example a scratch file NewFile was used for adding a new employee to the file (option #3), but if you have the procedure APPEND in your compiler, you should use it instead, as it will save you a lot of effort. This program is the nucleus of a database and can be modified to include more features, such as updating employees' information and removing unwanted records from the database.

9-7 Using the File Buffer Variable: GET and PUT

In standard Pascal, when you declare a file, a *file window* or a *file buffer variable* is created automatically. This buffer helps to compensate for the disk I/O transfers, which take a long time compared to memory transfers. The file window, a location in memory, is used to store the file items and transfer them to the external storage (the disk) while the other program statements are being executed. Today, however, with modern hardware, you may not encounter this problem.

If, for example, you declare a file variable DiskFile, the following file buffer variable is created:

```
DiskFile^
```

To use this buffer, you must use the predefined procedures GET for reading from the file, and PUT for writing to the file. These procedures are used instead of READ and WRITE. For example, consider the following declaration:

```
VAR
DiskFile: TEXT;
Ch: CHAR;
```

The statement WRITE(DiskFile, Ch), which is used to write data to the file, is equivalent to the following statements:

```
DiskFile^ := Ch;
PUT(DiskFile)
```

The first statement copies the data stored in Ch to the buffer, and the second statement transfers data from the buffer to the file variable.

Similarly, the statement READ(DiskFile, Ch), which is used to read from the file, is equivalent to the following statements:

```
Ch := DiskFile^;
GET(DiskFile)
```

The first statement copies the value of the buffer (which always contains the next file component) to the variable Ch, while the second one reads the next file component into the file variable.

You may try any of the previous examples using PUT and GET procedures. However, keep in mind that some versions of Pascal, including Turbo Pascal, do not provide the file buffer variable and, consequently, do not support GET or PUT.

Summary

In this chapter, you learned the main tools for handling data files:

1. You know that standard Pascal provided TEXT and non-TEXT sequential files, while modern versions also provide random/direct access files.

2. During your tour of sequential files, you learned how to declare, create, write to, and read from a file.

3. TEXT files are declared using the form:

    file-variable **:TEXT;**

4. Files of other types are declared using the forms:

    TYPE
        type-identifier = **FILE OF** component-type;
    VAR
        file-variable :type-identifier;

In standard Pascal the file-variable must be included as one of the file parameters or the file will be considered a temporary one and automatically deleted after the execution. In UCSD you must use the PURGE keyword to delete such a temporary file, and in Turbo the ERASE procedure.

5. The procedures used to open a file for either input or output are:

    RESET(file-variable);   (for input)
    REWRITE(file-variable);   (for output)

With modern versions of Pascal (such as Turbo) you can also open a sequential file for appending with the procedure APPEND, which has a similar form to those above.

6. With versions other than standard Pascal, the file-variable must be linked to the actual file name on the disk. In Turbo, this is done by using the procedure ASSIGN; in UCSD the actual file name comes as a second parameter of the RESET or REWRITE procedures. In these implementations the file must be closed after processing using the CLOSE procedure.

7. You learned the general form of the following input/output statements:

> READLN(file-variable, input-list);
> READ(file-variable, input-list);
> WRITELN(file-variable, output-list);
> WRITE(file-variable, output-list);

You also know that the READLN and WRITELN procedures may not be used with non-TEXT files. You also learned the standard Pascal procedures GET and PUT, which are used in conjunction with the file buffer variables to read from and write to data files. These procedures are not included in some versions of Pascal.

8. You also learned the general form of EOF and EOLN functions:

> EOF(file-variable)
> EOLN(file-variable)

Finally, you have had enough practice to enable you to create and manipulate files for different applications

Exercises

1. Modify Example 9-1 to count the number of vowels in the file CONFIG.SYS.

2. Write a program to open one of the Pascal files, and copy the contents of the file into a new text file. Add line numbers to each line in the new file. The input and output file names are provided at run time. In the following output, the example file 9-04.PAS was used as an input file:

```
 1: { ---------------------- Example 9-4 ---------------------- }
 2: PROGRAM ReadMultipleStrings1(OUTPUT,F);
 3: VAR
 4:     F                    :TEXT;
 5:     Str1,Str2,Str3 :STRING[5];
 6: BEGIN
 7:     ASSIGN(F,'test.txt');
 8:     RESET(F);
 9:     READLN(F,Str1,Str2,Str3);
10:     WRITELN('Str1= ', Str1);
11:     WRITELN('Str2= ', Str2);
12:     WRITELN('Str3= ', Str3);
13:     CLOSE(F);
14:     WRITELN('Press ENTER to continue..');
15:     READLN
16: END.
```

3. When reading a long program, sometimes you need to highlight the headers of procedures and functions to make the printed text scanable. Write a program to read a Pascal program file that contains some procedures and write the headers of those procedures into a separate file, along with their line numbers. The output from processing the file 9-09.PAS will look like this:

```
27: PROCEDURE GetInfo(VAR F :EmployeeFile);
38: PROCEDURE CalcWages(HoursWorked :REAL; VAR Wages :REAL);
46: PROCEDURE FilePayRoll(VAR P :TEXT; Wages :REAL);
63: PROCEDURE ReadPayRoll(VAR P:TEXT);
```

4. Modify Drill 9-3 to mark the records of the employees who received more than $1000.00 in this payroll period. Do this by adding * to the end of the record. The following is an example of the output file (PAYFILE.TXT):

```
122     Tammy M. Ockman    1234.75*
123     Tara S. Strahan     609.60
125     John G. Trainer    1427.50*
```

5. A publishing firm receives text from different writers, sometimes written in different styles. Some writers leave two spaces after the end of each sentence; other writers leave only one space. Write a program to scan a text file and convert any two spaces that follow a sentence to a single space.

Answers

1. Declare a SET variable, Vowels, to store the set of vowels, and add a counter to count the number of vowels.

   Assign the following set to the Vowels variable:

   ```
   Vowels := ['a','e','i','o','u','A','E','I','O','U'];
   ```

   Modify the IF statement to include counting the vowels as shown in this code segment:

   ```
   IF Ch IN Alphabet THEN
       BEGIN
           A := A + 1;
           IF Ch IN Vowels THEN
               V := V + 1;     { Vowel counter }
           IF Ch IN Small THEN
               S := S + 1;
           IF Ch IN Capital THEN
               C := C + 1;
       END
       ...
   ```

2. You can use the following code segment to copy MyFile to NewFile and add the line numbers to it. You may also open and display NewFile after the copying is finished.

   ```
   ASSIGN(MyFile, ReadFileName);
   RESET(MyFile);
   ASSIGN(NewFile, WriteFileName);
   REWRITE(NewFile);
   WHILE NOT EOF(MyFile) DO
       BEGIN
           READLN(MyFile,OneLine);
           Counter := Counter +1;
   ```

```
                    WRITELN(NewFile, Counter:3,': ', OneLine);
            END;
      CLOSE(MyFile);
      CLOSE(NewFile);
```

3. The following is the main algorithm that reads the Pascal file and copies the procedure lines (assuming that the word procedure is either uppercase or initial capped; you may add other casing possibilities).

```
WHILE NOT EOF(MyFile) DO
      BEGIN
            READLN(MyFile,OneLine);
            Counter := Counter +1;
            IF (COPY(OneLine,1,9) = 'PROCEDURE')
            OR
            (COPY(OneLine,1,9) = 'Procedure') THEN
                  WRITELN(NewFile, Counter:3,': ', OneLine);
      END;
```

4. The following is the required modification in the program DRL9-3:

```
WITH PayRec DO
      IF Wages >= 1000.0 THEN
            WRITELN(P, ID:3, Name:20, Wages:10:2, '*')
      ELSE
            WRITELN(P, ID:3, Name:20, Wages:10:2);
```

Using Variant Records

10-1 Variant Records

In real-life applications, employees in the same company may fall into different categories. Some employees are salaried, some are paid on an hourly basis, and others are paid by commission. The payroll for each of these categories uses different calculations. This is an example of a record for a salaried employee,

```
SalariedEmployee = RECORD
            ID              :STRING[5];
            Name            :STRING[20];
            Position        :STRING[20];
            SSN             :STRING[11];
            MonthlySalary   :REAL
          END;
```

while the following is an example of the record of an hourly employee,

```
HourlyEmployee = RECORD
                 ID           :STRING[5];
                 Name         :STRING[20];
                 Position     :STRING[20];
                 SSN          :STRING[11];
                 HourlyRate   :REAL
              END;
```

and this is an example of the record of a salesperson paid by commission:

```
CommissionEmployee = RECORD
                     ID           :STRING[5];
                     Name         :STRING[20];
                     Position     :STRING[20]
                     SSN          :STRING[11];
                     Commission   :REAL;
                     BasicSalary  :REAL;
                     Area         :STRING[20]
                  END;
```

It is not a good idea to use three different records in the same program to represent the employee record. In Pascal the variant record allows the programmer to store different types of data in the same memory location. The variant record, in this example, will have a fixed part which contains the fields that do not change from one employee to the other (such as ID, Name, and SSN), and a variant part which differs from one category to another (such as the payroll details). In order to differentiate between different types of records, the variant record must be declared using a CASE structure with one of the fields as the case expression. This field is called the *tag field*.

An example of the tag field that you can add to the record is a character variable that may contain the values '1', '2', or '3' to represent the following categories:

'1' = salaried employees
'2' = hourly paid employees
'3' = employees paid by commission

Here is the employee variant record:

```
SalariedEmployee = RECORD
                   ID                      :STRING[5];
                   Name, Position          :STRING[20];
                   SSN                     :STRING[11];
                   CASE Category           :CHAR OF
                      '1' :(MonthlySalary   :REAL);
                      '2' :(HourlyRate      :REAL);
                      '3' :(Commission,
                            BasicSalary      :REAL;
                            Area             :STRING[20])
                END;
```

The tag field here is Category. If the value of the tag field is '1,' it will transfer the control to the salaried employee and the variable MonthlySalary comes into effect. If it is '2,' the control is transferred to the hourly paid employee and the variable HourlyRate is in effect. If it is '3,' the three variables Commission, BasicSalary, and Area are all brought into action.

The variant record may contain a fixed part followed by a variant part, or may contain a variant part only. The declaration takes the following general form:

type-name = **RECORD**
> fixed field-list
> variant field-list
> **END;**

The variant field list takes the following form:

> **CASE** tag-field : type-definition **OF**
> label-1   : (field-list : type-definition);
> label-2   : (field-list : type-definition);
> ...
> label-*n*   : (field-list : type-definition);

Notice that the field list for each case is enclosed in parentheses, and the CASE structure does not contain an END statement.

10-2 Application: Enhanced Payroll System

In this program, you are going to read the records of different employees from a payroll file. The required record is retrieved using the Social Security Number which you enter from the keyboard. Before using this program, you have to create the text file PAYROLL.TXT which contains the employee records. You may use any text editor to create this file. The records in the file must be written sequentially without any gaps, and must be consistent with the record description. After the file is created (even with one record), you can use the program to append new records to it. For the purpose of testing the program, you may use the file PAYROLL.TXT on the companion CD.

Here are the contents of the file:

```
1MGT5
Tammy M. Ockman
Business Manager
232-65-1567
1                      → The tag field
3333.33
2STF1
Tara S. Strahan
Secretary II
```

```
404-38-1132
2                              → The tag field
8.24
3SAL4
John G. Trainer
Sales Representative
334-88-1234
3                              → The tag field
0.25                           → Notice additional fields
500.0                            in category 3
Baton Rouge, LA
1MGT4
Sally A. Abolrous
Technical Editor
434-65-6052
4343.88
1MGT1
James A. Abolrous
President
434-55-6666
1                              → The tag field
4343.88
```

Before we move to the discussion, let us take a look at the following program:

```
{ ---------------------- Example 10-1 -------------------------- }
PROGRAM EmployeeDataBase2(INPUT, OUTPUT, PayrollFile,  NewFile);
CONST
   FileName = 'payroll.txt';
   TempFile = 'temp.txt';
   Header = '------------- Main Menu -------------';
   Header1 = '---------- Employee DataBase ---------';
   Header2 = '--------- Employee Record ------------';
   Separator = '-----------------------------------';
TYPE
   EmployeeRecord = RECORD
                       ID              :STRING[5];
                       Name, Position  :STRING[20];
                       SSN             :STRING[11];
                       CASE Category   :CHAR OF
                         '1'   :(MonthlySalary    :REAL);
                         '2'   :(HourlyRate       :REAL);
                         '3'   :(Commission,
                                 BasicSalary      :REAL;
                                 Area             :STRING[20])
                    END;

VAR
   NewFile, PayrollFile  :TEXT;
   EmployeeRec           :EmployeeRecord;
   Title                 :ARRAY [1..9] OF STRING[20];
```

```pascal
   OneLine            :STRING[80];

{ ---------------------- Procedure ReadRec ---------------------- }
PROCEDURE ReadRec(VAR PayrollFile :TEXT; Employee :EmployeeRecord);
VAR
   SSNumber            :STRING[11];
   Found       :INTEGER;
BEGIN
   Found := 0;            {Reset the flag}
   ASSIGN(PayrollFile, FileName);
   RESET(PayrollFile);
   WRITELN;
   WRITE('Please enter the SSN of the employee: ');
   READLN(SSNumber);
   WHILE NOT EOF(PayrollFile) DO
     BEGIN
       WITH Employee DO
         BEGIN
           READLN(PayrollFile, ID);
           READLN(PayrollFile, Name);
           READLN(PayrollFile, Position);
           READLN(PayrollFile, SSN);
           READLN(PayrollFile, Category);
           CASE Category OF
            '1' : READLN(PayrollFile, MonthlySalary);
            '2' : READLN(PayrollFile, HourlyRate);
            '3' : BEGIN
                    READLN(PayrollFile, Commission);
                    READLN(PayrollFile, BasicSalary);
                    READLN(PayrollFile, Area)
                  END
           END;   { End of CASE structure }
           IF SSNumber = SSN THEN
             BEGIN
               WRITELN(Header2);
               WRITELN(Title[1], ID);
               WRITELN(Title[2], Name);
               WRITELN(Title[3], Position);
               WRITELN(Title[4], SSN);
                 CASE Category OF
                   '1' : WRITELN(Title[5], MonthlySalary:0:2);
                   '2' : WRITELN(Title[6], HourlyRate:0:2);
                   '3' : BEGIN
                           WRITELN(Title[7], Commission:0:2);
                           WRITELN(Title[8], BasicSalary:0:2);
                           WRITELN(Title[9], Area)
                         END
                 END;          { End of CASE structure }
               Found := 1
             END
```

```
            END              { End of WITH block }
          END;
        CLOSE(PayrollFile);
        IF Found <> 1 THEN
          BEGIN
            WRITELN('SSN not found in file.');
            WRITELN('Please try again.');
            WRITELN
          END
    END;


{ ---------------------- Procedure AddRec ---------------------- }
PROCEDURE AddRec(VAR NewFile, PayrollFile :TEXT;
                                          Employee: EmployeeRecord);
BEGIN
     ASSIGN(PayrollFile, FileName);
     RESET(PayrollFile);
     ASSIGN(NewFile, TempFile);
     REWRITE(NewFile);
{ Check for the end of the text file }
     WHILE NOT EOF(PayrollFile) DO
         BEGIN
{ Copy each record from PayrollFile to the NewFile }
           READLN(PayrollFile, OneLine);
           WRITELN(NewFile, OneLine);
         END;
{ Accept a new record from the keyboard }
     WITH Employee DO
       BEGIN
         WRITE('Please enter Employee ID: ');
         READLN(ID);
         WRITE('Name: ');              READLN(Name);
         WRITE('Position: ');          READLN(Position);
         WRITE('SSN (xxx-xx-xxxx): '); READLN(SSN);
         WRITE('Payroll category: ');  READLN(Category);
           CASE Category OF
             '1' : BEGIN
                     WRITE('Monthly Salary: ');
                     READLN(MonthlySalary);
                   END;
             '2' : BEGIN
                     WRITE('Rate: ');
                     READLN(HourlyRate);
                   END;
             '3' : BEGIN
                     WRITE('Commission: ');
                     READLN(Commission);
                     WRITE('Basic salary: ');
                     READLN(BasicSalary);
                     WRITE('Area: ');
```

```
                        READLN(Area)
            END
        END;
{ Store the information in NewFile }
    WRITELN(NewFile, ID);
    WRITELN(NewFile, Name);
    WRITELN(NewFile, Position);
    WRITELN(NewFile, SSN);
    WRITELN(NewFile, Category);
    CASE Category OF
      '1' : WRITELN(NewFile, MonthlySalary:0:2);
      '2' : WRITELN(NewFile, HourlyRate:0:2);
      '3' : BEGIN
               WRITELN(NewFile, Commission:0:2);
               WRITELN(NewFile, BasicSalary:0:2);
               WRITELN(NewFile, Area)
            END
    END
  END;
  CLOSE(NewFile);
  CLOSE(PayrollFile);
{ Copy NewFile back to Payroll File }
  ASSIGN(PayrollFile, FileName);
  REWRITE(PayrollFile);
  ASSIGN(NewFile, TempFile);
  RESET(NewFile);
  WHILE NOT EOF(NewFile) DO
    BEGIN
      READLN(NewFile, OneLine);
      WRITELN(PayrollFile, OneLine)
    END;
  CLOSE(NewFile);
  ERASE(NewFile);    { Erase the temporary file }
  CLOSE(PayrollFile)
END;


{ ----------------------- Procedure Menu ----------------------- }
PROCEDURE Menu;
VAR
  Option :INTEGER;
BEGIN
  WRITELN(Header);
  WRITELN;
  WRITELN('1. Display an employee record.');
  WRITELN('2. Add a new employee.');
  WRITELN('3. Exit.');
  WRITELN(Separator);
  WRITE('Make a choice and press a number: ');
  READLN(Option);
  CASE Option OF
```

```
      1 : ReadRec(PayrollFile, EmployeeRec);
      2 : AddRec(NewFile, PayrollFile, EmployeeRec);
      3 : Exit
  END;
  Menu
END;


{ ----------------------- Main Program ----------------------- }
BEGIN
{ Assign titles }
  Title[1] := 'ID: ';
  Title[2] := 'Name: ';
  Title[3] := 'Position: ';
  Title[4] := 'SSN: ';
  Title[5] := 'Salary: ';
  Title[6] := 'Rate: ';
  Title[7] := 'Commission: ';
  Title[8] := 'Basic Salary: ';
  Title[9] := 'Area: ';
  Menu
END.
{ ---------------------------------------------------------------- }
```

Sample Runs:

(1) Reading records from the file: In this sample run, three records for three different categories of employees are read from the file. In the fourth attempt to read a record, we entered a Social Security Number which is not in the file, and the message "SSN not found in file" was received. Notice that the data entered from the keyboard are bolded for clarity.

```
--------------- Main Menu ---------------
1. Display an employee record.
2. Add a new employee.
3. Exit.
-----------------------------------------
Make a choice and press a number: 1
Please enter the SSN of the employee: 434-55-6666

------------ Employee Record ------------
ID: 1MGT1
Name: James A. Abolrous
Position: President
SSN: 434-55-6666
Salary: 4343.88

--------------- Main Menu ---------------
1. Display an employee record.
2. Add a new employee.
3. Exit.
```

```
----------------------------------------
Make a choice and press a number: 1
Please enter the SSN of the employee: 404-38-1132

------------ Employee Record ------------
ID: 2STF1
Name: Tara S. Strahan
Position: Secretary II
SSN: 404-38-1132
Rate: 8.24

-------------- Main Menu --------------
1. Display an employee record.
2. Add a new employee.
3. Exit.
----------------------------------------
Make a choice and press a number: 1
Please enter the SSN of the employee: 334-88-1234

----------- Employee Record ------------
ID: 3SAL4
Name: John G. Trainer
Position: Sales Representative
SSN: 334-88-1234
Commission: 0.25
Basic Salary: 500.00
Area: Baton Rouge, LA

-------------- Main Menu --------------
1. Display an employee record.
2. Add a new employee.
3. Exit.
----------------------------------------
Make a choice and press a number: 1
Please enter the SSN of the employee: 555-55-5555
SSN not found in file.
Please try again.

-------------- Main Menu --------------
1. Display an employee record.
2. Add a new employee.
3. Exit.
----------------------------------------
Make a choice and press a number: 3
```

(2) Appending records to the file: In the following run, a new record is appended to the payroll file:

```
-------------- Main Menu --------------
1. Display an employee record.
2. Add a new employee.
```

```
3. Exit.
-----------------------------------------
Make a choice and press a number: 2
Please enter Employee ID: 3SAL6
Name: Barbara Ortiz
Position: Sales Representative
SSN (xxx-xx-xxxx): 347-12-3456
Payroll category:  3
Commission: .15
Basic salary: 450.0
Area: New Orleans, LA


-------------- Main Menu ----------------
1. Display an employee record.
2. Add a new employee.
3. Exit.
-----------------------------------------
Make a choice and press a number: 3
```

At this point, the new record of Barbara Ortiz has been appended to the payroll file and may be displayed using option 1. Needless to say, you can also add a record at the end of the file using any text editor.

Remarks

There are some important points in the program:

1. This program is divided into three procedures:

Menu:	to display and accept the menu options.
ReadRec:	to read the file.
AddRec:	to append records to the file.

2. When dealing with a variant record, either by reading or writing, you must use the CASE structure.

3. The flag Found is used in the ReadRec procedure to check the existence of the required record in the file, and to issue the proper message in each case. Notice that the flag is reset at the beginning of the procedure (Found := 0). When the required record is found, the flag is assigned the value 1; otherwise, it retains the value 0 and the message "SSN not found in file" is issued after the end-of-file has been reached.

Drill 10-1

Write a program to create the payroll file used in the previous example. You understand that this program may be used only once, because each time you run it, a new file is created. You may refer to the program on the companion CD under the name DRL10-1.PAS. The program is designed to create a file with the name PR.TXT in order to avoid rewriting the file PAYROLL.TXT.

10-3 Deleting Records from the File

The algorithm to delete an employee record from the payroll file is as follows:

1. Enter the Social Security Number of the employee to be removed.
2. Open the payroll file for reading and a temporary file for writing.
3. Read the payroll file up to the end-of-file. For each record, check the SSN field against the Social Security Number.
4. Copy each record, except the one that matches, to the temporary file.
5. Copy the temporary file into the original payroll file.
6. Delete the temporary file.

To do that you need to add the following procedure to the previous program. (The source code of this procedure is on the companion CD under the name DEL-PROC.PAS).

```
{ ---------------------- Procedure DelRec ---------------------- }
PROCEDURE DelRec(VAR NewFile, PayrollFile :TEXT;
                              Employee :EmployeeRecord);
VAR
   SSNumber :STRING[11];
BEGIN
   ASSIGN(PayrollFile, FileName);
   RESET(PayrollFile);
   ASSIGN(NewFile, TempFile);
   REWRITE(NewFile);
   WRITE('Please enter the SSN of the employee to be deleted: ');
   READLN(SSNumber);
   WHILE NOT EOF(PayrollFile) DO
     BEGIN
       WITH Employee DO
         BEGIN
           READLN(PayrollFile, ID);
           READLN(PayrollFile, Name);
           READLN(PayrollFile, Position);
           READLN(PayrollFile, SSN);
           READLN(PayrollFile, Category);
           CASE Category OF
             '1' : READLN(PayrollFile, MonthlySalary);
             '2' : READLN(PayrollFile, HourlyRate);
             '3' : BEGIN
                     READLN(PayrollFile, Commission);
                     READLN(PayrollFile, BasicSalary);
                     READLN(PayrollFile, Area)
                   END
         END;  { End of CASE structure }
         IF SSNumber <> SSN THEN
           BEGIN
```

```
                    WRITELN(NewFile, ID);
                    WRITELN(NewFile, Name);
                    WRITELN(NewFile, Position);
                    WRITELN(NewFile, SSN);
                    WRITELN(NewFile, Category);

                      CASE Category OF
                        '1' : WRITELN(NewFile, MonthlySalary:0:2);
                        '2' : WRITELN(NewFile, HourlyRate:0:2);
                        '3' : BEGIN
                                WRITELN(NewFile, Commission:0:2);
                                WRITELN(NewFile, BasicSalary:0:2);
                                WRITELN(NewFile, Area)
                              END
                      END;           { End of CASE structure }
                  END
          END          { End of WITH block }
        END;
    CLOSE(NewFile);
    CLOSE(PayrollFile);
  { Copy NewFile back to Payroll File }
    ASSIGN(PayrollFile, FileName);
    REWRITE(PayrollFile);
    ASSIGN(NewFile, TempFile);
    RESET(NewFile);
    WHILE NOT EOF(NewFile) DO
      BEGIN
        READLN(NewFile, OneLine);
        WRITELN(PayrollFile, OneLine)
      END;
    CLOSE(NewFile);
    ERASE(NewFile);        { Erase the temporary file }
    CLOSE(PayrollFile);
    WRITELN('The employee ', SSNumber, ' is removed from file.')
    END;
{ ------------------------------------------------------------------ }
```

In order to have the Delete Record option as one of the menu items, you need to modify the Menu procedure. It may look similar to the procedure below (this procedure is on the companion CD under the name MNU-PROC.PAS).

```
{ ---------------------- Procedure Menu ------------------------- }
PROCEDURE Menu;
VAR
   Option :INTEGER;
BEGIN
   WRITELN(Header);
   WRITELN;
   WRITELN('1. Display an employee record.');
   WRITELN('2. Add a new employee.');
   WRITELN('3. Delete an employee.');
```

```
   WRITELN('4. Exit.');
   WRITELN(Separator);
   WRITE('Make a choice and press a number: ');
   READLN(Option);
   CASE Option OF
      1 : ReadRec(PayrollFile, EmployeeRec);
      2 : AddRec(NewFile, PayrollFile, EmployeeRec);
      3 : DelRec(NewFile, PayrollFile, EmployeeRec);
      4 : Exit
   END;
   Menu
END;
{ ---------------------------------------------------------------- }
```

Here are all the modules of the program brought together:

```
{ ---------------------- Example 10-2 -------------------------- }
PROGRAM EmployeeDataBase2(INPUT, OUTPUT, PayrollFile,  NewFile);
CONST
   FileName = 'payroll.txt';
   TempFile = 'temp.txt';
   Header = '-------------- Main Menu --------------';
   Header1 = '--------- Employee DataBase ----------';
   Header2 = '---------- Employee Record -----------';
   Separator = '------------------------------------';
TYPE
   EmployeeRecord = RECORD
                     ID                 :STRING[5];
                     Name, Position     :STRING[20];
                     SSN                :STRING[11];
                     CASE Category      :CHAR OF
                        '1'    :(MonthlySalary :REAL);
                        '2'    :(HourlyRate    :REAL);
                        '3'    :(Commission,
                                 BasicSalary   :REAL;
                                 Area          :STRING[20])
                  END;


VAR
   NewFile, PayrollFile  :TEXT;
   EmployeeRec           :EmployeeRecord;
   Title                 :ARRAY [1..9] OF STRING[20];
   OneLine               :STRING[80];


{ ---------------------- Procedure ReadRec ---------------------- }
PROCEDURE ReadRec(VAR PayrollFile :TEXT; Employee :EmployeeRecord);
VAR
   SSNumber   :STRING[11];
   Found      :INTEGER;
BEGIN
   Found := 0;           {Reset the flag}
```

```
ASSIGN(PayrollFile, FileName);
RESET(PayrollFile);
WRITELN;
WRITE('Please enter the SSN of the employee: ');
READLN(SSNumber);
WHILE NOT EOF(PayrollFile) DO
  BEGIN
    WITH Employee DO
      BEGIN
        READLN(PayrollFile, ID);
        READLN(PayrollFile, Name);
        READLN(PayrollFile, Position);
        READLN(PayrollFile, SSN);
        READLN(PayrollFile, Category);
        CASE Category OF
         '1' : READLN(PayrollFile, MonthlySalary);
         '2' : READLN(PayrollFile, HourlyRate);
         '3' : BEGIN
                 READLN(PayrollFile, Commission);
                 READLN(PayrollFile, BasicSalary);
                 READLN(PayrollFile, Area)
               END
        END;   { End of CASE structure }
        IF SSNumber = SSN THEN
          BEGIN
            WRITELN(Header2);
            WRITELN(Title[1], ID);
            WRITELN(Title[2], Name);
            WRITELN(Title[3], Position);
            WRITELN(Title[4], SSN);
              CASE Category OF
                '1' : WRITELN(Title[5], MonthlySalary:0:2);
                '2' : WRITELN(Title[6], HourlyRate:0:2);
                '3' : BEGIN
                        WRITELN(Title[7], Commission:0:2);
                        WRITELN(Title[8], BasicSalary:0:2);
                        WRITELN(Title[9], Area)
                      END
              END;           { End of CASE structure }
            Found := 1
          END
    END            { End of WITH block }
  END;
CLOSE(PayrollFile);
IF Found <> 1 THEN
  BEGIN
    WRITELN('SSN not found in file.');
    WRITELN('Please try again.');
    WRITELN
  END
```

```
END;

{ ----------------------- Procedure AddRec ----------------------- }
PROCEDURE AddRec(VAR NewFile, PayrollFile :TEXT;
                                      Employee: EmployeeRecord);
BEGIN
   ASSIGN(PayrollFile, FileName);
   RESET(PayrollFile);
   ASSIGN(NewFile, TempFile);
   REWRITE(NewFile);
{ Check for the end of the text file }
   WHILE NOT EOF(PayrollFile) DO
      BEGIN
{ Copy each record from PayrollFile to the NewFile }
         READLN(PayrollFile, OneLine);
         WRITELN(NewFile, OneLine)
      END;
{ Accept a new record from the keyboard }
   WITH Employee DO
     BEGIN
       WRITE('Please enter Employee ID: ');
       READLN(ID);
       WRITE('Name: ');                  READLN(Name);
       WRITE('Position: ');              READLN(Position);
       WRITE('SSN (xxx-xx-xxxx): ');     READLN(SSN);
       WRITE('Payroll category: ');      READLN(Category);
         CASE Category OF
          '1' : BEGIN
                  WRITE('Monthly Salary: ');
                  READLN(MonthlySalary);
                END;
          '2' : BEGIN
                  WRITE('Rate: ');
                  READLN(HourlyRate);
                END;
          '3' : BEGIN
                  WRITE('Commission: ');
                  READLN(Commission);
                  WRITE('Basic salary: ');
                  READLN(BasicSalary);
                  WRITE('Area: ');
                  READLN(Area)
                END
        END
     END;
{ Store the information in NewFile }
   WRITELN(NewFile, ID);
   WRITELN(NewFile, Name);
   WRITELN(NewFile, Position);
   WRITELN(NewFile, SSN);
   WRITELN(NewFile, Category);
```

```
   CASE Category OF
     '1' : WRITELN(NewFile, MonthlySalary:0:2);
     '2' : WRITELN(NewFile, HourlyRate:0:2);
     '3' : BEGIN
              WRITELN(NewFile, Commission:0:2);
              WRITELN(NewFile, BasicSalary:0:2);
              WRITELN(NewFile, Area)
           END
   END
  END;
  CLOSE(NewFile);
  CLOSE(PayrollFile);
{ Copy NewFile back to Payroll File }
  ASSIGN(PayrollFile, FileName);
  REWRITE(PayrollFile);
  ASSIGN(NewFile, TempFile);
  RESET(NewFile);
  WHILE NOT EOF(NewFile) DO
    BEGIN
      READLN(NewFile, OneLine);
      WRITELN(PayrollFile, OneLine)
    END;
  CLOSE(NewFile);
  ERASE(NewFile);    { Erase the temporary file }
  CLOSE(PayrollFile)
END;


{ ----------------------- Procedure DelRec ----------------------- }

PROCEDURE DelRec(VAR NewFile, PayrollFile :TEXT;
Employee :EmployeeRecord);
VAR
   SSNumber :STRING[11];
BEGIN
   ASSIGN(PayrollFile, FileName);
   RESET(PayrollFile);
   ASSIGN(NewFile, TempFile);
   REWRITE(NewFile);
   WRITE('Please enter the SSN of the employee to be deleted: ');
   READLN(SSNumber);

   WHILE NOT EOF(PayrollFile) DO
     BEGIN
       WITH Employee DO
         BEGIN
           READLN(PayrollFile, ID);
           READLN(PayrollFile, Name);
           READLN(PayrollFile, Position);
           READLN(PayrollFile, SSN);
           READLN(PayrollFile, Category);
```

```
            CASE Category OF
              '1' : READLN(PayrollFile, MonthlySalary);
              '2' : READLN(PayrollFile, HourlyRate);
              '3' : BEGIN
                        READLN(PayrollFile, Commission);
                        READLN(PayrollFile, BasicSalary);
                        READLN(PayrollFile, Area)
                    END
            END;  { End of CASE structure }
            IF SSNumber <> SSN THEN
              BEGIN
                WRITELN(NewFile,ID);
                WRITELN(NewFile,Name);
                WRITELN(NewFile,Position);
                WRITELN(NewFile,SSN);
                WRITELN(NewFile,Category);

                  CASE Category OF
                    '1' : WRITELN(NewFile,MonthlySalary:0:2);
                    '2' : WRITELN(NewFile,HourlyRate:0:2);
                    '3' : BEGIN
                            WRITELN(NewFile,Commission:0:2);
                            WRITELN(NewFile,BasicSalary:0:2);
                            WRITELN(NewFile,Area)
                          END
                  END;  { End of CASE structure }
              END
          END { End of WITH block }
        END;
    CLOSE(NewFile);
    CLOSE(PayrollFile);
{ Copy NewFile back to Payroll File }
    ASSIGN(PayrollFile, FileName);
    REWRITE(PayrollFile);
    ASSIGN(NewFile, TempFile);
    RESET(NewFile);
    WHILE NOT EOF(NewFile) DO
      BEGIN
        READLN(NewFile,OneLine);
        WRITELN(PayrollFile,OneLine)
      END;
    CLOSE(NewFile);
    ERASE(NewFile);        { Erase the temporary file }
    CLOSE(PayrollFile);
    WRITELN('The employee ', SSNumber, ' is removed from file.')
    END;

{ ------------------------ Procedure Menu ------------------------ }
PROCEDURE Menu;
VAR
```

```
      Option :INTEGER;
BEGIN
   WRITELN(Header);
   WRITELN;
   WRITELN('1. Display an employee record.');
   WRITELN('2. Add a new employee.');
   WRITELN('3. Delete an employee.');
   WRITELN('4. Exit.');
   WRITELN(Separator);
   WRITE('Make a choice and press a number: ');
   READLN(Option);
   CASE Option OF
      1 : ReadRec(PayrollFile, EmployeeRec);
      2 : AddRec(NewFile, PayrollFile, EmployeeRec);
      3 : DelRec(NewFile, PayrollFile, EmployeeRec);
      4 : Exit
   END;
   Menu
END;


{ ------------------------- Main Program ------------------------- }
BEGIN
{ Assign titles }
   Title[1] := 'ID: ';
   Title[2] := 'Name: ';
   Title[3] := 'Position: ';
   Title[4] := 'SSN: ';
   Title[5] := 'Salary: ';
   Title[6] := 'Rate: ';
   Title[7] := 'Commission: ';
   Title[8] := 'Basic Salary: ';
   Title[9] := 'Area: ';
   Menu
END.
{ ------------------------------------------------------------------- }
```

Sample Run:

The following is a sample run to delete the record of the employee whose SSN is 347-12-3456. The user input is bolded for clarity.

```
      -------------- Main Menu --------------
      1. Display an employee record.
      2. Add a new employee.
      3. Delete an employee.
      4. Exit.
      ---------------------------------------
      Make a choice and press a number: 3
      Please enter the SSN of the employee to be deleted: 347-12-3456
      The employee 347-12-3456 is removed from file.
```

```
-------------- Main Menu --------------
1. Display an employee record.
2. Add a new employee.
3. Delete an employee.
4. Exit.
----------------------------------------
Make a choice and press a number: 4
```

Drill 10-2

The previous program will send the message "The employee ... is removed from file," whether or not the SSN is in the file.

Add the necessary code to make the program send the proper message in each case.

10-4 Updating Records

The algorithm to update records in the file is as follows:

1. Enter the Social Security Number of the employee whose record is to be updated.

2. Open the payroll file for reading and a temporary file for writing.

3. Read the payroll file up to the end-of-file. For each record, check the SSN field against the Social Security Number.

4. Copy each record to the temporary file until you reach the record to be updated.

5. For the record to be updated, read the new data from the keyboard and write them to the temporary file.

6. Copy the rest of the records into the temporary file.

7. Copy the temporary file into the original payroll file.

8. Delete the temporary file.

You may add the following procedure to the program (this procedure is on the companion CD under the name UPD-PROC.PAS).

```
{ -------------------- Procedure UpdateRec ---------------------- }
PROCEDURE UpdateRec(VAR NewFile, PayrollFile :TEXT;
                                    Employee :EmployeeRecord);
VAR
    SSNumber    :STRING[11];
    Found       :INTEGER;
BEGIN
    Found := 0;
    ASSIGN(PayrollFile, FileName);
    RESET(PayrollFile);
    ASSIGN(NewFile, TempFile);
```

```
REWRITE(NewFile);
WRITE('Please enter the SSN of the employee to be updated: ');
READLN(SSNumber);
WHILE NOT EOF(PayrollFile) DO
  BEGIN
    WITH Employee DO
      BEGIN
        READLN(PayrollFile, ID);
        READLN(PayrollFile, Name);
        READLN(PayrollFile, Position);
        READLN(PayrollFile, SSN);
        READLN(PayrollFile, Category);
        CASE Category OF
         '1' : READLN(PayrollFile, MonthlySalary);
         '2' : READLN(PayrollFile, HourlyRate);
         '3' : BEGIN
                 READLN(PayrollFile, Commission);
                 READLN(PayrollFile, BasicSalary);
                 READLN(PayrollFile, Area)
               END
        END;  { End of CASE structure }
        IF SSNumber <> SSN THEN
          BEGIN
            WRITELN(NewFile, ID);
            WRITELN(NewFile, Name);
            WRITELN(NewFile, Position);
            WRITELN(NewFile, SSN);
            WRITELN(NewFile, Category);
              CASE Category OF
                '1' : WRITELN(NewFile, MonthlySalary:0:2);
                '2' : WRITELN(NewFile, HourlyRate:0:2);
                '3' : BEGIN
                        WRITELN(NewFile, Commission:0:2);
                        WRITELN(NewFile, BasicSalary:0:2);
                        WRITELN(NewFile, Area);
                      END
              END;  { End of CASE structure }
          END
        ELSE
          BEGIN
            Found := 1;
            WRITELN('Please enter the updated information:');
            WRITE('ID: ');           READLN(ID);
            WRITELN(NewFile, ID);
            WRITE('Name: ');         READLN(Name);
            WRITELN(NewFile, Name);
            WRITE('Position: ');   READLN(Position);
            WRITELN(NewFile, Position);
            WRITELN(NewFile, SSN);
            WRITE('Category: ');   READLN(Category);
```

```
                    WRITELN(NewFile, Category);
                      CASE Category OF
                        '1' : BEGIN
                                WRITE('Salary: ');
                                READLN(MonthlySalary);
                                WRITELN(NewFile, MonthlySalary:0:2)
                              END;
                        '2' : BEGIN
                                WRITE('Hourly Rate: ');
                                READLN(HourlyRate);
                                WRITELN(NewFile, HourlyRate:0:2)
                              END;
                        '3' : BEGIN
                                WRITE('Commission: ');
                                READLN(Commission);
                                WRITELN(NewFile, Commission:0:2);
                                WRITE('Basic Salary: ');
                                READLN(BasicSalary);
                                WRITELN(NewFile, BasicSalary:0:2);
                                WRITE('Area: ');
                                READLN(Area);
                                WRITELN(NewFile, Area)
                              END
                      END;  { End of CASE structure }
                  END
            END { End of WITH block }
        END;
    CLOSE(NewFile);
    CLOSE(PayrollFile);
  { Copy NewFile back to Payroll File }
    ASSIGN(PayrollFile, FileName);
    REWRITE(PayrollFile);
    ASSIGN(NewFile, TempFile);
    RESET(NewFile);
    WHILE NOT EOF(NewFile) DO
      BEGIN
        READLN(NewFile, OneLine);
        WRITELN(PayrollFile, OneLine)
      END;
    CLOSE(NewFile);
    ERASE(NewFile);         { Erase the temporary file }
    CLOSE(PayrollFile);
  { User Messages }
    IF Found =1 THEN
      WRITELN('The employee ', SSNumber, ' is updated.')
    ELSE
      BEGIN
        WRITELN('The SSN ', SSNumber, ' is not found.');
        WRITELN('Check the number and try again.');
        WRITELN
```

```
      END
    END;
  { ------------------------------------------------------------------ }
```

The Found flag is of the INTEGER type. However, you may use any other type such as BOOLEAN which makes your program more readable. With a Boolean flag, you may use statements like IF Found and IF NOT Found.

You also need to modify the menu procedure in order to incorporate the update option, as follows (this procedure is on the companion CD under the name MNU-PRO2.PAS).

```
{ ---------------------- Procedure Menu ------------------------ }
PROCEDURE Menu;
VAR
   Option :INTEGER;
BEGIN
   WRITELN(Header);
   WRITELN;
   WRITELN('1. Display an employee record.');
   WRITELN('2. Add a new employee.');
   WRITELN('3. Delete an employee.');
   WRITELN('4. Update an employee record.');
   WRITELN('5. Exit.');
   WRITELN(Separator);
   WRITE('Make a choice and press a number: ');
   READLN(Option);
   CASE Option OF
      1 : ReadRec(PayrollFile, EmployeeRec);
      2 : AddRec(NewFile, PayrollFile, EmployeeRec);
      3 : DelRec(NewFile, PayrollFile, EmployeeRec);
      4 : UpdateRec(NewFile, PayrollFile, EmployeeRec);
      5 : Exit
   END;
   Menu
END;
{ ------------------------------------------------------------------ }
```

Drill 10-3

Bring procedures together in order to build a complete program containing the capabilities to display, add, delete, and update an employee record.

10-5 Enhance the Program Modularity

Now that you've added more procedures to your program, you may need to take a second look at the modularity of the program. One disadvantage of the program is that the flag Found is used in three procedures to check the existence of the required record.

Another disadvantage is that the PAYROLL.TXT file is being copied into the temporary file whether or not the required record exists. This redundancy could be avoided
by building a new procedure to search the file and set (or reset) the Found flag. Thus,
when any of the other procedures is entered, the procedure knows in advance
whether or not the record exists. Therefore, all the steps can be included inside an IF
block as shown below:

```
READLN(SSNumber);
   SearchRec(PayrollFile, EmployeeRec, SSNumber, Found);
   IF Found =1 THEN
     BEGIN
     ...
     { open files and carry out the required chores }
     ...
     END
   ELSE
      { send the proper message }

   END;
```

The new procedure SearchRec is invoked after the value of the SSNumber is entered
from the keyboard. The procedure opens the file, searches for the required employee,
and returns the proper value of the flag Found. If the record is found, the regular
chores (updating, deleting, or reading) are carried on by the other procedures; otherwise, the proper message is sent and no files have to be reopened.

The following are some important points of the SearchRec procedure:

■ The SSNumber and the flag are both passed as parameters to the procedure.

■ Because the value of the flag is expected to be modified by the procedure, it has to
be passed using the VAR keyword.

■ In order to pass the string variable (SSNumber), the parameter has to be TYPEd;
for this reason, a new type is declared in the TYPE section as follows:

```
             SSNstring = STRING[11];
```

This is the program in its final shape:

```
{ ------------------------- Example 10-3 ------------------------- }
PROGRAM EmployeeDataBase2(INPUT, OUTPUT, PayrollFile, NewFile);
CONST
   FileName = 'payroll.txt';
   TempFile = 'temp.txt';
   Header = '-------------- Main Menu --------------';
   Header1 = '----------- Employee DataBase -----------';
   Header2 = '------------ Employee Record ------------';
   Separator = '-----------------------------------------';
TYPE
   EmployeeRecord = RECORD
                    ID                :STRING[5];
```

```
                     Name, Position    :STRING[20];
                     SSN               :STRING[11];
                     CASE Category     :CHAR OF
                        '1'   :(MonthlySalary  :REAL);
                        '2'   :(HourlyRate     :REAL);
                        '3'   :(Commission,
                               BasicSalary    :REAL;
                               Area           :STRING[20])
                  END;

   SSNstring = STRING[11];
VAR
   NewFile, PayrollFile :TEXT;
   EmployeeRec          :EmployeeRecord;
   Title                :ARRAY [1..9] OF STRING[20];
   OneLine              :STRING[80];

{ ----------------------- Procedure SearchRec -------------------- }
PROCEDURE SearchRec(VAR PayrollFile :TEXT;
                        Employee :EmployeeRecord;
                        SSNumber :SSNstring;
                        VAR Found :INTEGER);
BEGIN
   Found := 0;
   ASSIGN(PayrollFile, FileName);
   RESET(PayrollFile);
   WHILE NOT EOF(PayrollFile) DO
      BEGIN
         WITH Employee DO
            BEGIN
               READLN(PayrollFile, ID);
               READLN(PayrollFile, Name);
               READLN(PayrollFile, Position);
               READLN(PayrollFile, SSN);
               READLN(PayrollFile, Category);
               CASE Category OF
                 '1' : READLN(PayrollFile, MonthlySalary);
                 '2' : READLN(PayrollFile, HourlyRate);
                 '3' : BEGIN
                          READLN(PayrollFile, Commission);
                          READLN(PayrollFile, BasicSalary);
                          READLN(PayrollFile, Area)
                       END
               END;  { End of CASE structure }
               IF SSNumber = SSN THEN
                  Found := 1;
            END { End of WITH block }
      END;
   CLOSE(PayrollFile);
END;
```

```
{ --------------------- Procedure ReadRec ----------------------- }
PROCEDURE ReadRec(VAR PayrollFile :TEXT;
Employee :EmployeeRecord);
VAR
   SSNumber  :STRING[11];
   Found     :INTEGER;
BEGIN
   WRITELN;
   WRITE('Please enter the SSN of the employee: ');
   READLN(SSNumber);
   SearchRec(PayrollFile, EmployeeRec, SSNumber, Found);
   IF Found =1 THEN
     BEGIN
       ASSIGN(PayrollFile, FileName);
       RESET(PayrollFile);
       WHILE NOT EOF(PayrollFile) DO
         BEGIN
           WITH Employee DO
             BEGIN
               READLN(PayrollFile, ID);
               READLN(PayrollFile, Name);
               READLN(PayrollFile, Position);
               READLN(PayrollFile, SSN);
               READLN(PayrollFile, Category);
               CASE Category OF
                 '1' : READLN(PayrollFile, MonthlySalary);
                 '2' : READLN(PayrollFile, HourlyRate);
                 '3' : BEGIN
                         READLN(PayrollFile, Commission);
                         READLN(PayrollFile, BasicSalary);
                         READLN(PayrollFile, Area)
                       END
             END;  { End of CASE structure }
               IF SSNumber = SSN THEN
                 BEGIN
                   WRITELN(Header2);
                   WRITELN(Title[1],ID);
                   WRITELN(Title[2],Name);
                   WRITELN(Title[3],Position);
                   WRITELN(Title[4], SSN);
                   CASE Category OF
                     '1' : WRITELN(Title[5], MonthlySalary:0:2);
                     '2' : WRITELN(Title[6], HourlyRate:0:2);
                     '3' : BEGIN
                             WRITELN(Title[7], Commission:0:2);
                             WRITELN(Title[8], BasicSalary:0:2);
                             WRITELN(Title[9], Area)
                           END
                 END;  { End of CASE structure }
               END
```

```
                    END { End of WITH block }
        END;
        CLOSE(PayrollFile)
        END
     ELSE     { If not found }
       BEGIN
         WRITELN('SSN not found in file.');
         WRITELN('Please try again.');
         WRITELN
       END
END;

{ ----------------------- Procedure DelRec ------------------------ }
PROCEDURE DelRec(VAR NewFile, PayrollFile :TEXT;
Employee :EmployeeRecord);
VAR
   SSNumber :STRING[11];
   Found    :INTEGER;
BEGIN
   WRITE('Please enter the SSN of the employee to be deleted: ');
   READLN(SSNumber);
   SearchRec(PayrollFile, EmployeeRec, SSNumber, Found);
   IF Found =1 THEN
     BEGIN
       ASSIGN(NewFile, TempFile);
       REWRITE(NewFile);
       ASSIGN(PayrollFile, FileName);
       RESET(PayrollFile);
       WHILE NOT EOF(PayrollFile) DO
         BEGIN
           WITH Employee DO
             BEGIN
               READLN(PayrollFile, ID);
               READLN(PayrollFile, Name);
               READLN(PayrollFile, Position);
               READLN(PayrollFile, SSN);
               READLN(PayrollFile, Category);
               CASE Category OF
                 '1' : READLN(PayrollFile, MonthlySalary);
                 '2' : READLN(PayrollFile, HourlyRate);
                 '3' : BEGIN
                         READLN(PayrollFile, Commission);
                         READLN(PayrollFile, BasicSalary);
                         READLN(PayrollFile, Area)
                       END
               END;  { End of CASE structure }
               IF SSNumber <> SSN THEN
                 BEGIN
                   WRITELN(NewFile, ID);
                   WRITELN(NewFile, Name);
```

```
                        WRITELN(NewFile, Position);
                        WRITELN(NewFile, SSN);
                        WRITELN(NewFile, Category);
                        CASE Category OF
                          '1' : WRITELN(NewFile, MonthlySalary:0:2);
                          '2' : WRITELN(NewFile, HourlyRate:0:2);
                          '3' : BEGIN
                                    WRITELN(NewFile, Commission:0:2);
                                    WRITELN(NewFile, BasicSalary:0:2);
                                    WRITELN(NewFile, Area)
                                END
                        END;  { End of CASE structure }
                    END;
                END { End of WITH block }
            END;  {End of DO }
        CLOSE(NewFile);
        CLOSE(PayrollFile);
{ Copy NewFile back to Payroll File }
        ASSIGN(PayrollFile, FileName);
        REWRITE(PayrollFile);
        ASSIGN(NewFile, TempFile);
        RESET(NewFile);
        WHILE NOT EOF(NewFile) DO
          BEGIN
          READLN(NewFile, OneLine);
          WRITELN(PayrollFile, OneLine)
          END;
        CLOSE(NewFile);
        ERASE(NewFile);          { Erase the temporary file }
        CLOSE(PayrollFile);
{ User Messages }
        WRITELN('The employee ', SSNumber,
                              ' is removed from file.')
      END { End of the "IF Found.." block }
    ELSE  { IF not found }
     BEGIN
       WRITELN('The SSN ', SSNumber, ' is not found.');
       WRITELN('Check the number and try again.');
       WRITELN
     END
  END;


{ ----------------------- Procedure AddRec ----------------------- }
PROCEDURE AddRec(VAR NewFile, PayrollFile :TEXT;
                              Employee: EmployeeRecord);
BEGIN
   ASSIGN(PayrollFile, FileName);
   RESET(PayrollFile);
   ASSIGN(NewFile, TempFile);
   REWRITE(NewFile);
```

```
      WHILE NOT EOF(PayrollFile) DO
        BEGIN
{ Copy each record from PayrollFile to the NewFile }
          READLN(PayrollFile, OneLine);
          WRITELN(NewFile, OneLine)
        END;
{ Accept a new record from the keyboard }
    WITH Employee DO
      BEGIN
        WRITE('Please enter Employee ID: ');
        READLN(ID);
        WRITE('Name: ');                READLN(Name);
        WRITE('Position: ');            READLN(Position);
        WRITE('SSN (xxx-xx-xxxx): ');   READLN(SSN);
        WRITE('Payroll category: ');    READLN(Category);
          CASE Category OF
            '1' : BEGIN
                    WRITE('Monthly Salary: ');
                    READLN(MonthlySalary)
                  END;
            '2' : BEGIN
                    WRITE('Rate: ');
                    READLN(HourlyRate)
                    END;
            '3' : BEGIN
                    WRITE('Commission: ');
                    READLN(Commission);
                    WRITE('Basic salary: ');
                    READLN(BasicSalary);
                    WRITE('Area: ');
                    READLN(Area)
          END
      END;
{ Store the information in NewFile }
      WRITELN(NewFile, ID);
      WRITELN(NewFile, Name);
      WRITELN(NewFile, Position);
      WRITELN(NewFile, SSN);
      WRITELN(NewFile, Category);
      CASE Category OF
        '1' : WRITELN(NewFile, MonthlySalary:0:2);
        '2' : WRITELN(NewFile, HourlyRate:0:2);
        '3' : BEGIN
                WRITELN(NewFile, Commission:0:2);
                WRITELN(NewFile, BasicSalary:0:2);
                WRITELN(NewFile, Area)
            END
    END
  END;
  CLOSE(NewFile);
```

```
    CLOSE(PayrollFile);
{ Copy NewFile back to Payroll File }
  ASSIGN(PayrollFile, FileName);
  REWRITE(PayrollFile);
  ASSIGN(NewFile, TempFile);
  RESET(NewFile);
  WHILE NOT EOF(NewFile) DO
    BEGIN
      READLN(NewFile, OneLine);
      WRITELN(PayrollFile, OneLine)
    END;
  CLOSE(NewFile);
  ERASE(NewFile);    { Erase the temporary file }
  CLOSE(PayrollFile)
END;


{ -------------------- Procedure UpdateRec ----------------------- }
PROCEDURE UpdateRec(VAR NewFile, PayrollFile :TEXT;
                    Employee :EmployeeRecord);
VAR
   SSNumber      :STRING[11];
   Found         :INTEGER;
BEGIN
   WRITE('Please enter the SSN of the employee to be updated: ');
   READLN(SSNumber);
   SearchRec(PayrollFile, EmployeeRec, SSNumber, Found);
   IF Found =1 THEN
     BEGIN
       ASSIGN(PayrollFile, FileName);
       RESET(PayrollFile);
       ASSIGN(NewFile, TempFile);
       REWRITE(NewFile);
       WHILE NOT EOF(PayrollFile) DO
         BEGIN
           WITH Employee DO
             BEGIN
               READLN(PayrollFile, ID);
               READLN(PayrollFile, Name);
               READLN(PayrollFile, Position);
               READLN(PayrollFile, SSN);
               READLN(PayrollFile, Category);
               CASE Category OF
                 '1' : READLN(PayrollFile, MonthlySalary);
                 '2' : READLN(PayrollFile, HourlyRate);
                 '3' : BEGIN
                         READLN(PayrollFile, Commission);
                         READLN(PayrollFile, BasicSalary);
                         READLN(PayrollFile, Area)
                       END
             END;   { End of CASE structure }
```

```
IF SSNumber <> SSN THEN
  BEGIN
    WRITELN(NewFile, ID);
    WRITELN(NewFile, Name);
    WRITELN(NewFile, Position);
    WRITELN(NewFile, SSN);
    WRITELN(NewFile, Category);
    CASE Category OF
      '1' : WRITELN(NewFile, MonthlySalary:0:2);
      '2' : WRITELN(NewFile, HourlyRate:0:2);
      '3' : BEGIN
              WRITELN(NewFile, Commission:0:2);
              WRITELN(NewFile, BasicSalary:0:2);
              WRITELN(NewFile, Area)
            END
    END   { End of CASE structure }
  END   { End of IF block }
ELSE
  BEGIN
    WRITELN('Please enter the updated information:');
    WRITE('ID: ');          READLN(ID);
    WRITELN(NewFile, ID);
    WRITE('Name: ');          READLN(Name);
    WRITELN(NewFile, Name);
    WRITE('Position: ');   READLN(Position);
    WRITELN(NewFile, Position);
    WRITELN(NewFile, SSN);
    WRITE('Category: ');   READLN(Category);
    WRITELN(NewFile, Category);
    CASE Category OF
      '1' : BEGIN
              WRITE('Salary: ');
              READLN(MonthlySalary);
              WRITELN(NewFile, MonthlySalary:0:2)
            END;
      '2' : BEGIN
              WRITE('Hourly Rate: ');
              READLN(HourlyRate);
              WRITELN(NewFile, HourlyRate:0:2)
            END;
      '3' : BEGIN
              WRITE('Commission: ');
              READLN(Commission);
              WRITELN(NewFile, Commission:0:2);
              WRITE('Basic Salary: ');
              READLN(BasicSalary);
              WRITELN(NewFile, BasicSalary:0:2);
              WRITE('Area: ');
              READLN(Area);
              WRITELN(NewFile, Area)
```

```
                                 END
                          END    { End of CASE structure }
                       END  { End of ELSE block }
                    END { End of WITH block }
                 END; { End of DO }
             CLOSE(NewFile);
             CLOSE(PayrollFile);
{ Copy NewFile back to Payroll File }
             ASSIGN(PayrollFile, FileName);
             REWRITE(PayrollFile);
             ASSIGN(NewFile, TempFile);
             RESET(NewFile);
             WHILE NOT EOF(NewFile) DO
               BEGIN
                 READLN(NewFile, OneLine);
                 WRITELN(PayrollFile, OneLine)
               END;
             CLOSE(NewFile);
             ERASE(NewFile);  { Erase the temporary file }
             CLOSE(PayrollFile);
{ User Messages }
             WRITELN('The employee ', SSNumber, ' is updated.')
           END { End of IF block }
        ELSE
         BEGIN
           WRITELN('The SSN ', SSNumber, ' is not found.');
           WRITELN('Check the number and try again.');
           WRITELN
         END
      END;


{ ---------------------- Procedure Menu ----------------------- }
PROCEDURE Menu;
VAR
   Option :INTEGER;
BEGIN
   WRITELN(Header);
   WRITELN;
   WRITELN('1. Display an employee record.');
   WRITELN('2. Add a new employee.');
   WRITELN('3. Delete an employee.');
   WRITELN('4. Update an employee record.');
   WRITELN('5. Exit.');
   WRITELN(Separator);
   WRITE('Make a choice and press a number: ');
   READLN(Option);
   CASE Option OF
       1 : ReadRec(PayrollFile, EmployeeRec);
       2 : AddRec(NewFile, PayrollFile, EmployeeRec);
       3 : DelRec(NewFile, PayrollFile, EmployeeRec);
```

```
        4 : UpdateRec(NewFile, PayrollFile, EmployeeRec);
        5 : Exit
    END;
    Menu
END;


{ ----------------------- Main Program ------------------------ }
BEGIN
{ Assign titles }
    Title[1] := 'ID: ';
    Title[2] := 'Name: ';
    Title[3] := 'Position: ';
    Title[4] := 'SSN: ';
    Title[5] := 'Salary: ';
    Title[6] := 'Rate: ';
    Title[7] := 'Commission: ';
    Title[8] := 'Basic Salary: ';
    Title[9] := 'Area: ';
    Menu
END.
{ ---------------------------------------------------------------- }
```

Suggestions

In order to make the program more reliable, you may add the following features:

1. When you enter the SSN for a new employee, the program does not check the data format, which means a wrong number such as 12345-678 will be accepted. You can add the necessary statements to check for the exact number of digits as well as the hyphens.

2. If you enter a value other than 1, 2, or 3, it will be accepted as a Category. Consequently, the salary will not be processed by the CASE structure. You can add the necessary steps to check the valid values of the Category variable.

3. If you added the same employee to the file twice, this program would not know that the record already exists. Therefore, you need to check the SSN before you add a new record.

4. If you are using Turbo Pascal, you use *units*. With units you can put each procedure in a separate file called a unit. The units you build could be usable by more than one program.

These enhancements are left for you as a drill.

Summary

1. In this chapter you learned how to use variant records to store your data into an efficient data structure.

2. You can declare a variant record type using the following format:

   type-name = **RECORD**
       fixed field-list
   variant field-list
   END;

   The variant field list takes the following form:

   CASE tag-field : type-definition **OF**
   label-1 : (field-list : type-definition);
   label-2 : (field-list : type-definition);

   ...

   label-*n* : (field-list : type-definition);

3. The variant record may contain a fixed part followed by a variant part, or a variant part only.

4. You learned how to read, write, update, and delete variant records stored in files, using the CASE structure.

Exercises

1. Write a variant record declaration for a person that includes the following information:
   - ID
   - Name
   - SSN
   - Marital status includes three cases:
     - Married: Required information is spouse name and number of kids.
     - Single: No additional information required.
     - Divorced: The required information is the name of former spouse, divorce date, and the number of kids living with the person.

2. Write a variant record declaration for a geometric shape that can be used to calculate the area and/or the volume of the following shapes:
   - Circle: The required information is the radius.
   - Cylinder: The required information is the radius and the height.
   - Sphere: The required information is the radius.
   - Cube: The required information is the side.

Answers

1. Person = RECORD

```
                ID                        :STRING[5];
                Name                      :STRING[20];
                SSN                       :STRING[11];
                CASE Status               : CHAR OF
                   'M': (SpouseName        : STRING[20];
                         NumberOfKids      : INTEGER);
                   'S'                     : ();
                   'D': (FormerSpouseName  : STRING[20];
                         DivorceDate       : STRING[10];
                         CustKids          : INTEGER)
           END;
```

2. FigureName = (Circle, Cylinder, Sphere, Cube);
ShapeInformation = RECORD

```
                CASE Figure     : FigureName  OF
                     Circle    :(Radius   : REAL);
                     Cylinder  :(CylRadius: REAL;
                                 Height: REAL );
                     Sphere    :(SphRadius: REAL);
                     Cube      :(Side: REAL)
           END;
```

Chapter 11

Pointers and Linked Lists

Chapter Topics:

- **Declaring and using pointers**
- **Passing pointers as parameters to subprograms**
- **Building linked lists**
- **Storing lists in files**
- **Reading lists from files**
- **Searching lists**
- **Adding and deleting nodes**
- **Ordered linked lists**
- **Linked list applications**

11-1 Dynamic Memory Allocation

The variables already used so far are called *static variables*. The relationship between the static variable and the memory location to which it refers is established compilation time and does not change during the program execution. *A dynamic variable*, on the contrary, is created or disposed during the execution. In other words, the necessary memory location for a dynamic variable is allocated while the program is running, and may be released and allocated to another variable. In Pascal, you may create a simple dynamic variable or a complex *dynamic data structure* such as a *linked list*. A linked list may be needed in some situations when you cannot predict your memory requirements. As opposed to the linked list, the array is an example of *static data structures*. The memory locations associated with the array elements are allocated at the time of compilation. The disadvantage of using arrays, in such situations, is the need to allocate enough space for the maximum possible number of elements. Defining a huge array which may exceed your needs is a waste of memory; and using a small array will limit your program to a specific number of elements. The problem occurs when you need to insert a new element in the array. Dynamic data structures may expand or shrink during the program execution, and so does the associated memory. Dynamic memory allocation is accomplished by using *pointers*. In the following sections you learn how to declare and use pointers.

11-2 Pointers

A pointer is a special type of variable that does not hold data; instead, it holds the address of a data location. Therefore, it is said that it points to a data location. In your program, it is possible to redirect the pointer to make it point to another memory location, or to no memory location. It is also possible to release the memory associated with a specific pointer and make it available to other variables. Pointers can point to any type of data, from CHARs and INTEGERs to complex data structures such as records and linked lists.

A pointer to an integer is declared as follows:

```
VAR
PtrVariable    : ^INTEGER;
```

In order to use the pointer, you must allocate memory using the procedure NEW:

```
NEW(PtrVariable);
```

This assigns a memory address to the pointer variable PtrVariable (e.g., 709Ch). The value stored in this address is the actual data. To refer to the location pointed to by the pointer PtrVariable, use the variable name:

```
PtrVariable^
```

which is treated like a regular variable. For example, you may assign it a numeric value:

```
PtrVariable^ := 500;
```

or assign it to another static variable:

```
AnotherVariable := PtrVariable^ ;
```

This is demonstrated in the following diagram:

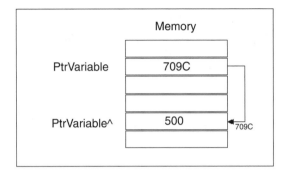

The memory allocated to the pointer may be released using the procedure DISPOSE:

```
DISPOSE(PtrVariable);
```

Once a pointer is disposed it becomes *undefined*.

In the following program, these features are demonstrated. An integer variable (MyInteger), and an integer pointer (MyIntegerPointer) are declared. The contents of the allocated location MyIntegerPointer ⌃ are assigned to the variable MyInteger. Both, when printed, should give the same value (500).

```
{ ----------------------- Example 11-1 ------------------------ }
PROGRAM PointerExample(OUTPUT);

VAR
MyIntegerPointer     :^INTEGER;
MyInteger            :INTEGER;
BEGIN

MyInteger := 50;
NEW(MyIntegerPointer);
MyIntegerPointer^ := 500;
MyInteger := MyIntegerPointer^;

WRITELN('The value of MyInteger is: ', MyInteger);
WRITELN('The value pointed to by MyIntegerPointer is: '
                                , MyIntegerPointer^);
DISPOSE(MyIntegerPointer);
WRITELN('Press any key to continue...');
READLN
END.
{ ------------------------------------------------------------- }
```

Notice that the procedure DISPOSE is not necessary in this program, because the memory is deallocated automatically when the program ends. It is used only for demonstration.

In the same way, you can declare pointers to other types, for example:

```
VAR
MyCharPointer        :^CHAR;
MyStringPointer      :^STRING;
MyRealPointer        :^REAL;
```

Before you try to use any of these pointers, remember to use the procedure NEW to allocate memory for each one:

```
NEW(MyCharPointer);
NEW(MyStringPointer);
NEW(MyRealPointer);
```

When you are finished, you may use DISPOSE to deallocate memory associated with each of them:

```
DISPOSE(MyCharPointer);
DISPOSE(MyStringPointer);
DISPOSE(MyRealPointer);
```

11-3 Pointer Operations

The operations performed on pointers are limited to assignment and comparison.

Assignment

If two pointers ptr1 and ptr2 are of the same type, then the following statement is valid:

```
ptr1 :=  ptr2;
```

The effect of this statement is to redirect the pointer ptr1 to make it point to the same location pointed to by ptr2. The location which was pointed to by ptr1, before the assignment, is now inaccessible (unless it was pointed to by another pointer).

When you dispose of these pointers, you need to dispose only one of them, because they point to the same location. A second DISPOSE statement will result in an error message.

Obviously, the previous assignment is totally different from the following assignment:

```
ptr1^ := ptr2^;
```

which means copying the contents of the location pointed to by ptr2 into the location pointed to by ptr1. The two pointers, however, may still be pointing to the same original locations.

Comparison

You may use the Boolean operators = or < > to compare two pointers:

```
IF ptr1 = ptr2 THEN ..
```

The Boolean expression ptr1 = ptr2 is true if the two pointers are pointing to the same memory location.

These features are demonstrated in the following program.

```
{ ----------------------- Example 11-2 -------------------------- }
PROGRAM PointerExample2(OUTPUT);

TYPE
intptr  = ^INTEGER;
realptr = ^REAL;

VAR
MyIntegerPointer, AnotherIntPointer :intptr;
MyRealPointer                       :realptr;

BEGIN
NEW(MyIntegerPointer);
NEW(MyRealPointer);
NEW(AnotherIntPointer);

MyRealPointer^ := 2.25;
MyIntegerPointer^ := 500;
AnotherIntPointer^ := 400;

{ Copy contents of locations:}
MyRealPointer^ := MyIntegerPointer^;

{ Redirect MyIntegerPointer:}
MyIntegerPointer := AnotherIntPointer;

{ Display results }
WRITELN('MyRealPointer is pointing to: ', MyRealPointer^:2:2);
WRITELN;

{Check if the two pointers point to the same location:}
IF (MyIntegerPointer = AnotherIntPointer) THEN
WRITELN('Yes, The two integer pointers are pointing to the same location.');

WRITELN('MyIntegerPointer is pointing to: ', MyIntegerPointer^);
WRITELN('AnotherIntPointer is pointing to: ', AnotherIntPointer^);
```

```
WRITELN;

{ Note: The DISPOSE procedure is not necessary for any pointer in
this program. }
DISPOSE(MyIntegerPointer);
DISPOSE(MyRealPointer);
{DISPOSE(AnotherIntPointer);} {illegal now..}

WRITELN('Press any key to continue...');
READLN
END.
```

When you run this program, it will display the following messages:

```
MyRealPointer is pointing to: 500.00
Yes, The two integer pointers are pointing to the same location.
MyIntegerPointer is pointing to: 400
AnotherIntPointer is pointing to: 400

Press any key to continue...
```

Remarks:

The following are the operations that took place in the program (also refer to the diagram below):

■ The variable MyRealPointer ^ is assigned the value 2.25.

■ The variable MyIntegerPointer ^ is assigned the value 500.

■ The variable AnotherIntPointer ^ is assigned the value 400.

■ The contents of MyIntegerPointer ^ are copied into MyRealPointer ^; therefore, its stored value becomes 500.00.

■ The pointer MyIntegerPointer is redirected to point to the same location pointed to by AnotherIntPointer, which contains the value 400.

Note: You cannot read a pointer value. You can only read the contents pointed to by the pointer.

11-4 Pointers to Records

You can declare a pointer to a record in the same way you do with other types of data. It is preferred to define the pointer type in the TYPE section:

```
TYPE
emprec = RECORD
           ID   :INTEGER;
           Wage : REAL;
         END;
empptr = ^emprec;
```

then declare the pointer variables in the VAR section:

```
VAR
ptr1, ptr2 :empptr;
```

With records, you may use all pointer operations in the same way you do with other pointer types. But there are some restrictions:

1. When you create a pointer to a record, the pointer is bound to this specific record type and may not be used with another record type.

2. The relational expression

```
ptr1^ = ptr2^
```

is invalid, as records cannot be compared using relational expressions. You may, however, compare the two pointers to check if they are pointing to the same record.

```
ptr1 = ptr2, or
ptr1 <> ptr2
```

3. The field contents are accessed using fielded variables:

```
ptr1^.ID
ptr1^.Wage
ptr2^.ID
ptr2^.Wage
```

or using a WITH statement:

```
WITH ptr1^ DO
ID := 123;
Wage := 22.5;
...
```

In the following program, the two record pointers, ptr1 and ptr2, are used to access the record fields; then, one of the pointers is redirected to point to the same record as the other one does.

```
{ -------------------------- Example 11-3 -------------------------- }
PROGRAM PointersToRecords(OUTPUT);
TYPE
emprec = RECORD
            ID   : INTEGER;
            Wage : REAL;
         END;
empptr = ^emprec;

VAR
ptr1, ptr2 : empptr;

BEGIN
NEW(ptr1);
NEW(ptr2);
{ Assign values to the fields }
ptr1^.ID := 123;
ptr1^.Wage := 25.5;
ptr2^.ID := 456;
ptr2^.Wage := 33.25;

{Print contents:}
WRITELN('Before redirection of ptr1:');
WRITELN('Ptr1 points to ID: ', ptr1^.ID,
                    ', and Wage: $', ptr1^.Wage:2:2);
WRITELN('Ptr2 points to ID: ', ptr2^.ID,
                    ', and Wage: $', ptr2^.Wage:2:2);

{Redirect ptr1:}
ptr1 := ptr2;

{Print contents:}
WRITELN;
WRITELN('After redirection of ptr1:');
WRITELN('Ptr1 points to ID: ', ptr1^.ID,
                    ', and Wage: $', ptr1^.Wage:2:2);
WRITELN('Ptr2 points to ID: ', ptr2^.ID,
                    ', and Wage: $', ptr2^.Wage:2:2);
WRITELN('Press any key to continue...');
READLN
END.
{ -------------------------------------------------------------- }
```

Output:

```
Before redirection of ptr1:
Ptr1 points to ID: 123, and Wage: $25.50
```

```
Ptr2 points to ID: 456, and Wage: $33.25

After redirection of ptr1:
Ptr1 points to ID: 456, and Wage: $33.25
Ptr2 points to ID: 456, and Wage: $33.25
Press any key to continue...
```

Drill 11-1

Write a program to create the payroll file used in Chapter 10, using a pointer to the employee record. You may modify the file DRL10-1.PAS on the companion CD.

11-5 Passing Pointers as Parameters

You may pass pointers as parameters to functions and procedures, in the same way you do with static variables. You can pass pointers either as value or variable parameters. Remember that both actual and formal parameters must be of the same type; in case of record pointers, they must point to the same record type.

Drill 11-2

Make the necessary modifications to the program 10-02.PAS on the companion CD, in order to apply pointer parameters to the procedures.

11-6 Basics of Linked Lists

A linked list is a collection of data items called *nodes*. Each node contains a pointer to the next one. The linked list may be used to store any data type, but is usually used to hold records. In the following diagram a linked list is demonstrated.

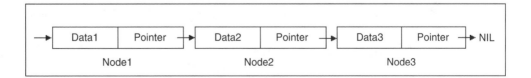

As you can see in the diagram, each node in the linked list contains two items, the data and a pointer to the next node. The pointer in the last node points to the constant NIL, which indicates the end of the list.

List Declaration

The following is a declaration of a linked list that contains an integer data field:

```
TYPE
     ListPointer = ^ListRecord;
     ListRecord = RECORD
                       DataField :INTEGER;
                       NextField :ListPointer;
                   END;
```

Each node in the linked list (ListRecord) has the structure of a record. It contains a *data field* (DataField), which holds the actual data, and a *pointer field* (NextField), also referred to as a *link field*, which keeps track of the order of the list. Notice that the pointer definition (ListPointer) precedes the record definition (ListRecord). This is actually the only situation in which you can use an identifier before it is defined. You can declare a linked list in which to store records in the same way; however, it is best to start with simple ones.

Building a List

To build a linked list, you need to declare two pointers: one to point to the first node (e.g., FirstPointer), and another to use temporarily in the construction process (e.g., ToolPointer). Both pointers are obviously of the type ListPointer.

```
VAR
     FirstPointer, ToolPointer     :ListPointer;
```

These are the steps to build the list:

1. Initialize an empty list by assigning the FirstPointer the NIL value:

```
FirstPointer := NIL;
```

2. Create a node using the temporary pointer:

```
NEW(ToolPointer);
```

3. Read the integer from the keyboard (or any other medium) and store it into the data field of this node:

```
READLN(ToolPointer^.DataField);
```

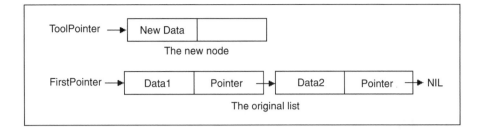

4. Add the node to the list by setting the pointer field so that it points to the same location as the FirstPointer:

```
ToolPointer^.NextField := FirstPointer;
```

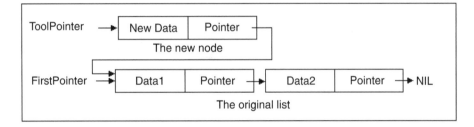

5. Redirect the FirstPointer to the new node (which is the beginning of the list):

```
FirstPointer   := ToolPointer;
```

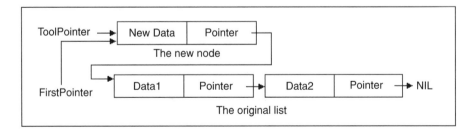

Repeat the preceding steps until all the data are read. The last data item you read will be in the first node of the linked list.

The same procedure, except for the first step, is used to add new nodes to an existing list (as you do not need to create an empty list).

The following is the procedure segment that creates the list:

```
FirstPointer := NIL;
WHILE { Boolean Expression } DO
```

```
BEGIN
    NEW(ToolPointer);
    READLN(ToolPointer^.DataField);
    ToolPointer^.NextField := FirstPointer;
    FirstPointer  := ToolPointer;
END;
```

Reading a List

To read a linked list, you need two pointers: the FirstPointer, which points to the first node on the list, and the CurrentPointer, which moves from one node to the other across the entire list.

The following are the steps to read and display the contents of a list:

1. Make the CurrentPointer point to the first node by assigning it the same direction as the FirstPointer:

```
CurrentPointer := FirstPointer;
```

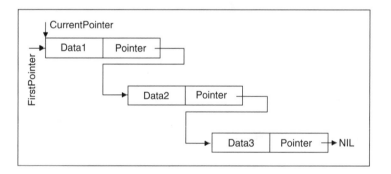

2. Use the CurrentPointer to access and display the contents of the data field:

```
WRITELN(CurrentPointer^.DataField);
```

3. Move the CurrentPointer to the next node by assigning it the direction of the pointer field (NextField) of the same node:

```
CurrentPointer := CurrentPointer^.NextField;
```

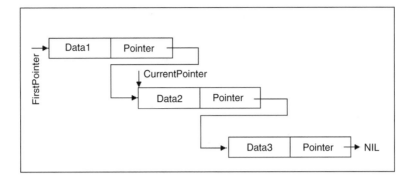

4. Repeat steps 2 and 3 until you get to the last node. This occurs when the following condition is TRUE:

```
CurrentPointer = NIL
```

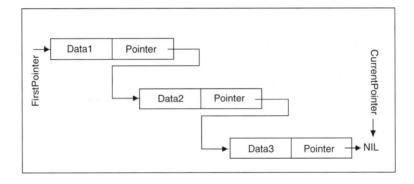

The following is a program segment to read a list:

```
VAR
CurrentPointer :ListPointer;
BEGIN
  CurrentPointer := FirstPointer;
  WHILE CurrentPointer <> NIL DO
    BEGIN
      WRITELN(CurrentPointer^.DataField);
      CurrentPointer := CurrentPointer^.NextField
    END;
    WRITELN
END
```

Application: A Linked List Demo

In the following program, you are going to build a linked list which stores names of people, then read the list and display its contents. The program contains the following procedures:

- Menu   to display and accept user options.
- GetData   to accept data from the keyboard.
- BuildList   to create and add nodes to the list.
- ReadList   to read the contents of the list.
- DisplayInfo   to display the list on the screen.

```
{ ----------------------- Example 11-4 ------------------------ }
PROGRAM LinkedListDemo(INPUT, OUTPUT);

CONST
Header = '-------------- Main Menu --------------';
Separator = '-----------------------------------------';

TYPE
   DataString = STRING[30];
   ListPointer = ^ListRecord;
   ListRecord = RECORD
                   DataField :DataString;
                   NextField :ListPointer;
                END;
VAR
   FirstPointer :ListPointer;


{ --------------------- Procedure BuildList --------------------- }
PROCEDURE BuildList(VAR FirstPointer :ListPointer;
                    DataItem :DataString);
{Note: The FirstPointer is passed using the VAR keyword because it will be
updated by this procedure.}

VAR
  ToolPointer :ListPointer;

BEGIN
  NEW(ToolPointer);
  ToolPointer^.DataField := DataItem;
  ToolPointer^.NextField := FirstPointer;
  FirstPointer := ToolPointer
END;


{ --------------------- Procedure ReadList --------------------- }
PROCEDURE ReadList(FirstPointer :ListPointer);

VAR
```

```
    CurrentPointer :ListPointer;
BEGIN
  CurrentPointer := FirstPointer;
  WHILE CurrentPointer <> NIL DO
    BEGIN
      WRITELN(CurrentPointer^.DataField);
      CurrentPointer := CurrentPointer^.NextField
    END;
    WRITELN
END;
{ ---------------------- Procedure GetData ----------------------- }
PROCEDURE GetData(VAR FirstPointer :ListPointer);
{Note: The FirstPointer is passed using the VAR keyword because it will be
updated when passed to BuildList procedure.}

VAR
  Name :DataString;

BEGIN
  WRITELN('Enter the names to be added to the list,',
                     ' when finished hit ENTER.');
{ Read the first data item }
  READLN(Name);
{ Check for end-of-data }
  WHILE LENGTH(Name) <> 0 DO
    BEGIN
      BuildList(FirstPointer, Name);
      READLN(Name)
    END
END;

{ -------------------- Procedure DisplayInfo --------------------- }
PROCEDURE DisplayInfo(FirstPointer :ListPointer);

BEGIN
  WRITELN(Separator);
  WRITELN('The contents of the list: ');
  ReadList(FirstPointer);
  WRITE('Hit any key to continue...');
  READLN
END;
{ ----------------------- Procedure Menu ------------------------- }
PROCEDURE Menu;

VAR
    Option :INTEGER;

BEGIN
  WRITELN(Header);
  WRITELN('1. Store data in a list.');
```

```
      WRITELN('2. Display the list.');
      WRITELN('3. Exit.');
      WRITELN(Separator);
      WRITE('Make a choice and press a number: ');
      READLN(Option);
      CASE Option OF
         1 : GetData(FirstPointer);
         2 : DisplayInfo(FirstPointer);
         3 : Exit
      END;
      Menu
  END;
END;
{ ---------------------- Main Program ------------------------- }
BEGIN
{ Initialize an empty list }
  FirstPointer := NIL;
  menu
END.
{ ---------------------------------------------------------------- }
```

Sample Run:

When you run this program and choose to store data in a list (option 1), you will be asked to enter some names; when you are finished just hit Enter (without writing any text). At this point, the name list is built into memory and may be displayed. Notice that the last name you entered from the keyboard will appear first on the screen, because you always insert nodes at the beginning of the list. In this sample run, the data entered by the user are bolded for clarity.

```
------------- Main Menu --------------
1. Store data in a list.
2. Display the list.
3. Exit.
----------------------------------------
Make a choice and press a number: 1
Enter the names to be added to the list, when finished hit ENTER.
John Smith        <ENTER> → Names entered from the keyboard
Jean Murdock      <ENTER> →
Sally Bedford     <ENTER> →
Deanna Loerwold  <ENTER> →
<ENTER>
------------- Main Menu --------------
1. Store data in a list.
2. Display the list.
3. Exit.
----------------------------------------
Make a choice and press a number: 2
----------------------------------------
The contents of the list:
Deanna Loerwold      → Notice the sequence of names
```

```
Sally Bedford     →
Jean Murdock      →
John Smith        →

Hit any key to continue...
------------- Main Menu -------------
1. Store data in a list.
2. Display the list.
3. Exit.
-------------------------------------
Make a choice and press a number: 3
```

Notice the following in the program:

1. The VAR keyword is used in the procedure BuildList as it updates the direction of the FirstPointer with the statement:

```
FirstPointer := ToolPointer;
```

The procedure GetData does not update the FirstPointer explicitly, but passes it to the procedure BuildList; therefore, the VAR keyword still has to be used.

2. Note that the empty list is initialized only once in the main program:

```
FirstPointer := NIL;
```

This means that you can keep adding items to the same list if you choose option 1 more than once. The list is reinitialized only if you exit and start over. If you like to initialize an empty list each time you choose option 1, then move the statement FirstPointer := NIL to the GetData procedure.

3. Although three pointers were used in the program, the procedure NEW is used only with the ToolPointer. This procedure is only needed to allocate memory when nodes are created.

11-7 Storing Lists in Files

To store a linked list in a file, follow these steps:

1. Open the file for writing.

2. Make the CurrentPointer point to the first node:

```
CurrentPointer := FirstPointer;
```

3. Read the data field (CurrentPointer ^ .DataField), and write it to the file:

```
WRITE(MyListFile, CurrentPointer^.DataField);
```

4. Move the CurrentPointer to the next node by updating its direction to point to the pointer field (NextField):

```
CurrentPointer := CurrentPointer^.NextField;
```

5. Repeat steps 3 and 4 until you reach the end of the list. At this point, the CurrentPointer will be NIL.

```
    Close the file.
```

The following program segment summarizes the preceding steps:

```
VAR
    CurrentPointer :ListPointer;
BEGIN
  ASSIGN(MyListFile, FileName);
  REWRITE(MyListFile);
  CurrentPointer := FirstPointer;
  WHILE CurrentPointer <> NIL DO
    BEGIN
      WRITE(MyListFile, CurrentPointer^.DataField);
      CurrentPointer := CurrentPointer^.NextField
    END;
  CLOSE(MyListFile)
END;
```

11-8 Reading Lists from Files

When you store a linked list in a file, you only store the data. The list pointers are only used in memory to control the list. Therefore, when the file is written to the disk, it becomes a regular data file, and may be read using the regular procedures. After reading the file, it is your preference to build the data as a linked list. To add the data read from a file to a linked list, do the following:

1. Open the file for reading.

2. Read a data item from the file.

3. Add the item to the list using the procedure BuildList explained earlier.

In the following segment, the data item Name is read from the file MyListFile and added to the list:

```
    WHILE NOT EOF (MyListFile) DO
        BEGIN
          READ(MyListFile, Name);
          BuildList(FirstPointer, Name);
        END;
```

4. Repeat steps 2 and 3 until you reach end-of-file.

Drill 11-3

Modify Example 11-4 to add the two options:

■ Save the list to a file.

■ Add data from file.

For the type of data you are currently using, you may use either a TEXT or a non-TEXT file.

Application: Building a List of Records

In this section, you are going to work with a more practical linked list, a list of employee records. Look at these types:

```
TYPE
{Declaration of data type }
   SSNstring  = STRING[11];
   DataRecord = RECORD
                   ID                    :STRING[5];
                   Name, Position        :STRING[20];
                   SSN                   :SSNstring;
                   Rate                  :REAL
               END;
{Declaration of the list }
   ListPointer = ^ListRecord;
   ListRecord = RECORD
                   DataField :DataRecord;
                   NextField :ListPointer
                END;
   EmpFile = FILE OF DataRecord;
```

These declarations are divided into two main parts:

1. The definition of the data type (the record), which is used as a data field in the linked list.

2. The linked list definition.

Note in these declarations that the SSNstring type comes first, because it is used in the definition of the employee record (DataRecord). Note also that the data field (DataField) in the linked list is of the type DataRecord.

A file of DataRecords, in which you are going to store the list, is also defined. Using a file of records makes the file handling much easier.

The global variables you are going to use are a list pointer, a file variable, and a record variable:

```
VAR
   FirstPointer :ListPointer;
```

```
MyListFile   :EmpFile;
EmpRecord    :DataRecord;
```

When you deal with a list of records, use the same procedures used with simple lists, because you are still dealing with nodes. Only remember to use fielded variables to read the fields. For example, in a list of strings, refer to each string using the variable:

```
CurrentPointer^.DataField
```

In a list of records, refer to the SSN field (as an example) using the variable:

```
CurrentPointer^.DataField.SSN
```

or you may use a WITH statement to do the same thing:

```
WITH CurrentPointer^.DataField DO
       BEGIN
         WRITE(ID :7);
         WRITE(Name :22); ...
```

11-9 Searching Lists

In real applications, displaying the whole list on the screen is not useful, because the list may be too long. Instead, you need to display a specific record. To do this, you have to search in the list for a unique field such as the Social Security Number SSN. These are the steps to search a list:

1. Start from the first node by setting up the CurrentPointer so that it points to the first node:

```
CurrentPointer := FirstPointer;
```

2. Match the Social Security Number entered from the keyboard (SSNumber) with the SSN field in the node. If they match, set a flag such as Found:

```
IF CurrentPointer^.DataField.SSN = SSNumber THEN
Found := TRUE
```

The CurrentPointer, in this case, is just pointing to the required node, and may be used to read the information.

3. If the required record is not found, move the CurrentPointer to the next node:

```
CurrentPointer := CurrentPointer^.NextField;
```

4. Repeat steps 2 and 3 until you either find the matching record (Found = TRUE), or you reach the end of the list (CurrentPointer = NIL). Thus, your WHILE loop will be using these two conditions:

```
WHILE (CurrentPointer <> NIL) AND (NOT Found) DO
 ....
```

The following is a program segment that includes the preceding steps:

```
CurrentPointer := FirstPointer;
  WHILE (CurrentPointer <> NIL) AND (NOT Found) DO
      IF CurrentPointer^.DataField.SSN = SSNumber THEN
          Found := TRUE
    ELSE
        CurrentPointer := CurrentPointer^.NextField;
```

To display the information in the required node, you may use the following segment:

```
WITH CurrentPointer^.DataField DO
    BEGIN
      WRITELN('ID: ',ID);
      WRITELN('Name: ',Name);
      WRITELN('Position: ', Position);
      WRITELN('Social Security Number: ',SSN);
      WRITELN('Hourly Rate: ',Rate :2:2)
    END;
```

The following program is the linked list version of the employee database. It includes the options to search for and display a specific record, in addition to better file processing. The program includes the following procedures:

- SearchList   to search for a specific record.
- BuildList   to add records to the list.
- ReadList   to display the whole list.
- GetData   to accept data from the keyboard.
- DisplayRec   to display a specific record.
- DisplayItAll   to display the headers of the fields and invoke ReadList.
- ReadFile   to read records from the data file and invoke BuildList.
- SaveList   to save the list to a file.
- Menu   to display the user menu.

```
{ ---------------------- Example 11-5 ---------------------- }
PROGRAM LinkedListDB(INPUT, OUTPUT, MyListFile);
{ This program processes an employee database as list of records. }

CONST
   FileName = 'emplist.bin';
   Header = '-------------- Main Menu --------------';
   Separator = '---------------------------------------';

TYPE
{Declaration of data type }
   SSNstring = STRING[11];
   DataRecord = RECORD
```

```
                    ID                     :STRING[5];
                    Name, Position         :STRING[20];
                    SSN                    :SSNstring;
                    Rate                   :REAL
                END;
{Declaration of the list }
   ListPointer = ^ListRecord;
   ListRecord = RECORD
                      DataField :DataRecord;
                      NextField :ListPointer
                   END;
   EmpFile = FILE OF DataRecord;

VAR
   FirstPointer :ListPointer;
   MyListFile   :EmpFile;
   EmpRecord    :DataRecord;


{ -------------------- Procedure SearchList ---------------------- }
PROCEDURE SearchList(FirstPointer :ListPointer;
                     VAR CurrentPointer :ListPointer;
                     SSNumber :SSNstring;
                     VAR Found :BOOLEAN);
{ This procedure searches the linked list for an employee's SSN. If found, the
value of the Boolean flag Found becomes TRUE, and the CurrentPointer points to
the required node. }

BEGIN
  CurrentPointer := FirstPointer;
  WHILE (CurrentPointer <> NIL) AND (NOT Found) DO
     IF CurrentPointer^.DataField.SSN = SSNumber THEN
        Found := TRUE
    ELSE
      CurrentPointer := CurrentPointer^.NextField;
END;


{ -------------------- Procedure BuildList ----------------------- }
PROCEDURE BuildList(VAR FirstPointer :ListPointer;
                    DataItem :DataRecord);
{ This procedure builds the linked list, or adds nodes to it.}
{Note: The FirstPointer is passed using the VAR keyword as it will be updated
by this procedure. }

VAR
  ToolPointer :ListPointer;
BEGIN
  NEW(ToolPointer);
  ToolPointer^.DataField := DataItem;
  ToolPointer^.NextField := FirstPointer;
  FirstPointer := ToolPointer
```

```
END;
{ --------------------- Procedure ReadList --------------------- }
PROCEDURE ReadList(FirstPointer :ListPointer);
{ This procedure reads and displays the contents of the list. }

VAR
  CurrentPointer :ListPointer;

BEGIN
  CurrentPointer := FirstPointer;
  WHILE CurrentPointer <> NIL DO
    BEGIN
      WITH CurrentPointer^.DataField DO
        BEGIN
          WRITE(ID :7);
          WRITE(Name :22);
          WRITE(Position :22);
          WRITE(SSN :13);
          WRITELN(' $' ,Rate :0:2)
        END;
        CurrentPointer := CurrentPointer^.NextField
    END;
    WRITELN
END;
{ --------------------- Procedure GetData ----------------------- }
PROCEDURE GetData(VAR FirstPointer :ListPointer);
{ This procedure receives the employee data from the keyboard, and passes the
record information to the procedure BuildList to be added to the linked list. }

VAR
   Item :DataRecord;

BEGIN
    WRITELN('Please enter the record information,',
                        ' when finished hit ENTER.');
{ Read the first data item }
  WITH Item DO
      BEGIN
        WRITE('ID: ');            READLN(ID);
        WRITE('Name: ');          READLN(Name);
        WRITE('Position: ');      READLN(Position);
        WRITE('SSN: ');           READLN(SSN);
        WRITE('Rate: ');          READLN(Rate);
        WRITE(Separator)
      END;
      BuildList(FirstPointer, Item);
END;


{ ------------------- Procedure DisplayItAll --------------------- }
PROCEDURE DisplayItAll(FirstPointer :ListPointer);
```

```
{ This procedures displays the headers of the fields in the proper format and
calls the procedure ReadList to display the contents of the list. }

BEGIN
  WRITELN(Separator);
  WRITELN('The contents of the list: ');
  WRITELN('ID' :7, 'Name' :22, 'Position' :22, 'SSN' :13,
          'Rate' :7);
  WRITELN;
  ReadList(FirstPointer);
  WRITE('Hit any key to continue...');
  READLN
END;


{ -------------------- Procedure DisplayRec ---------------------- }
PROCEDURE DisplayRec(FirstPointer :ListPointer);
{ This procedure displays the information for a specific employee. It calls the
procedure SearchList to search the list using the Social Security Number of the
employee. If found, the information is displayed, otherwise a "not found" error
message is issued. }

VAR
    CurrentPointer :ListPointer;
    SSNumber       :SSNstring;
    Found          :BOOLEAN;

BEGIN
  Found := FALSE;
  WRITELN(Separator);
  WRITE('Enter the SSN for the employee:'); READLN(SSNumber);
  SearchList(FirstPointer, CurrentPointer, SSNumber, Found);
  IF NOT Found THEN
     WRITELN('SSN: ', SSNumber, ' Not Found')
  ELSE
    WITH CurrentPointer^.DataField DO
      BEGIN
        WRITELN('ID: ',ID);
        WRITELN('Name: ',Name);
        WRITELN('Position: ', Position);
        WRITELN('Social Security Number: ',SSN);
        WRITELN('Hourly Rate: ',Rate :2:2)
      END;
  WRITE('Hit any key to continue...');
  READLN
END;


{ -------------------- Procedure SaveList ----------------------- }
PROCEDURE SaveList(FirstPointer :ListPointer;
                                VAR MyListFile: EmpFile);
```

```
{This procedure saves the data fields in the linked list to a file of the type
RECORD. }

VAR
   CurrentPointer :ListPointer;

BEGIN
  ASSIGN(MyListFile, FileName);
  REWRITE(MyListFile);
  CurrentPointer := FirstPointer;
  WHILE CurrentPointer <> NIL DO
    BEGIN
      WRITE(MyListFile, CurrentPointer^.DataField);
      CurrentPointer := CurrentPointer^.NextField
    END;
  CLOSE(MyListFile)
END;


{ --------------------- Procedure ReadFile --------------------- }
PROCEDURE ReadFile(VAR FirstPointer :ListPointer;
                              VAR MyListFile: EmpFile);
{This procedure reads data from the file EMPLIST.BIN and adds the data to the
linked list. }

VAR
   Item   :DataRecord;

BEGIN
  ASSIGN(MyListFile, FileName);
  RESET(MyListFile);
  WHILE NOT EOF (MyListFile) DO
    BEGIN
      READ(MyListFile, Item);
      BuildList(FirstPointer, Item);
    END;
  CLOSE(MyListFile)
END;


{ ------------------------ Procedure Menu ------------------------ }
PROCEDURE Menu;

VAR
   Option :INTEGER;

BEGIN
  WRITELN(Header);
  WRITELN('1. Add records to the list.');
  WRITELN('2. Display the whole list.');
  WRITELN('3. Display an employee record.');
  WRITELN('4. Add records from file.');
```

```
      WRITELN('5. Save the list to a file.');
      WRITELN('6. Exit.');
      WRITELN(Separator);
      WRITE('Make a choice and press a number: ');
      READLN(Option);
      CASE Option OF
          1 : GetData(FirstPointer);
          2 : DisplayItAll(FirstPointer);
          3 : DisplayRec(FirstPointer);
          4 : ReadFile(FirstPointer, MyListFile);
          5 : SaveList(FirstPointer, MyListFile);
          6 : Exit
      END;
      Menu
END;


{ ----------------------- Main Program ------------------------ }

BEGIN
{ Initialize an empty list. }
  FirstPointer := NIL;
  menu
END.
{ ----------------------------------------------------------------- }
```

Sample Run:

A sample of the file EMPLIST.BIN is included on the companion CD. When you run the program, you may start with loading records from the file by choosing option 4, then display the list using option 2. In the following sample run, the user input is bolded for clarity.

```
-------------- Main Menu --------------
1. Add records to the list.
2. Display the whole list.
3. Display an employee record.
4. Add records from file.
5. Save the list to a file.
6. Exit.
----------------------------------------
Make a choice and press a number: 4    → At this point, the list is loaded into memory.
-------------- Main Menu --------------
1. Add records to the list.
2. Display the whole list.
3. Display an employee record.
4. Add records from file.
5. Save the list to a file.
6. Exit.
----------------------------------------
Make a choice and press a number: 2
```

```
--------------------------------------
The contents of the list:
    ID                Name              Position         SSN    Rate

   456          Mark Poche      Staff Assistant  999-99-9999 $23.00
   345      Deanna Bedford          Secretary I  444-44-4444 $12.55
   123   John Martin Smith        Sales Manager  111-11-1111 $22.50
   234      James Strahan  Sales Representative  222-22-2222 $11.50
   987      Charles Berlin            President  333-33-3333 $60.50

Hit any key to continue...
```

For your convenience, the Social Security Numbers in the file are made easy to remember when you search for a certain employee. Here is an example:

```
-------------- Main Menu --------------
1. Add records to the list.
2. Display the whole list.
3. Display an employee record.
4. Add records from file.
5. Save the list to a file.
6. Exit.
--------------------------------------
Make a choice and press a number: 3
--------------------------------------
Enter the SSN for the employee: 111-11-1111
ID: 123
Name: John Martin Smith
Position: Sales Manager
Social Security Number: 111-11-1111
Hourly Rate: 22.50

Hit any key to continue...
-------------- Main Menu --------------
1. Add records to the list.
2. Display the whole list.
3. Display an employee record.
4. Add records from file.
5. Save the list to a file.
6. Exit.
--------------------------------------
Make a choice and press a number: 6
```

Notice the following points in the search procedure:

1. The call to the search procedure takes the form:

```
SearchList(FirstPointer, CurrentPointer, SSNumber, Found);
```

where the SSNumber is the Social Security Number to be matched with the field SSN.

2. Both the CurrentPointer and the flag Found are passed using the keyword VAR, because their values are expected to change after the search process:

```
PROCEDURE SearchList(FirstPointer :ListPointer;
        VAR CurrentPointer :ListPointer;
        SSNumber :SSNstring;
        VAR Found :BOOLEAN);
```

Drill 11-4

Add a procedure to the previous program to incorporate the Update record option in your menu. To update a record, search for it, accept the new information from the keyboard, and write the record to the data field in the current node. Remember to update the menu options as well, by adding the option Update a record.

11-10 Deleting Nodes from Lists

To delete a node from a linked list, you need to declare three pointers:

- FirstPointer   which points to the first node.
- CurrentPointer   which points to the current node.
- PreviousPointer   which points to the previous node.

The algorithm to delete a node depends on its relative position in the link. There are two cases to consider:

A. If the node is the first node in the list:

The procedure to delete the node in this case is simple, and requires only the two pointers FirstPointer and CurrentPointer:

1. Set the CurrentPointer to point to the node to be deleted (the first node).

2. Set the FirstPointer to point to the second node in the list:

```
FirstPointer := FirstPointer^.NextField;
```

3. Dispose of the CurrentPointer:

```
DISPOSE(CurrentPointer);
```

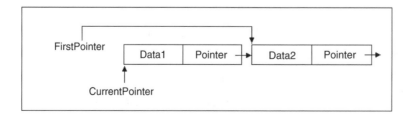

B. If the node has a predecessor:

This is the case in which you need the third pointer that points to the previous node. The following is the algorithm to delete the node:

1. Set the CurrentPointer to point to the node to be deleted.
2. Set the PreviousPointer to point to the successor of the current node:

```
PreviousPointer^.NextField := CurrentPointer^.NextField;
```

3. Dispose of the CurrentPointer:

```
DISPOSE(CurrentPointer);
```

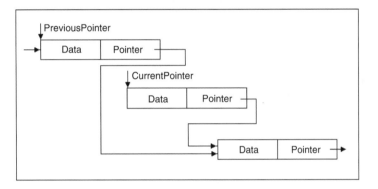

The previous steps imply that the algorithm of the search procedure must be changed so that the PreviousPointer follows the CurrentPointer step by step through the list.

This is the new version of the procedure SearchList:

```
{ -------------------- Procedure SearchList ---------------------- }
PROCEDURE SearchList(FirstPointer :ListPointer;
                     VAR CurrentPointer :ListPointer;
                     VAR PreviousPointer :ListPointer;
                     SSNumber :SSNstring;
                     VAR Found :BOOLEAN);

BEGIN
  PreviousPointer := NIL;
  CurrentPointer := FirstPointer;
  WHILE (CurrentPointer <> NIL) AND (NOT Found) DO
      IF CurrentPointer^.DataField.SSN = SSNumber THEN
        Found := TRUE
    ELSE
      BEGIN
        PreviousPointer := CurrentPointer;
        CurrentPointer := CurrentPointer^.NextField
      END
```

```
END;
```

The procedure header is changed to:

```
PROCEDURE SearchList(FirstPointer :ListPointer;
                VAR CurrentPointer :ListPointer;
                VAR PreviousPointer :ListPointer;
                SSNumber :SSNstring;
                VAR Found :BOOLEAN);
```

Because the PreviousPointer follows the CurrentPointer and its value is expected to change, it has to be preceded by the keyword VAR.

The following is the DelRecord Procedure:

```
{ -------------------- Procedure DelRecord ---------------------- }
PROCEDURE DelRecord(VAR FirstPointer :ListPointer);

VAR
  CurrentPointer, PreviousPointer :ListPointer;
  Found :BOOLEAN;
  SSNumber: SSNstring;

BEGIN
  Found := FALSE;
  WRITELN(Separator);
  WRITE('Enter the SSN of the employee to be removed:');
  READLN(SSNumber);
  SearchList(FirstPointer, CurrentPointer, PreviousPointer,
            SSNumber, Found);
  IF NOT Found THEN
    WRITELN('SSN: ', SSNumber, ' Not Found')
  ELSE
    BEGIN
      IF PreviousPointer = NIL THEN
{ The node to be deleted is the first node. }
        FirstPointer := FirstPointer^.NextField
      ELSE
{ The node to be deleted has a predecessor. }
        PreviousPointer^.NextField := CurrentPointer^.NextField;
      DISPOSE(CurrentPointer);
      WRITELN('The record has been deleted from the list.')
    END;
  WRITE('Hit any key to continue...');
  READLN
END;
{ ---------------------------------------------------------------- }
```

The changes made on the SearchList procedure will affect other procedures. Any call to the SearchList must include the new pointer parameter PreviousPointer as shown in the following call:

```
SearchList(FirstPointer, CurrentPointer, PreviousPointer,
                                      SSNumber, Found);
```

In the previous program (Example 11-5) the DisplayRec procedure calls SearchList using two pointer parameters only. This is obvious because PreviousPointer is not used in the DisplayRec procedure. In order to incorporate the new SearchList procedure into the program, the calls to the SearchList must be modified. In the procedure DisplayRec, you may declare a dummy pointer which has no work to do except being passed as a parameter to the search procedure. This is an example of the new call:

```
SearchList(FirstPointer, CurrentPointer, DummyPointer,
                                      SSNumber, Found);
```

In the following program, the employee database is almost completed. These are the main features of the program:

1. A call to the SearchList procedure is made before entering the data of a new employer. The Social Security Number is checked to see if it originally exists. If it does, no data are entered, and the proper message is issued.

2. The DelRecord procedure is added.

3. The UpdateRec procedure is added.

4. The SearchList procedure is used to reject any operation (e.g., delete, update, or display) if the SSN is not found.

```
{ ---------------------- Example 11-6 ---------------------- }
PROGRAM LinkedListDB(INPUT, OUTPUT, MyListFile);

CONST
    FileName = 'emplist.bin';
    Header = '-------------- Main Menu --------------';
    Separator = '----------------------------------------';

TYPE
{Declaration of data type }
    SSNstring   = STRING[11];
    DataRecord = RECORD
                    ID                        :STRING[5];
                    Name, Position            :STRING[20];
                    SSN                       :SSNstring;
                    Rate                      :REAL
                END;
{Declaration of the list }
    ListPointer = ^ListRecord;
    ListRecord = RECORD
                    DataField :DataRecord;
                    NextField :ListPointer
                END;
    EmpFile = FILE OF DataRecord;
```

```
VAR
   FirstPointer :ListPointer;
   MyListFile   :EmpFile;
   EmpRecord    :DataRecord;

{ ------------------- Procedure SearchList --------------------- }
PROCEDURE SearchList(FirstPointer :ListPointer;
                     VAR CurrentPointer :ListPointer;
                     VAR PreviousPointer :ListPointer;
                     SSNumber :SSNstring;
                     VAR Found :BOOLEAN);
{ This procedure searches the linked list for an employee's SSN. If found, the
value of the Boolean flag "Found" becomes TRUE. }

BEGIN
  PreviousPointer := NIL;
  CurrentPointer := FirstPointer;
  WHILE (CurrentPointer <> NIL) AND (NOT Found) DO
      IF CurrentPointer^.DataField.SSN = SSNumber THEN
         Found := TRUE
    ELSE
      BEGIN
         PreviousPointer := CurrentPointer;
         CurrentPointer := CurrentPointer^.NextField
      END
END;

{ --------------------- Procedure BuildList --------------------- }
PROCEDURE BuildList(VAR FirstPointer :ListPointer;
                    DataItem :DataRecord);
{ This procedure builds the linked list, or adds nodes to it.}
{Note: The FirstPointer is passed using the VAR keyword because it will be
updated by this procedure.}

VAR
  ToolPointer :ListPointer;
BEGIN
  NEW(ToolPointer);
  ToolPointer^.DataField := DataItem;
  ToolPointer^.NextField := FirstPointer;
  FirstPointer := ToolPointer
END;
{ --------------------- Procedure ReadList --------------------- }
PROCEDURE ReadList(FirstPointer :ListPointer);
{ This procedure reads and displays the contents of the list }

VAR
  CurrentPointer :ListPointer;

BEGIN
```

```
      CurrentPointer := FirstPointer;
      WHILE CurrentPointer <> NIL DO
        BEGIN
          WITH CurrentPointer^.DataField DO
            BEGIN
              WRITE(ID :7);
              WRITE(Name :22);
              WRITE(Position :22);
              WRITE(SSN :13);
              WRITELN(' $' ,Rate :0:2)
            END;
          CurrentPointer := CurrentPointer^.NextField
        END;
        WRITELN
END;
{ -------------------- Procedure DelRecord ----------------------- }
PROCEDURE DelRecord(VAR FirstPointer :ListPointer);
{ This procedure deletes a node from the list. If the node to be deleted is the
first node. The FirstPointer is moved to the next node; otherwise, the pointer
field of the previous node is updated to point to the next node. In both cases
the CurrentPointer is disposed. }

VAR
  CurrentPointer, PreviousPointer :ListPointer;
  Found :BOOLEAN;
  SSNumber: SSNstring;

BEGIN
  Found := FALSE;
  WRITELN(Separator);
  WRITE('Enter the SSN of the employee to be removed:');
  READLN(SSNumber);
  SearchList(FirstPointer, CurrentPointer, PreviousPointer,
             SSNumber, Found);
  IF NOT Found THEN
    WRITELN('SSN: ', SSNumber, ' Not Found')
  ELSE
    BEGIN
      IF PreviousPointer = NIL THEN
{ The node to be deleted is the first node. }
        FirstPointer := FirstPointer^.NextField
      ELSE
{ The node to be deleted has a predecessor. }
        PreviousPointer^.NextField := CurrentPointer^.NextField;
      DISPOSE(CurrentPointer);
      WRITELN('The record has been deleted from the list.')
    END;
  WRITE('Hit any key to continue...');
  READLN
END;
```

```
{ --------------------- Procedure GetData ----------------------- }
PROCEDURE GetData(VAR FirstPointer :ListPointer);
{ This procedure receives the employee data from the keyboard, and passes the
record information to the procedure BuildList to be added to the linked list. }

VAR
   CurrentPointer, DummyPointer :ListPointer;
   Item    :DataRecord;
   SSNumber: SSNstring;
   Found   :BOOLEAN;
BEGIN
   Found := FALSE;
   WRITE('Please enter the SSN of the employee: ');
   READLN(SSNumber);
   SearchList(FirstPointer, CurrentPointer, DummyPointer,
              SSNumber, Found);
   IF NOT Found THEN
     BEGIN
       WRITELN('Please enter the employee information:');
       WITH Item DO
         BEGIN
           SSN := SSNumber;
           WRITE('ID: ');          READLN(ID);
           WRITE('Name: ');        READLN(Name);
           WRITE('Position: ');    READLN(Position);
           WRITE('Rate: ');        READLN(Rate);
           WRITELN(Separator)
         END;
       BuildList(FirstPointer, Item);
       WRITELN('The employee has been added to the list.')
     END
       ELSE
       WRITELN('The SSN: ', SSNumber, ' is already in the list.');
   WRITE('Hit any key to continue...');
   READLN
END;


{ -------------------- Procedure DisplayItAll --------------------- }
PROCEDURE DisplayItAll(FirstPointer :ListPointer);
{ This procedures displays the headers of the fields in the proper format and
calls the procedure ReadList to display the contents of the list. }

BEGIN
  WRITELN(Separator);
  WRITELN('The contents of the list: ');
  WRITELN('ID' :7, 'Name' :22, 'Position' :22, 'SSN' :13,
          'Rate' :7);
  WRITELN;
  ReadList(FirstPointer);
  WRITE('Hit any key to continue...');
```

```
   READLN
END;


{ -------------------- Procedure DisplayRec --------------------- }
PROCEDURE DisplayRec(FirstPointer :ListPointer);
{ This procedure displays the information for a specific employee. It calls the
procedure SearchList to search the list using the Social Security Number of the
employee.}

VAR
   CurrentPointer, DummyPointer :ListPointer;
   SSNumber        :SSNstring;
   Found           :BOOLEAN;

{ Note: The DummyPointer is used to call the SearchList
  procedure (which takes three pointers as parameters), but this
  pointer is not required in this procedure. }

BEGIN
  Found := FALSE;
  WRITELN(Separator);
  WRITE('Enter the SSN of the employee:'); READLN(SSNumber);
  SearchList(FirstPointer, CurrentPointer,
            DummyPointer, SSNumber, Found);
  IF NOT Found THEN
    WRITELN('SSN: ', SSNumber, ' Not Found')
  ELSE
    WITH CurrentPointer^.DataField DO
      BEGIN
        WRITELN('ID: ',ID);
        WRITELN('Name: ',Name);
        WRITELN('Position: ', Position);
        WRITELN('Social Security Number: ', SSN);
        WRITELN('Hourly Rate: $', Rate :2:2)
      END;
  WRITE('Hit any key to continue...');
  READLN
END;


{ -------------------- Procedure UpdateRec --------------------- }
PROCEDURE UpdateRec(FirstPointer :ListPointer);
{ This procedure updates record information for a specific employee. It calls
the procedure SearchList to search the list using the Social Security Number of
the employee. The new information is accepted from the user, otherwise a "not
found" error message is issued. }

VAR
   CurrentPointer, DummyPointer :ListPointer;
   SSNumber        :SSNstring;
   Found           :BOOLEAN;
```

```
{ Note: The DummyPointer is used to call the SearchList
  procedure (which takes three pointers as parameters), but this
  pointer is not required in this procedure. }

BEGIN
  Found := FALSE;
  WRITELN(Separator);
  WRITE('Enter the SSN of the employee:'); READLN(SSNumber);
  SearchList(FirstPointer, CurrentPointer,
             DummyPointer, SSNumber, Found);
  IF NOT Found THEN
     WRITELN('SSN: ', SSNumber, ' Not Found')
  ELSE
    WITH CurrentPointer^.DataField DO
      BEGIN
        WRITELN('Please enter the now information for',
                ' the employee (SSN: ', SSNumber,'):');
        WRITE('ID: ');                   READLN(ID);
        WRITE('Name: ');                 READLN(Name);
        WRITE('Position: ');             READLN(Position);
        WRITE('Hourly Rate: ');          READLN(Rate);
        WRITELN('Record updated.')
      END;
  WRITE('Hit any key to continue...');
  READLN
END;
{ --------------------- Procedure SaveList ---------------------- }
PROCEDURE SaveList(FirstPointer :ListPointer;
                             VAR MyListFile: EmpFile);
{This procedure saves the data fields in the linked list to a file of the type
RECORD. }

VAR
   CurrentPointer :ListPointer;

BEGIN
  ASSIGN(MyListFile, FileName);
  REWRITE(MyListFile);
  CurrentPointer := FirstPointer;
  WHILE CurrentPointer <> NIL DO
    BEGIN
      WRITE(MyListFile, CurrentPointer^.DataField);
      CurrentPointer := CurrentPointer^.NextField
    END;
  CLOSE(MyListFile);
  WRITELN('The list has been saved to the file.');
  WRITE('Hit any key to continue...');
  READLN
END;
```

```
{ -------------------- Procedure ReadFile ---------------------- }
PROCEDURE ReadFile(VAR FirstPointer :ListPointer;
                                VAR MyListFile: EmpFile);
{This procedure reads data from the file EMPLIST.BIN and adds the data to the
linked list. }

VAR
   Item              :DataRecord;

BEGIN
  ASSIGN(MyListFile, FileName);
  RESET(MyListFile);
  WHILE NOT EOF (MyListFile) DO
    BEGIN
      READ(MyListFile, Item);
      BuildList(FirstPointer, Item);
    END;
  CLOSE(MyListFile);
  WRITELN('The employee list is ready in memory.');
  WRITE('Hit any key to continue...');
  READLN
END;

{ ---------------------- Procedure Menu ---------------------- }
PROCEDURE Menu;
VAR
   Option :INTEGER;

BEGIN
   WRITELN(Header);
   WRITELN('1. Add records to the list.');
   WRITELN('2. Display the whole list.');
   WRITELN('3. Display an employee record.');
   WRITELN('4. Add records from file.');
   WRITELN('5. Save the list to a file.');
   WRITELN('6. Delete a record.');
   WRITELN('7. Update a record.');
   WRITELN('8. Exit.');
   WRITELN(Separator);
   WRITE('Make a choice and press a number: ');
   READLN(Option);
   CASE Option OF
      1 : GetData(FirstPointer);
      2 : DisplayItAll(FirstPointer);
      3 : DisplayRec(FirstPointer);
      4 : ReadFile(FirstPointer, MyListFile);
      5 : SaveList(FirstPointer, MyListFile);
      6 : DelRecord(FirstPointer);
      7 : UpdateRec(FirstPointer);
      8 : Exit
```

```
    END;
    Menu
END;

{ ---------------------- Main Program -------------------------- }
BEGIN
{ Initialize an empty List }
  FirstPointer := NIL;
  menu
END.
{ ---------------------------------------------------------------- }
```

Sample Run:

In the following run, option 1 was chosen in order to add a new employee (SSN: 222-22-2222). However, the program refused to add it because the SearchList procedure found this SSN in the list. The user input is bolded for clarity.

```
-------------- Main Menu --------------
1. Add records to the list.
2. Display the whole list.
3. Display an employee record.
4. Add records from file.
5. Save the list to a file.
6. Delete a record.
7. Update a record.
8. Exit.
----------------------------------------
Make a choice and press a number: 4
The employee list is ready in memory.
Hit any key to continue...
-------------- Main Menu --------------
1. Add records to the list.
2. Display the whole list.
3. Display an employee record.
4. Add records from file.
5. Save the list to a file.
6. Delete a record.
7. Update a record.
8. Exit.
----------------------------------------
Make a choice and press a number: 1
Please enter the SSN of the employee: 222-22-2222
The SSN: 222-22-2222 is already in the list.
Hit any key to continue...
```

11-11 Arranging Nodes in Sequential Order

The linked list you have used so far is classified as an *unordered* linked list because you have no control over the sequence of nodes in the list. When you insert a new node, it goes directly to the beginning of the list. In an *ordered* linked list, items are stored in an ascending or descending order. Therefore, if the items are records, the ordering must be based on one of the data fields in the record such as the SSN or the last name. This data field is known as the *key field*. In an ordered linked list, the logic of insertion and searching procedures will be different from those used with unordered lists. However, the deletion procedure is essentially the same. Adding a record to an ordered list includes searching the list for the proper insertion point.

Inserting Nodes

To add a new item to an ordered list, use the following pointers:

- CurrentPointer   A pointer to the current node.
- PreviousPointer   A pointer to the predecessor node.
- NewItemPointer   A pointer to the new node that will
                          contain the item.

Assume that the new node will be inserted between the two nodes pointed to by PreviousPointer and CurrentPointer, as shown in the following figure:

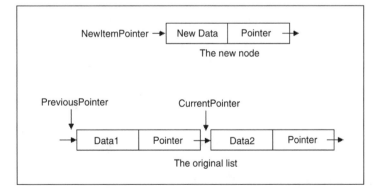

To insert the new node, do the following:

- Assign the CurrentPointer to the link field (NextField) of the new node:

        NewItemPointer^.NextField := CurrentPointer;

- Assign the NewItemPointer to the link field of the predecessor node:

        PreviousPonter^.NextField := NewItemPointer;

The result is shown in the following diagram:

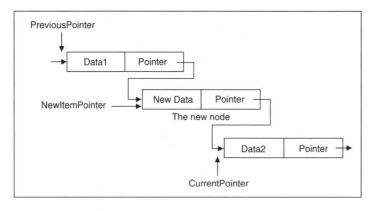

As you can see, inserting a new item is a straightforward task accomplished in two steps. However, the important part in this task is to locate the two nodes between which the new node will be inserted. This algorithm is explained in the next section.

Searching an Ordered List

The following terms are used in the search algorithm:

- ItemExists   A flag indicating that the item already exists in the list.
- FoundInsertionPoint   A flag indicating that a proper insertion point is found.
- FirstPointer   The pointer to the first node.
- CurrentPointer   The pointer to the current node.
- PreviousPointer   The pointer to the predecessor node.
- SSNumber   The Social Security Number in the record to be inserted.
- SSN   The Social Security Number field in any data node.

Assuming that the list is sorted in an ascending order based on the Social Security Number (SSN) key, the following steps indicate the algorithm for searching the list to locate the proper insertion point.

1. Start from the first node by setting up the CurrentPointer so that it points to the first node:

```
CurrentPointer := FirstPointer;
PreviousPointer := NIL;
```

2. Compare the Social Security Number in the record, which is to be inserted, to the SSN field in the current node:

```
IF CurrentPointer^.DataField.SSN >= SSNumber THEN ..
```

3. If the condition is true, one of two cases will occur.

- If the equality condition (=) is met, there is no need to insert the item into the list because it already exists. In this case, set the proper flag:

```
                             ItemExists := TRUE;
```

■ If the greater than condition (>) is met, then the CurrentPointer is pointing to the item next to the correct insertion point. In this case, set the flag ItemExists to FALSE, and set the FoundInsertionPoint flag to TRUE:

```
                    ItemExists := FALSE;
                    FoundInsertionPoint := TRUE;
```

4. If the >= condition is not met, move the CurrentPointer to the next node and continue searching:

```
           PreviousPointer := CurrentPointer;
           CurrentPointer := CurrentPointer^.NextField;
```

5. Special cases:

■ If you reach the end of the list (CurrentPointer = NIL) without meeting the >= condition, the item has to be inserted at the end of the list.

■ If the PreviousPointer is NIL, the item is inserted at the beginning of the list.

The following is the updated SearchList procedure that applies the preceding steps:

```
{ ------------------- Procedure SearchList ---------------------- }
PROCEDURE SearchList(FirstPointer :ListPointer;
                     VAR CurrentPointer  :ListPointer;
                     VAR PreviousPointer :ListPointer;
                     SSNumber            :SSNstring;
                     VAR ItemExists      :BOOLEAN);
{ This procedure searches the ordered linked list for an employee's SSN. If
found, the value of the Boolean flag ItemExists becomes TRUE }

VAR
FoundInsertionPoint :BOOLEAN;
BEGIN
  PreviousPointer := NIL;
  CurrentPointer := FirstPointer;
  ItemExists := FALSE;
  FoundInsertionPoint := FALSE;
  WHILE (CurrentPointer <> NIL) AND (NOT FoundInsertionPoint) DO
      IF CurrentPointer^.DataField.SSN >= SSNumber THEN
         BEGIN
            FoundInsertionPoint := TRUE;
            IF CurrentPointer^.DataField.SSN = SSNumber THEN
               ItemExists := TRUE
         END
      ELSE
         BEGIN
         PreviousPointer := CurrentPointer;
         CurrentPointer := CurrentPointer^.NextField
         END
END;
{ ---------------------------------------------------------------- }
```

The following is the insertion procedure that applies the new algorithm. It replaces the procedure BuildList in the previous version (Example 11-6):

```
{ ------------------- Procedure InsertInList -------------------- }
PROCEDURE InsertInList(VAR FirstPointer :ListPointer;
                           DataItem :DataRecord);
{ This procedure builds the linked list, or adds nodes to it.}

VAR
  NewItemPointer, PreviousPointer, CurrentPointer :ListPointer;
  ItemExists :BOOLEAN;

BEGIN
  SearchList(FirstPointer, CurrentPointer, PreviousPointer,
             DataItem.SSN, ItemExists);
  IF ItemExists THEN
    DuplicateMsg(DataItem.SSN)
  ELSE
    BEGIN
      NEW(NewItemPointer);
      NewItemPointer^.DataField := DataItem;
      IF PreviousPointer = NIL THEN
        { No Predecessor }
        BEGIN
          NewItemPointer^.NextField := FirstPointer;
          FirstPointer := NewItemPointer
        END
      ELSE
        BEGIN
          NewItemPointer^.NextField := CurrentPointer;
          PreviousPointer^.NextField := NewItemPointer
        END
    END
END;
{ -------------------------------------------------------------- }
```

Application: The Final Linked List Database

The following program brings all the pieces together. One of the glitches in the previous version (Example 11-6) is that when you load the linked list from a file, the SSN is not checked for duplication. Consequently, you can load the list from the file many times without any warning. In this program, each record in the file is checked to assure that it does not already exist. Also, the modularity of the program has been enhanced in this version by adding the new procedure DuplicateMsg to display a warning message about the duplicate record.

```
{ ---------------------- Example 11-7 ---------------------- }
PROGRAM OrderedLinkedListDB(INPUT, OUTPUT, MyListFile);
{ This program is used to process an ordered linked list, using the SSN as
```

```pascal
    the key field. }

CONST
   FileName = 'emplist1.bin';
   Header = '------------- Main Menu --------------';
   Separator = '-------------------------------------';
   Message = 'This record is already in the list.';

TYPE
{Declaration of data type }
   SSNstring  = STRING[11];
   DataRecord = RECORD
                   ID                    :STRING[5];
                   Name, Position        :STRING[20];
                   SSN                   :SSNstring;
                   Rate                  :REAL
               END;
{Declaration of the list }
   ListPointer = ^ListRecord;
   ListRecord = RECORD
                   DataField :DataRecord;
                   NextField :ListPointer
               END;
   EmpFile = FILE OF DataRecord;

VAR
   FirstPointer :ListPointer;
   MyListFile   :EmpFile;
   EmpRecord    :DataRecord;

{ ------------------- Procedure DuplicateMsg -------------------- }
PROCEDURE DuplicateMsg(SSNumber: SSNString);
{ This procedure prints an error message in case you attempt to insert the
  same SSN twice }

BEGIN
   WRITELN('SSN: ',SSNumber, '. ', Message);
   WRITELN(Separator)
END;


{ ------------------- Procedure SearchList --------------------- }
PROCEDURE SearchList(FirstPointer :ListPointer;
                     VAR CurrentPointer  :ListPointer;
                     VAR PreviousPointer :ListPointer;
                     SSNumber            :SSNstring;
                     VAR ItemExists      :BOOLEAN);
{ This procedure searches the ordered linked list for an employee's SSN. If
  found, the value of the Boolean flag ItemExists becomes TRUE.}
VAR
```

```
FoundInsertionPoint :BOOLEAN;

BEGIN
  PreviousPointer := NIL;
  CurrentPointer := FirstPointer;
  ItemExists := FALSE;
  FoundInsertionPoint := FALSE;
  WHILE (CurrentPointer <> NIL) AND (NOT FoundInsertionPoint) DO
      IF CurrentPointer^.DataField.SSN >= SSNumber THEN
         BEGIN
            FoundInsertionPoint := TRUE;
            IF CurrentPointer^.DataField.SSN = SSNumber THEN
               ItemExists := TRUE
         END
      ELSE
         BEGIN
         PreviousPointer := CurrentPointer;
         CurrentPointer := CurrentPointer^.NextField
         END
END;

{ ------------------- Procedure InsertInList --------------------- }
PROCEDURE InsertInList(VAR FirstPointer :ListPointer;
                    DataItem :DataRecord);
{ This procedure builds the linked list, or adds nodes to it.}
{ Note: The FirstPointer is passed using the VAR keyword as it will be
  updated by this procedure. }

VAR
  NewItemPointer, PreviousPointer, CurrentPointer :ListPointer;
  ItemExists :BOOLEAN;

BEGIN
  SearchList(FirstPointer, CurrentPointer, PreviousPointer,
           DataItem.SSN, ItemExists);
  IF ItemExists THEN
    DuplicateMsg(DataItem.SSN)
  ELSE
    BEGIN
       NEW(NewItemPointer);
       NewItemPointer^.DataField := DataItem;
       IF PreviousPointer = NIL THEN
          { No Predecessor }
          BEGIN
             NewItemPointer^.NextField := FirstPointer;
             FirstPointer := NewItemPointer
          END
       ELSE
          BEGIN
             NewItemPointer^.NextField := CurrentPointer;
```

```
                        PreviousPointer^.NextField := NewItemPointer
             END
       END
END;
{ -------------------- Procedure ReadList ---------------------- }
PROCEDURE ReadList(FirstPointer :ListPointer);
{ This procedure reads and displays the contents of the list }

VAR
  CurrentPointer :ListPointer;

BEGIN
  CurrentPointer := FirstPointer;
  WHILE CurrentPointer <> NIL DO
    BEGIN
      WITH CurrentPointer^.DataField DO
        BEGIN
          WRITE(ID :7);
          WRITE(Name :22);
          WRITE(Position :22);
          WRITE(SSN :13);
          WRITELN(' $' ,Rate :0:2)
      END;
      CurrentPointer := CurrentPointer^.NextField
    END;
    WRITELN
END;
{ -------------------- Procedure DelRecord ---------------------- }
PROCEDURE DelRecord(VAR FirstPointer :ListPointer);
{ This procedure deletes a node from the list. If the node to be deleted is
  the first node, the FirstPointer is moved to the next node; otherwise, the
  pointer field of the previous node is updated to point to the next node.
  In both cases the CurrentPointer is disposed. }

VAR
  CurrentPointer, PreviousPointer :ListPointer;
  Found :BOOLEAN;
  SSNumber: SSNstring;

BEGIN
  Found := FALSE;
  WRITELN(Separator);
  WRITE('Enter the SSN of the employee to be removed:');
  READLN(SSNumber);
  SearchList(FirstPointer, CurrentPointer, PreviousPointer,
             SSNumber, Found);
  IF NOT Found THEN
    WRITELN('SSN: ', SSNumber, ' Not Found')
  ELSE
    BEGIN
```

```
            IF PreviousPointer = NIL THEN
{ The node to be deleted is the first node. }
            FirstPointer := FirstPointer^.NextField
          ELSE
{ The node to be deleted has a predecessor. }
            PreviousPointer^.NextField := CurrentPointer^.NextField;
        DISPOSE(CurrentPointer);
        WRITELN('The record has been deleted from the list.')
      END
END;


{ --------------------- Procedure GetData ----------------------- }
PROCEDURE GetData(VAR FirstPointer :ListPointer);
{ This procedure receives the employee data from the keyboard, and passes
  the record information to the procedure InsertInList to be added to the
  linked list. }

VAR
   CurrentPointer, DummyPointer :ListPointer;
   Item     :DataRecord;
   SSNumber: SSNstring;
   Found    :BOOLEAN;
BEGIN
   Found := FALSE;
   WRITE('Please enter the SSN of the employee: ');
   READLN(SSNumber);
   SearchList(FirstPointer, CurrentPointer, DummyPointer,
              SSNumber, Found);
   IF NOT Found THEN
     BEGIN
       WRITELN('Please enter the employee information:');
       WITH Item DO
         BEGIN
           SSN := SSNumber;
           WRITE('ID: ');           READLN(ID);
           WRITE('Name: ');         READLN(Name);
           WRITE('Position: ');     READLN(Position);
           WRITE('Rate: ');         READLN(Rate);
           WRITELN(Separator)
         END;
       InsertInList(FirstPointer, Item);
       WRITELN('The employee has been added to the list.')
     END
       ELSE
         DuplicateMsg(SSNumber)
END;


{ -------------------- Procedure DisplayItAll -------------------- }
PROCEDURE DisplayItAll(FirstPointer :ListPointer);
{ This procedure displays the headers of the fields in the proper format and
```

calls the procedure ReadList to display the contents of the list. }

```
BEGIN
  WRITELN(Separator);
  WRITELN('The contents of the list: ');
  WRITELN('ID' :7, 'Name' :22, 'Position' :22, 'SSN' :13,
          'Rate' :7);
  WRITELN;
  ReadList(FirstPointer)
END;

{ ------------------- Procedure DisplayRec ---------------------- }
PROCEDURE DisplayRec(FirstPointer :ListPointer);
{ This procedure displays the information for a specific employee. It calls
  the SearchList procedure to search the list using the Social Security Number
  of the employee. }

VAR
   CurrentPointer, DummyPointer :ListPointer;
   SSNumber        :SSNstring;
   Found           :BOOLEAN;

{ Note: The DummyPointer is used to call the SearchList
  procedure (which takes three pointers as parameters), but this
  pointer is not required in this procedure. }

BEGIN
  Found := FALSE;
  WRITELN(Separator);
  WRITE('Enter the SSN of the employee:'); READLN(SSNumber);
  SearchList(FirstPointer, CurrentPointer,
             DummyPointer, SSNumber, Found);
  IF NOT Found THEN
    WRITELN('SSN: ', SSNumber, ' Not Found')
  ELSE
    WITH CurrentPointer^.DataField DO
      BEGIN
        WRITELN('ID: ',ID);
        WRITELN('Name: ',Name);
        WRITELN('Position: ', Position);
        WRITELN('Social Security Number: ',SSN);
        WRITELN('Hourly Rate: $',Rate :2:2)
      END
END;

{ ------------------- Procedure UpdateRec ---------------------- }
PROCEDURE UpdateRec(FirstPointer :ListPointer);
{ This procedure updates record information for a specific employee. It calls
  the procedure SearchList to search the list using the Social Security Number
  of the employee. The new information is accepted from the user; otherwise,
```

a message not found is issued.}

```
VAR
   CurrentPointer, DummyPointer :ListPointer;
   SSNumber        :SSNstring;
   Found           :BOOLEAN;
```

{ Note: The DummyPointer is used to call the SearchList procedure (which takes three pointers as parameters), but this pointer is not required in this procedure. }

```
BEGIN
  Found := FALSE;
  WRITELN(Separator);
  WRITE('Enter the SSN of the employee:'); READLN(SSNumber);
  SearchList(FirstPointer, CurrentPointer,
             DummyPointer, SSNumber, Found);
  IF NOT Found THEN
    WRITELN('SSN: ', SSNumber, ' Not Found')
  ELSE
    WITH CurrentPointer^.DataField DO
      BEGIN
        WRITELN('Please enter the new information for',
                ' the employee (SSN: ', SSNumber,'):');
        WRITE('ID: ');               READLN(ID);
        WRITE('Name: ');             READLN(Name);
        WRITE('Position: ');         READLN(Position);
        WRITE('Hourly Rate: ');      READLN(Rate);
        WRITELN('Record updated.')
      END
END;
{ --------------------- Procedure SaveList --------------------- }
PROCEDURE SaveList(FirstPointer :ListPointer;
                   VAR MyListFile: EmpFile);
{ This procedure saves the data fields in the linked list to a file of the type
RECORD. }

VAR
   CurrentPointer :ListPointer;

BEGIN
  ASSIGN(MyListFile, FileName);
  REWRITE(MyListFile);
  CurrentPointer := FirstPointer;
  WHILE CurrentPointer <> NIL DO
    BEGIN
      WRITE(MyListFile, CurrentPointer^.DataField);
      CurrentPointer := CurrentPointer^.NextField
    END;
  CLOSE(MyListFile);
```

```
      WRITELN('The list has been saved to the file.')
END;


{ ---------------------- Procedure ReadFile ---------------------- }
PROCEDURE ReadFile(VAR FirstPointer :ListPointer;
                   VAR MyListFile: EmpFile);
{ This procedure reads data from the file EMPLIST1.BIN and adds the data to the
linked list. }

VAR
   Item          :DataRecord;
   ToolPointer :ListPointer;
BEGIN
  ASSIGN(MyListFile, FileName);
  RESET(MyListFile);
  WHILE NOT EOF (MyListFile) DO
    BEGIN
      READ(MyListFile, Item);
      InsertInList(FirstPointer, Item);
    END;
  CLOSE(MyListFile)
END;


{ ---------------------- Procedure Menu ---------------------- }
PROCEDURE Menu;

VAR
   Option :INTEGER;

BEGIN
   WRITELN(Header);
   WRITELN('1. Add records to the list.');
   WRITELN('2. Display the whole list.');
   WRITELN('3. Display an employee record.');
   WRITELN('4. Add records from file.');
   WRITELN('5. Save the list to a file.');
   WRITELN('6. Delete a record.');
   WRITELN('7. Update a record.');
   WRITELN('8. Exit.');
   WRITELN(Separator);
   WRITE('Make a choice and press a number: ');
   READLN(Option);
   CASE Option OF
      1 : GetData(FirstPointer);
      2 : DisplayItAll(FirstPointer);
      3 : DisplayRec(FirstPointer);
      4 : ReadFile(FirstPointer, MyListFile);
      5 : SaveList(FirstPointer, MyListFile);
      6 : DelRecord(FirstPointer);
      7 : UpdateRec(FirstPointer);
```

```
      8 : Exit
   END;
   WRITELN('Hit any key to continue...');
   READLN;
   Menu
END;


{ ------------------------ Main Program ------------------------ }
BEGIN
{ Initialize an empty List }
  FirstPointer := NIL;
  menu
END.
{ ------------------------------------------------------------------ }
```

Sample Run:

Notice that the user input is bolded for clarity.

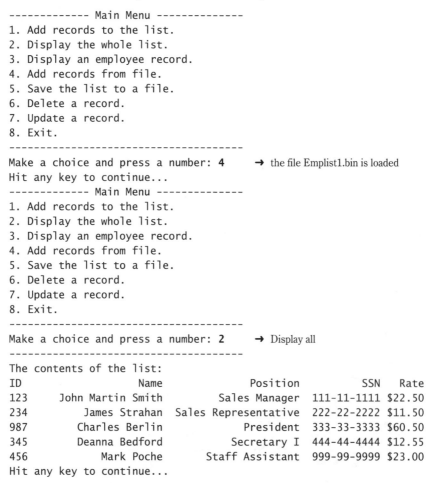

```
------------- Main Menu --------------
1. Add records to the list.
2. Display the whole list.
3. Display an employee record.
4. Add records from file.
5. Save the list to a file.
6. Delete a record.
7. Update a record.
8. Exit.
--------------------------------------
Make a choice and press a number: 4      → the file Emplist1.bin is loaded
Hit any key to continue...
------------- Main Menu --------------
1. Add records to the list.
2. Display the whole list.
3. Display an employee record.
4. Add records from file.
5. Save the list to a file.
6. Delete a record.
7. Update a record.
8. Exit.
--------------------------------------
Make a choice and press a number: 2      → Display all
--------------------------------------
The contents of the list:
ID            Name            Position          SSN    Rate
123     John Martin Smith    Sales Manager  111-11-1111 $22.50
234        James Strahan  Sales Representative 222-22-2222 $11.50
987        Charles Berlin        President  333-33-3333 $60.50
345       Deanna Bedford       Secretary I  444-44-4444 $12.55
456          Mark Poche     Staff Assistant  999-99-9999 $23.00
Hit any key to continue...
```

```
------------- Main Menu --------------
1. Add records to the list.
2. Display the whole list.
3. Display an employee record.
4. Add records from file.
5. Save the list to a file.
6. Delete a record.
7. Update a record.
8. Exit.
----------------------------------------
Make a choice and press a number: 1                    → Add a new record
Please enter the SSN of the employee: 111-11-1111      → This SSN already exists
SSN: 111-11-1111. This record is already in the list.  → Error message
----------------------------------------
Hit any key to continue...
------------- Main Menu --------------
1. Add records to the list.
2. Display the whole list.
3. Display an employee record.
4. Add records from file.
5. Save the list to a file.
6. Delete a record.
7. Update a record.
8. Exit.
----------------------------------------
Make a choice and press a number: 1                    → Add a new record
Please enter the SSN of the employee: 111-22-2222
Please enter the employee information:
ID: 122
Name: Craig Combel
Position: Manager
Rate: 88
----------------------------------------
The employee has been added to the list.
Hit any key to continue...
------------- Main Menu --------------
1. Add records to the list.
2. Display the whole list.
3. Display an employee record.
4. Add records from file.
5. Save the list to a file.
6. Delete a record.
7. Update a record.
8. Exit.
----------------------------------------
Make a choice and press a number: 2                              → Display all
----------------------------------------
The contents of the list:
ID                Name            Position        SSN      Rate
123     John Martin Smith         Sales Manager  111-11-1111 $22.50
```

```
122          Craig Combel          Manager  111-22-2222 $88.00  → New
234         James Strahan  Sales Representative  222-22-2222 $11.50
987         Charles Berlin         President  333-33-3333 $60.50
345        Deanna Bedford        Secretary I  444-44-4444 $12.55
456           Mark Poche    Staff Assistant  999-99-9999 $23.00
Hit any key to continue...
------------ Main Menu -------------
1. Add records to the list.
2. Display the whole list.
3. Display an employee record.
4. Add records from file.
5. Save the list to a file.
6. Delete a record.
7. Update a record.
8. Exit.
---------------------------------------
Make a choice and press a number: 4                → Load the file again
SSN: 333-33-3333. This record is already in the list.  → error
---------------------------------------
SSN: 222-22-2222. This record is already in the list.  → error
---------------------------------------
SSN: 111-11-1111. This record is already in the list.  → error
---------------------------------------
SSN: 444-44-4444. This record is already in the list.  → error
---------------------------------------
SSN: 999-99-9999. This record is already in the list.  → error
---------------------------------------
Hit any key to continue...
------------ Main Menu -------------
1. Add records to the list.
2. Display the whole list.
3. Display an employee record.
4. Add records from file.
5. Save the list to a file.
6. Delete a record.
7. Update a record.
8. Exit.
---------------------------------------
Make a choice and press a number: 8                → Exit
```

Summary

In this chapter you learned the following features of pointers:

1. A pointer may be used to point to any data type.

2. A pointer to a specific data type is bound to this type.

3. You cannot read or display the value of a pointer. You can only read or display the value pointed to by the pointer.

4. The operations you may apply on pointers are assignment and comparison (= or < >). The only values you may assign to a pointer are the constant NIL or the value of another pointer bound to the same type.

5. To declare a pointer type use the general form:

> **TYPE**
> Pointer-Type = ^ type-definition;

where type-definition is a standard or user-defined type.

6. The procedure NEW is used to allocate memory for a pointer, while the procedure DISPOSE is used to release the allocated memory. The following two procedures use the pointer as a parameter:

> NEW(PtrVariable);
> DISPOSE(PtrVariable);

You also learned how to use linked lists as advanced data structures that expand or shrink dynamically during the execution of the program. The following are the most important features of linked lists:

1. In a linked list, data are stored in nodes. Each node contains a data-field and a pointer-field. The pointer-field points to the second node.

2. The nodes in a linked list may store any type of data; however, they are used most often to store records.

3. To declare a linked list use the general form:

> **TYPE**
> Data-Type = type-definition;
> ListPointer = ^ ListRecord;
> ListRecord = **RECORD**
> DataField : Data-Type;
> NextField :ListPointer;
> **END;**

4. Linked lists are constructed and manipulated using pointers.

5. You may add or delete nodes to or from a linked list. In unordered linked lists, nodes can only be added at the beginning of the list. In ordered linked lists, the nodes are kept in sequence, and a new node is inserted in the proper sequential position.

Exercises

1. Given the following type and variable declarations:

```
TYPE
    PI = ^INTEGER;
```

```
      PR = ^REAL;
      PS = ^STRING;
VAR
      P1, P4    :PI;
      P2        :PR;
      P3        :PS;
      I         : INTEGER;
```

determine which of the following statements are valid and which are not:

```
{a} NEW(P1);
{b} NEW(P4);
{c} NEW (I);
{d} P3^ := 'Hello there!';
{e} WRITELN(P1^:4, P2^:4:00, P3^:15);
{f} WRITELN(P1, P2, P3);
{g} P1 := P4;
{h} P2^ := P1^;
{i} P4 := P1 + P4;
{j} WRITELN(P1=P4);
{k} WRITELN(P1^=P3^);
```

2. Given the following declarations:

```
TYPE
Employee = RECORD
                ID:INTEGER;
                Wage: REAL;
            END;
Empptr = ^Employee;
Person = RECORD
                Name :STRING[25];
                SSN  :STRING[11];
            END;
Personptr = ^person;

VAR
Ptr1, Ptr2    : Empptr;
Ptr3          : Personptr;
```

determine which of these operations are valid and which are invalid:

```
{a} Ptr1 := Ptr2;
{b} WRITELN(Ptr1=Ptr2);
{c} Ptr1 := Ptr3;
{d} WRITELN(Ptr1=Ptr3);
```

3. Using the declarations in the preceding exercise, write statements to display the fields of both Employee and Person records.

4. Write a type declaration for a linked list of inventory items to store Item Number, Item Name, Quantity, and Invoice Price. Also declare the necessary variables to process the list and store it into a file:

- Item Number: May contain letters and numbers.
- Item Name: May contain letters and numbers.
- Quantity: Integer number.
- Invoice Price: Real number.

Answers

1.

```
{a} Valid
{b} Valid
{c} Invalid - NEW is used with pointers only
{d} Valid
{e} Valid
{f} Invalid - cannot print pointers
{g} Valid
{h} Valid
{i} Invalid - cannot add pointers
{j} Valid
{k} Invalid - Type mismatch
```

2.

```
{a} Valid
{b} Valid
{c} Invalid - Type mismatch
{d} Invalid - Type mismatch
```

4. The following are the record and list declarations:

```
TYPE
    InventoryItem = RECORD
        ItemNo        :STRING[10];
        ItemName      :STRING[20];
        Quantity      :INTEGER;
        InvoicePrice  :REAL
    END;
    {Declaration of the list: }
    ListPointer = ^ListRecord;
    ListRecord =   RECORD
                        DataField :InventoryItem;
                        NextField :ListPointer
                    END;
    {Declare a file of records: }
    InventoryFile = FILE OF InventoryItem;
VAR
    FirstPointer        :ListPointer;
    MyFile              :InventoryFile;
    MyRecord            :InventoryItem;
```

Chapter 12

Advanced Programming Algorithms

Chapter Topics:

- Searching algorithms
- Sorting algorithms
- Binary search trees

12-1 Sorting Algorithms

In Chapter 5, you learned how to sort an array using the bubble sort method, which depends on comparing each element to the other elements, and swapping elements if necessary. The bubble sort algorithm is efficient only for sorting arrays of small sizes because the computing time increases with the array size. The fastest sorting algorithm that can be used with large arrays is called *quicksort*. In this section, the bubble sort algorithm is revisited and the quicksort is introduced.

12-2 Bubble Sort—Enhanced Version

The main feature of this version is that the program is divided into specialized procedures as follows:

■ The main program: reads and displays the array, in addition to calling the sort
procedure.

■ The bubble sort (BubbleSort) procedure: performs the comparisons between the
array elements. The array is passed to this procedure as a parameter.

■ The Swap procedure: swaps two elements of the array. This procedure is called
from the BubbleSort procedure.

You already know that using fewer global variables and relying on procedures and local
variables enhance the modularity of the program. In the examples and drills of this
chapter, you are going to use these modules (procedures) as building blocks of the programs. In this version of the bubble sort example, you can enter the number of elements at run time.

The Swap Procedure

The following code shows the Swap procedure used to exchange two integers X and Y.
For the swapping operation to be successful, the parameters X and Y have to be
passed by reference (using the VAR keyword); otherwise the operation will be performed on local copies of the variables X and Y, leaving the original variables
untouched.

```
{ ---------------------- Procedure Swap ----------------------- }
PROCEDURE Swap(VAR X, Y: INTEGER);
{ This procedure swaps two integers  }
VAR
Pot     :INTEGER;
BEGIN
    Pot := X;
    X := Y;
    Y := Pot
END;
{ ------------------------------------------------------------- }
```

The Bubble Sort Procedure

This procedure does the actual work to sort an array in an ascending order by comparing each array element to the other elements and calling the Swap procedure if necessary. In this procedure too, the array has to be passed by reference (VAR Arr) in order
to process the original array elements instead of processing a copy of the array. As
mentioned before, if you want to sort the array in a descending order, change the
greater than operator (>) to the less than operator (<).

```
{ -------------------- Procedure BubbleSort -------------------- }
PROCEDURE BubbleSort(VAR Arr: NumbersArray);
{ Sort the array }
VAR
I, J    :INTEGER;
BEGIN
   FOR I := 1 TO ArraySize-1 DO
      BEGIN
         FOR J := I+1 TO ArraySize DO
               IF Arr[I] > Arr[J] THEN
                  Swap(Arr[I], Arr[J])
      END
END;
{ ---------------------------------------------------------------- }
```

The Bubble Sort Program

The following is the complete program that reads an array of integers, sorts it, and displays it. With minor changes, you can modify the program to sort any type of data.

```
{ ------------------------ Example 12-1 ------------------------ }
PROGRAM BubbleSortProgram(INPUT,OUTPUT);
CONST
   MAXSIZE = 100;
TYPE
   Range        = 1..MAXSIZE;
   NumbersArray = ARRAY[Range] OF INTEGER;
VAR
   Arr          :NumbersArray;
   I, ArraySize :INTEGER;
{ ---------------------- Procedure Swap ------------------------ }
PROCEDURE Swap(VAR X, Y: INTEGER);
{ This procedure swaps two integers  }
VAR
Pot     :INTEGER;
BEGIN
     Pot := X;
     X := Y;
     Y := Pot
END;
{ -------------------- Procedure BubbleSort -------------------- }
PROCEDURE BubbleSort(VAR Arr: NumbersArray);
{ Sort the array }
VAR
I, J    :INTEGER;
BEGIN
   FOR I := 1 TO ArraySize-1 DO
      BEGIN
         FOR J := I+1 TO ArraySize DO
               IF Arr[I] > Arr[J] THEN
```

```
                        Swap(Arr[I], Arr[J])
        END
END;
{ --------------------- Main Program -------------------------- }
BEGIN
{ Read the array }
   WRITE('Enter the number of elements in the list: ');
   READLN(ArraySize);
   FOR I := 1 TO ArraySize DO
      BEGIN
         WRITE('Enter element #', I,': ');
         READLN(Arr[I])
      END;
{ Sort the Array }
   BubbleSort(Arr);
{ Display Results }
   WRITELN;
   WRITELN('The sorted array is:');
   FOR I := 1 TO ArraySize DO
      WRITELN(Arr[I]);
   WRITELN('Press ENTER to continue..');
   READLN
END.
{ ---------------------------------------------------------------- }
```

Sample Run:

```
Enter the number of elements in the list: 6
Enter element #1: 21
Enter element #2: 4
Enter element #3: 56
Enter element #4: 7
Enter element #5: 34
Enter element #6: 26

The sorted array is:
4
7
21
26
34
56
Press ENTER to continue..
```

> ### *Drill 12-1*
>
> Write a bubble sort program capable of sorting names. The following is a sample run of the required program:
>
> ```
> Enter the number of names in the list: 4
> Enter name #1: Sam Adams
> Enter name #2: Sam Abolrous
> Enter name #3: Clara Bui
> Enter name #4: Shankar Pal
>
> The sorted array is:
> Clara Bui
> Sam Abolrous
> Sam Adams
> Shankar Pal
> Press ENTER to continue..
> ```

12-3 Quicksort Algorithm

The quicksort algorithm is based on two operations:

- Splitting the array into two sub-arrays by placing the first array element in a middle position such that all the numbers to the right are greater than all numbers to the left.

- Repeating the previous step recursively by dividing each sub-array into two sub-arrays in the same manner until an empty sub-array is reached.

To demonstrate, consider the list 10, 2, 17, 7, 16, 3, 9. The following steps represent the quicksort algorithm to sort this array (notice that the number being processed is underlined):

- Place the first number in the middle such that all the numbers to the left are less than 10, and all the numbers to the right are greater than 10, that is:

  3, 9, 2, 7   **10**   16, 17

- Now, you have two sub-arrays, one to the left and one to the right. Split the left one by using the same method:

  2   **3**   9,7

- The left array cannot be split any further because it contains one number (2).

  2   3   9,7

- Now, switch to the right sub-array:

  7   **9**   blank

- The right sub-array is now empty, and cannot be split any more, and the left sub-array concluded to one number (7):

  <u>7</u> 9

- Look at the result that you got in the left list by reading the processed numbers (the bold numbers):

  2, 3, 7, 9 **10** 16, 17

- Now process the right sub-array in step 1, by spliting it, and positioning the first number 16 in the middle of the list:

  blank, <u>**16**</u> 17

- This gives you two sub-arrays, one empty, to the left, and one that contains one element (17) to the right:

  16 <u>**17**</u>

- That means that this list cannot be processed any further and the sorting is complete. Now look at the final result by writing all the underlined numbers in the new sequence:

  2, 3, 7, 9, 10, 16, 17

The following figure demonstrates the sorting process graphically. The sub-arrays are shown inside boxes while the final numbers are shown as bolded text.

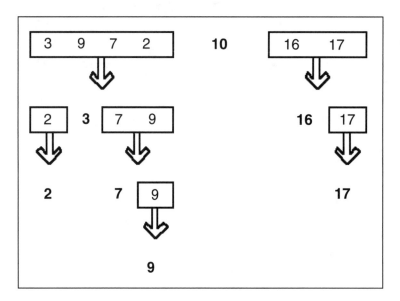

You can accomplish this process by using two procedures, one to split the array (let us call it DivideAndConquer), and one to call this procedure in a recursive manner (let us call it QuickSort) until an empty list is reached.

The Divide and Conquer Procedure

The DivideAndConquer procedure is shown below. The array to be sorted is passed by reference as a parameter Arr. The indexes of the array range from Arr[First] to Arr[Last]. After dividing the array (or the sub-array) the first element takes the location Mid.

```
{ ----------------- Procedure DivideAndConquer ------------------- }
PROCEDURE DivideAndConquer(VAR Arr:NumbersArray;
                          First, Last: INTEGER; VAR Mid: INTEGER);
{ This procedure rearranges the array passed as a parameter such that
Arr[First] is preceded by all the lower numbers and followed by the higher
numbers. The procedure returns the new position of the first number in the
variable Mid. This procedure is called from the QuickSort procedure. }

VAR
   Left, Right: INTEGER;
BEGIN
   Left := First;  { Initialize Left by the first element index }
   Right := Last;  { initialize Right by the last element index }
{ Search the list until Left meets Right }
WHILE Left < Right DO
   BEGIN
      { Search from the right side }
      WHILE Arr[Right] > Arr[First] DO
         Right := Right - 1;  { Move to the left }
      { Search from the Left side }
      WHILE (Left < Right) AND (Arr[Left] <= Arr[First]) DO
         Left := Left + 1;  { Move to the right }
      {Swap values if the search is not met}
      IF Left < Right THEN
         Swap(Arr[Left], Arr[Right]);
   END;
{ Place the selected item in the middle position Mid }
Mid := Right;
{ Swap the first and the middle elements }
Swap(Arr[Mid], Arr[First])
END;
{ ---------------------------------------------------------------- }
```

Notice the following points in the DivideAndConquer procedure:

■ Two search operations started together, one from the left, and one from the right.

■ At the beginning of the search operations, the index Left is the same as First, and the index Right is the same as Last. During the operation, Right moves to the left, and Left moves to the right.

■ The search operations continue as long as the two search operations do not meet. This occurs when Right=Left. At this point, the WHILE loop ends and the first element takes a new position stored in the index Mid.

- The DivideAndConquer procedure does the main process, which is arranging the array passed to it. This procedure is called from the quicksort procedure (QuickSort).

The QuickSort Procedure

This procedure calls the DivideAndConquer procedure to arrange one array. It also calls itself twice to process the two halves of the array, the right sub-array and the left sub-array.

```
{ -------------------- Procedure QuickSort --------------------- }
PROCEDURE QuickSort(VAR Arr: NumbersArray; First, Last: INTEGER);
{ The QuickSort procedure calls the DivideAndConquer procedure, and calls
itself to repeat processing sub-arrays recursively }

VAR
   Mid : INTEGER;
BEGIN
   IF First < Last THEN  { If the sub-array contains more than one item }
      BEGIN
         DivideAndConquer(Arr, First, Last, Mid);
         QuickSort(Arr, First, Mid-1);
         QuickSort(Arr, Mid+1, Last)
      END
END;
{ -------------------------------------------------------------- }
```

Notice the following points of this procedure:

- The array being processed uses the range: Arr[First] .. Arr[Last].
- The element between the two sub-arrays uses the variable Mid.
- The left sub-array uses the range: Arr[First] .. Arr[Mid–1].
- The right sub-array uses the range: Arr[Mid+1].. Arr[Last].

The QuickSort Program

The following is the complete quicksort program, which includes the DivideAndConquer, QuickSort, and Swap procedures.

```
{ ----------------------- Example 12-2 ------------------------- }
PROGRAM QuickSortProgram(INPUT,OUTPUT);
CONST
   MAXSIZE = 100;
TYPE
   Range        = 1..MAXSIZE;
   NumbersArray = ARRAY[Range] OF INTEGER;
VAR
   Element      :NumbersArray;
   ArraySize, I :INTEGER;
```

```
{ ----------------------- Procedure Swap ----------------------- }
PROCEDURE Swap(VAR X, Y: INTEGER);
{ This procedure swaps two integers  }
VAR
Pot     :INTEGER;
BEGIN
     Pot := X;
     X := Y;
     Y := Pot
END;
{ ---------------- Procedure DivideAndConquer ------------------- }
PROCEDURE DivideAndConquer(VAR Arr:NumbersArray;
                          First, Last: INTEGER; VAR Mid: INTEGER);
{ The procedure rearranges the array passed as a parameter such that Arr[First]
is preceded by all the lower numbers and proceeded by the
higher numbers. The procedure returns the new position of the first
number in the variable Mid. This procedure is called from the QuickSort
procedure. }

VAR
   Left, Right: INTEGER;
BEGIN
   Left := First;  { Initialize Left by the first element index }
   Right := Last;  { initialize Right by the last element index }
{ Search the list until Left meets Right }
WHILE Left < Right DO
   BEGIN
      { Search from the right side }
      WHILE Arr[Right] > Arr[First] DO
         Right := Right - 1;  { Move to the left }
      { Search from the Left side }
      WHILE (Left < Right) AND (Arr[Left] <= Arr[First]) DO
         Left := Left + 1;  { Move to the right }
      {Swap values if the search is not met}
      IF Left < Right THEN
         Swap(Arr[Left], Arr[Right]);
   END;
{ Place the selected item in the middle position Mid }
Mid := Right;
{ Swap the first and the middle elements }
Swap(Arr[Mid], Arr[First])
END;
{ -------------------- Procedure QuickSort ---------------------- }
PROCEDURE QuickSort(VAR Arr: NumbersArray; First, Last: INTEGER);
{ The QuickSort procedure calls the DivideAndConquer procedure, and calls
itself to repeat processing sub-arrays recursively }

VAR
   Mid : INTEGER;
BEGIN
```

```
        IF First < Last THEN   { If the sub-array contains more than one item }
           BEGIN
              DivideAndConquer(Arr, First, Last, Mid);
              QuickSort(Arr, First, Mid-1);
              QuickSort(Arr, Mid+1, Last)
           END
END;
{ ------------------------ Main Program ------------------------ }
BEGIN
{ Read the array }
   WRITE('Enter the number of elements in the list: ');
   READLN(ArraySize);
   FOR I := 1 TO ArraySize DO
      BEGIN
         WRITE('Enter element #', I,': ');
         READLN(Element[I])
      END;
{ Sort the array }
   QuickSort(Element, 1, ArraySize);
{ Print results }
   WRITELN;
   WRITELN('The sorted array is:');
   FOR I := 1 TO ArraySize DO
      WRITELN(Element[I]);
   WRITELN('Press ENTER to continue..');
   READLN
END.
{ ----------------------------------------------------------------- }
```

Sample Run:

```
     Enter the number of elements in the list: 7
     Enter element #1: 11
     Enter element #2: 2
     Enter element #3: 44
     Enter element #4: 25
     Enter element #5: 6
     Enter element #6: 77
     Enter element #7: 8

     The sorted array is:
     2
     6
     8
     11
     25
     44
     77
     Press ENTER to continue..
```

Drill 12-2

Make the necessary changes to the preceding program to make it useful for sorting names.

12-4 Searching Algorithms

In the preceding chapters, we searched arrays, linked lists, and files for a specific data item or array element. The search algorithm that we used so far is called the linear search. The linear search is good for small lists or files that contain a limited number of records. When it comes to lists that contain a huge amount of data, the *binary search* algorithm is faster. In the following sections, the following topics are introduced:

■ A review of the linear search algorithm

■ The binary search algorithm

■ Examples on using the binary search logic in programs

12-5 Linear Search

The following is the pseudo-code that represents the logic for searching an array of size ArraySize by using the linear search method:

■ Set the flag Found to FALSE.

■ Start from index #1.

■ Do the following until Found becomes TRUE or the index becomes greater than ArraySize:

    a. If the sought item = the current array element, set Found to TRUE and exit.

    b. Otherwise, increment the index counter.

12-6 Binary Search

The binary search algorithm may only be used with a sorted array. You start by comparing the sought item to the middle element in the array. According to the result of this comparison, you can decide if the item is in the upper half or the lower half of the array. Therefore, you search only one half of the array. By using the same method repeatedly, you divide any sub-array into smaller sub-arrays, and search another half until you find the sought item. The following is the pseudo code for searching an array Arr of the size ArraySize:

- Set the flag Found to FALSE.
- Set the variable First to index #1 and the variable Last to the number of elements.
- Do the following until Found becomes TRUE or First becomes greater than Last:
  a. Locate the sequence of middle element by using the formula:
  $Mid = (First + Last)/2$.
  b. Compare the sought item to Mid. The comparison renders one of three results:

  If the item is found, then the sought item is Arr[Mid]. Set Found to TRUE.

  If the item > Arr[Mid], the sought item is in the upper half. Set First to Mid+1.

  If the item < Arr[Mid], the sought item is in the lower half. Set Last to Mid–1.

The BinarySearch Procedure

The following procedure is the Pascal code for the binary search algorithm. Notice that the array must be sorted for the search to work.

```
{ ------------------------ Binary Search ------------------------ }
PROCEDURE BinarySearch(VAR Arr: NumbersArray; ArraySize: INTEGER;
                        Element: INTEGER; VAR Found: BOOLEAN);
{ This procedure searches a sorted array for a specific element using the
binary search algorithm }

VAR
First, Last, Mid    :INTEGER;
BEGIN
   First := 1;
   Last := ArraySize;
   Found := FALSE;
   WHILE (First <= Last) AND (NOT Found) DO
      BEGIN
        Mid := (First + Last) DIV 2;
        IF Element = Arr[Mid] THEN
           Found := TRUE
        ELSE IF Element > Arr[Mid] THEN
           First := Mid + 1   { Search the second half }
        ELSE IF Element < Arr[Mid] THEN
           Last := Mid - 1   { Search the first half }
      END
END;
{------------------------------------------------------------------}
```

The Binary Search Program

In order to build the complete binary search program, you need to add the following procedures, which you already used in this chapter:

- A procedure to sort the array (BubbleSort): In this program the bubble sort procedure is used. Of course, you can replace it by the quicksort procedure, if you are processing large lists.

- A procedure to exchange elements (Swap): This procedure is used by other sorting procedures.

You also need a text file that contains some numbers. You can create this file by using any text editor such as the NOTEPAD.EXE, or use the file on the companion CD.

In this program, you are going to read the numbers from the file, store them in an array, and search the array for an item. For simplicity, the following test file NUMBERS.TXT (which is on the companion CD) is used:

The File NUMBERS.TXT:

```
10
8
9
6
7
4
3
2
1
5
```

Searching the array for a single number is the same as searching it for a complete record. In the case of records, once you locate the sequence of the record in the records array, then you can easily retrieve the rest of the information using the key field.

```
{ ------------------------ Example 12-3 ------------------------ }
PROGRAM BinarySearchProgram(INPUT,OUTPUT,DiskFile);
{ This program reads a list of numbers from a text file, sorts the list using
the bubble sort algorithm, and then applies the binary search algorithm to
search for an element in the array. }
{ Note: The file NUMBERS.TXT must be in the same folder with the program,
otherwise you must change the pathname. }

CONST
   MAXSIZE  = 100;
   FileName = 'Numbers.txt'; TYPE
   Range        = 1..MAXSIZE;
   NumbersArray = ARRAY[Range] OF INTEGER;
VAR
```

```
    Arr          :NumbersArray;
    I, ArraySize :INTEGER;
    DiskFile     :TEXT;
    Item         :INTEGER;
    Found        :BOOLEAN;
{ ---------------------- Procedure Swap ----------------------- }
PROCEDURE Swap(VAR X, Y: INTEGER);
{ This procedure swaps two integers  }
VAR
Pot      :INTEGER;
BEGIN
     Pot := X;
     X := Y;
     Y := Pot
END;
{ -------------------- Procedure BubbleSort --------------------- }
PROCEDURE BubbleSort(VAR Arr: NumbersArray);
{ Sort the array }
VAR
I, J     :INTEGER;
BEGIN
   FOR I := 1 TO ArraySize-1 DO
      BEGIN
         FOR J := I+1 TO ArraySize DO
            IF Arr[I] > Arr[J] THEN
               Swap(Arr[I], Arr[J])
      END
END;
{ ----------------------- Binary Search ----------------------- }
PROCEDURE BinarySearch(VAR Arr: NumbersArray; ArraySize: INTEGER;
                       Element: INTEGER; VAR Found: BOOLEAN);
{ This procedure searches a sorted array for a specific element using the
binary search algorithm }
VAR
First, Last, Mid    :INTEGER;
BEGIN
   First := 1;
   Last := ArraySize;
   Found := FALSE;
   WHILE (First <= Last) AND (NOT Found) DO
      BEGIN
        Mid := (First + Last) DIV 2;
        IF Element = Arr[Mid] THEN
           Found := TRUE
        ELSE IF Element > Arr[Mid] THEN
           First := Mid + 1   { Search the second half }
        ELSE IF Element < Arr[Mid] THEN
           Last := Mid - 1   { Search the first half }
      END
END;
```

```
{-------------------------- Main Program -------------------------}
BEGIN
   ASSIGN(DiskFile, FileName);
   RESET(DiskFile);
   I := 1;
   WHILE NOT EOF(DiskFile) DO
      BEGIN
{ Read one line from the text file }
         READLN(DiskFile, Item);
         Arr[I] := Item;
         I := I + 1
      END;
{ Store the counter I into the array size }
{ Notice that I was incremented after the last read }
   ArraySize := I-1;
   CLOSE(DiskFile);
{ Sort the array }
   BubbleSort(Arr);
   WRITE('Please enter the number you are searching for: ');
   READLN(Item);
{ Search the list }
   BinarySearch(Arr, ArraySize, Item, Found);
   IF Found THEN
      WRITELN('Item ', Item, ' found in the list')
   ELSE
       WRITELN('Item not found, sorry.');
   WRITELN('Press ENTER to continue..');
   READLN
END.
{----------------------------------------------------------------}
```

Sample Run:

```
Please enter the number you are searching for: 3
Item 3 found in the list
Press ENTER to continue..

Please enter the number you are searching for: 55
Item not found, sorry
Press ENTER to continue..
```

> ## Drill 12-3
>
> Make the necessary changes to the preceding program to make it search for names. You can test the program by creating a text file NAMES.TXT that contains one name on each line. You can also use the text file NAMES.TXT on the companion CD. In this program, you need to enter the complete name of the person. The following is a sample run:
>
> ```
> Please enter the name you are searching for: Sally Suttleworth
> The name Sally Suttleworth not found, sorry.
> Press ENTER to continue..
>
> Please enter the name you are searching for: Sally Shuttleworth
> The name Sally Shuttleworth found in the list
> Press ENTER to continue..
> ```

12-7 Binary Search Trees

The binary search tree, also referred to as *multiply linked structure*, is a special kind of linked list that enables *binary* searching. Like a linked list, a tree consists of nodes. Unlike linked lists, each node consists of three fields, a data field and two link fields or pointers. The data field may be a simple type such as an integer or a string, or a complete record that contains many fields.

The Binary Tree Structure

A simple representation of a binary tree, which contains some numbers, is shown in the following figure. Each node in the tree can have two pointers, a left and a right pointer. Each pointer is a link to another node.

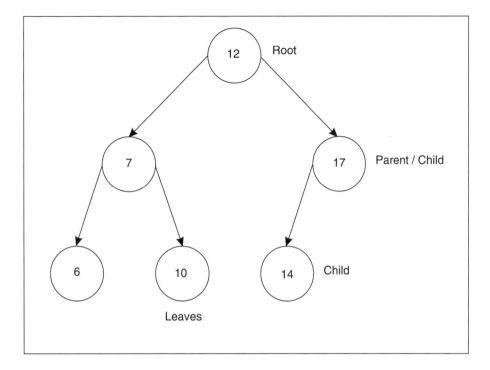

The *root* of the tree, which is the number 12 in this example, is the first node in the tree. The root has two pointers, one to the left and one to the right. Each pointer is pointing to a *subtree* (or a child). Any *node* in the binary tree can have a maximum of two children; in which case it is called a parent node (for example, 12, 7, and 17). Except for the root, a node can be a child and a parent at the same time (for example, 7 and 17). The children that are not parents to other nodes are called *leaves* (for example, 6, 10, and 14). You must have noticed that the tree looks like a real tree, except that it is drawn upside down. In many applications, the left and right children are used to represent binary data such as TRUE or FALSE, 1 or 0, YES or NO, and so forth.

The record representation of a tree node is shown in the following figure. The node contains the following three fields:

■ The data field (which can be a record made up of many fields)

■ The pointer to the left child

■ The pointer to the right child

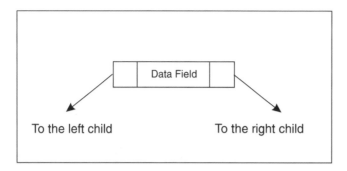

As you can see in the graph, the two link fields contain pointers to left and right children. If any of the pointers is NIL, the node does not have a corresponding child. If both pointers are NIL, the node is a leaf.

In the following figure, the same binary tree example is illustrated as records.

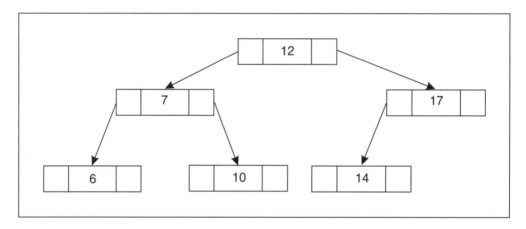

Searching the Tree

One way to search a binary tree is to start at the root and traverse the tree in the following order:

- Visit each node
- Visit the left subtree
- Visit the right subtree

In the current example, notice that the data are organized in the tree in such a way that at any node, the larger number is to the right, while the smaller number is to the left. This kind of tree is called a *binary search tree* (BST). To search the tree for the number 10, for example, proceed as follows:

- Start at the root and compare the number 10 to the data field 12. The result is FALSE. Because 10 is less than 12, it must be in the left subtree.

- Visit the left child and compare the number 10 to the data field 7. Because the number 10 is greater than 7, it must be in the right child.
- Visit the right child (10) and compare the number 10 to the data field; the result is TRUE.

As you can see, in the previous search, there was no need to visit all the nodes to find the number 10, which lies at the bottom of the tree. Actually, you visited only one half of the tree; this is because of the logical way in which data are organized in the tree.

Another example is to search for the number 13, which does not exist in the tree. In this case, only three comparisons are made:

- Compare the number 13 to the root (12). The result is FALSE. Because the number 13 is larger than 12, the next comparison should be done in the right subtree.
- Compare the number 13 to the right child (17). Because the number 13 is less than 17, the next comparison should be done in the left subtree.
- Compare the number 13 to the left child (14). Because the number 13 is less than 14, it is not expected to be found by going any further in the tree.

Drill 12-4

Write a pseudo-code algorithm to search the following tree for the number 61:

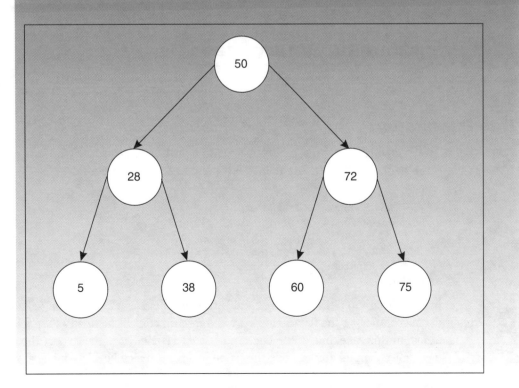

Traversing the Tree

You can traverse a binary tree using one of the following sequences:

- Left child-**N**ode-**R**ight child (*LNR*)
- **N**ode-**L**eft child-**R**ight child (*NLR*)
- **L**eft child-**R**ight child-**N**ode (*LRN*)

You may use any one of these methods to search for items in the tree. However, to retrieve the data from the tree in a sequential order, you have to use the first method (LNR), which is known as the *inorder* traversal method.

Try to experiment with these methods in traversing the tree in the figure on page 307. The results should be:

- The LNR method: 6, 7, 10, 12, 14, 17
- The NLR method: 12, 7, 6, 10, 17, 14
- The LRN method: 6, 10, 7, 14, 17, 12

Drill 12-5

Traverse the tree in Drill 12-4 using each of the three methods: LNR, NLR, and LRN. Then list the results in each case.

12-8 Programming Binary Trees

In this section, you learn how to declare, build, and test a binary search tree.

Tree Declaration

The following program segment is used to declare a binary tree, whose nodes contain three fields, an integer data field, a left pointer, and a right pointer:

```
TYPE
   NodePointer = ^TreeRecord;
   TreeRecord  = record
      DataKey         :INTEGER;
      LeftChild       :NodePointer;
      RightChild      :NodePointer
END;
```

In this declaration, the DataKey field is the only field that contains data. It is possible, of course, to have the data field as a whole record consisting of any number of data items. In this case, one of the data items must be used as a key to sort the data in the tree. For example, you can use the name of a person as a key, in which case the data are sorted alphabetically. If you use a numeric field as a key, it has to be unique such as an ID number. In this example, the integer field, which is the only data field in the node, is the sort key.

Building a Binary Search Tree

To build a binary search tree, you have to insert the nodes in a sequential order. The following procedure is an example of building the binary search tree that contains an integer in each node. The procedure uses a tree pointer (NodePointer) as a parameter. In the process of creating the tree, two tree pointers, Current and Previous, are used to point to the current and the previous nodes. The first number is accepted from the keyboard, and inserted in the root node. Then, the rest of the numbers are read and inserted in the proper sequence by comparing each number to the previous number.

```
{ -------------------- Procedure BuildBT ----------------------- }
PROCEDURE BuildBT(VAR Node :NodePointer);
{ This procedure is used to build a binary search tree (BST). Each node
contains one number, and two pointers, LeftChild and RightChild.
Two pointers, Current and Previous, are used to point to the current and
previous nodes. }

VAR
    Current, Previous :NodePointer;
    Number            :INTEGER;
BEGIN
{Read the first number and insert it into a node to start the root
of a tree.}
    Node := NIL;
    NEW(Node);
    READLN(Node^.DataKey);
    Node^.LeftChild  := NIL;
    Node^.RightChild := NIL;
    Current  := Node;
    Previous := Node;
{Read the rest of the numbers until the EOF is encountered.}
    WHILE NOT EOF DO
       BEGIN
          Current := Node;
          READLN(Number);
{Traverse the tree to find the proper location to insert the number.}
          WHILE (Number <> Previous^.DataKey) and (Current <> NIL)  DO
             BEGIN
                Previous := Current;
                IF Number < Previous^.DataKey THEN
                   Current := Previous^.LeftChild
                ELSE
                   Current := Previous^.RightChild
             END;
{Check if the number is previously inserted in the tree.}
```

```
                    IF Number = Previous^.DataKey THEN
                        WRITELN('The number ', Number, ' already exists.')
                    ELSE
                        BEGIN
{Insert the number.}
                            New(Current);
                            Current^.DataKey     := Number;
                            Current^.LeftChild  := NIL;
                            Current^.RightChild := NIL;
{Add the new node to the tree.}
                            IF Number < Previous^.DataKey THEN
                                Previous^.LeftChild  := Current
                            ELSE
                                Previous^.RightChild := Current
                        END
            END
END;
{ ----------------------------------------------------------------- }
```

Testing the Tree

In order to test the binary tree, you can write a procedure to read the tree the contents of each node. The following is a recursive procedure that reads and displays the contents of the binary tree by using the inorder traversal method (LNR). You should expect to see the output sorted sequentially.

```
{ -------------------- Procedure ReadLNR ----------------------- }
PROCEDURE ReadLNR(Node: NodePointer);
{ This procedure reads the tree using the sequence LNR, and prints the contents
of the data field in each node. }

BEGIN
    IF Node <> NIL THEN
        BEGIN
            ReadLNR(Node^.LeftChild);
            WRITELN(Node^.DataKey);
            ReadLNR(Node^.RightChild)
        END
END;
{ ----------------------------------------------------------------- }
```

12-9 Application: Building and Printing a Binary Tree

In this program, the two procedures are brought together to give you experience in using a binary tree. When you run this program, you are asked to enter the data elements of the tree from the keyboard. When you are done, the data are sorted and displayed.

```
{ ----------------------- Example 12-4 ------------------------ }
Program BuildaTree(INPUT, OUTPUT);
{ This program is used to build a tree of numbers and print the data field in
each node to check the validity of the tree. }

TYPE
   NodePointer = ^TreeRecord;
   TreeRecord  = record
      DataKey        :INTEGER;
      LeftChild      :NodePointer;
      RightChild     :NodePointer
END;
VAR
   TreePointer        :NodePointer;
{ --------------------- Procedure BuildBT ----------------------- }
PROCEDURE BuildBT(VAR Node :NodePointer);
{ This procedure is used to build a binary search tree (BST).
Each node contains one number, and two pointers, LeftChild and RightChild. Two
pointers, Current and Previous, are used to point to the current and previous
nodes. }

VAR
   Current, Previous :NodePointer;
   Number            :INTEGER;
BEGIN
{Read the first number and insert it into a node to start the root
of a tree.}
   Node := NIL;
   NEW(Node);
   READLN(Node^.DataKey);
   Node^.LeftChild  := NIL;
   Node^.RightChild := NIL;
   Current  := Node;
   Previous := Node;
{Read the rest of the numbers until the EOF is encountered.}
   WHILE NOT EOF DO
      BEGIN
         Current := Node;
         READLN(Number);
{Traverse the tree to find the proper location to insert the number.}
         WHILE (Number <> Previous^.DataKey) and (Current <> NIL)  DO
            BEGIN
               Previous := Current;
               IF Number < Previous^.DataKey THEN
                  Current := Previous^.LeftChild
               ELSE
                  Current := Previous^.RightChild
            END;
{Check if the number is previously inserted in the tree.}
         IF Number = Previous^.DataKey THEN
```

```
                    WRITELN('The number ', Number, ' already exists.')
            ELSE
                BEGIN
{Insert the number.}
                    New(Current);
                    Current^.DataKey    := Number;
                    Current^.LeftChild  := NIL;
                    Current^.RightChild := NIL;
{Add the new node to the tree.}
                    IF Number < Previous^.DataKey THEN
                        Previous^.LeftChild  := Current
                    ELSE
                        Previous^.RightChild := Current
                END
        END
END;
{ --------------------- Procedure ReadLNR ---------------------- }
PROCEDURE ReadLNR(Node: NodePointer);
{ This procedure reads the tree according to the sequence LNR, and prints the
contents of each data field. }

BEGIN
    IF Node <> NIL THEN
        BEGIN
            ReadLNR(Node^.LeftChild);
            WRITELN(Node^.DataKey);
            ReadLNR(Node^.RightChild)
        END
END;
{ ----------------------- Main Program ----------------------- }
BEGIN
    WRITELN('Please enter the numbers to be inserted into the tree.');
    WRITELN('Press <Enter> after each number. Press <Ctrl+Z> when done.');
{Build the tree }
    BuildBT(TreePointer);
{List the data fields in the tree }
    WRITELN('The contents of the binary tree are:');
    ReadLNR(TreePointer);
    WRITELN('Press <ENTER> to go back...');
    READLN
END.
{ ----------------------------------------------------------------- }
```

Sample Run:

```
    Please enter the numbers to be inserted into the tree.
    Press <Enter> after each number. Press <Ctrl+Z> when done.
    5
    11
    8
    5        → Notice that the number 5 has been inserted before
```

```
The number 5 already exists.
6
88
66
^Z
The contents of the binary tree are:
5
6
8
11
66
88
Press <ENTER> to go back...
```

The following are important notes on the preceding program:

■ In this program, the data are entered from the keyboard. By making minor changes to the program, you can read the data from a disk file as explained in Chapters 9 and 10.

■ Notice that the root of the tree is determined by the first number that you enter. Consequently, the shape of the tree will change according to the value of the root. This is because all the smaller numbers go to the left subtree and all the larger ones go to the right subtree.

■ Regardless of the shape of the tree, when you traverse it using the inorder traversal method (LNR), you always get a sorted list of numbers as shown in the sample run.

■ In addition to printing the tree contents as part of checking and validating the tree, you can add a debugging statement that prints on the screen the value stored in the previous node each time you add a new node to the tree. This way, you can almost watch the branches as they grow. The following is an example of the debugging statement that you can add right after attaching a new node (see the complete program, 12-4A.pas, on the companion CD):

```
...
{Add the new node to the tree.}
        IF Number < Previous^.DataKey THEN
            Previous^.LeftChild  := Current
        ELSE
            Previous^.RightChild := Current
        END;
{ The debugging statement }
WRITELN('Previous Node= ',Previous^.DataKey)   → Add this line
...
```

This feature will make it easy to visualize the tree while it is being built. For example, consider the following run:

```
Please enter the numbers to be inserted into the tree.
Press <Enter> after each number. Press <Ctrl+Z> when done.
```

```
5
11
Previous Node= 5
4
Previous Node= 5
88
Previous Node= 11
66
Previous Node= 88
^Z
Press <ENTER> to go back...
```

The following graphs show you how the tree was built step by step according to the preceding data entries. Notice that the previous node is marked with a small bold circle:

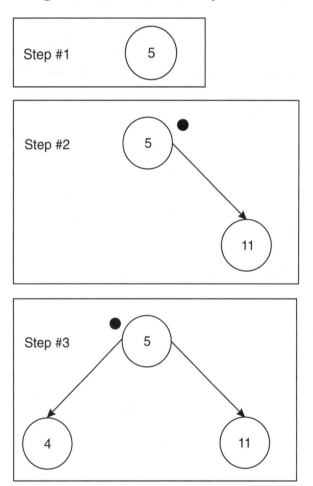

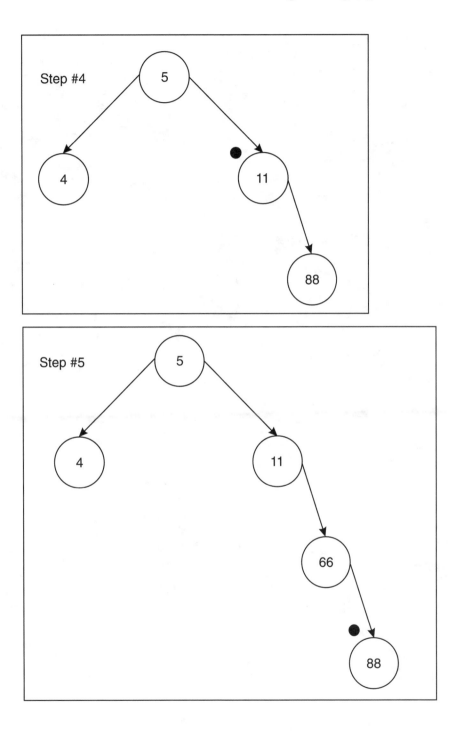

Drill 12-6

Draw the tree produced by the following sample runs of Example 12-4:

Sample Run 1:

```
Please enter the numbers to be inserted into the tree.
Press <Enter> after each number. Press <Ctrl+Z> when done.
1      → the root
2
3
4
5
^Z
The contents of the binary tree are:
1
2
3
4
5
Press <ENTER> to go back...
```

Sample Run 2:

In this sample run, the output of the debugging statement shows you the last node visited each time you add a new number.

```
Please enter the numbers to be inserted into the tree.
Press <Enter> after each number. Press <Ctrl+Z> when done.
50     → the root
5
Previous Node= 50
28
Previous Node= 5
65
Previous Node= 50
38
Previous Node= 28
60
Previous Node= 65
^Z
The contents of the binary tree are:
5
28
38
50
60
65
Press <ENTER> to go back...
```

12-10 Application: Sorting Data Files Using Binary Trees

The program in this example reads data from files and sorts them in memory in the form of a binary tree. The data file TREE.TXT contains a list of numbers, each written on a separate line. This program is modified from the previous example and has the following features:

■ Data are read from a disk file instead of the keyboard. You may create a text file for yourself or use the file TREE.TXT on the companion CD. You can also modify the program to make it read a file of records.

■ The program issues a warning message if it encounters a repeated number in the file, and ignores it. If the number is a key field, you must check the data file for redundancy. However, because this error is not likely to happen in real-life databases, you may want to disable this feature by removing the IF block that checks for repetition.

■ When you run a program that uses data files, you should place the data file and the source code in the same directory (or include the data file pathname explicitly in the program).

```
{ ---------------------- Example 12-5 -------------------------- }
Program BuildTreeFromFile(INPUT, OUTPUT, DiskFile);
{ This program reads a data file that contains numbers, builds a tree
of the numbers, and prints the data field in each node. }

CONST
    FileName = 'Tree.txt';

TYPE
    NodePointer        = ^TreeRecord;
    TreeRecord         = record
        DataKey        :INTEGER;
        LeftChild      :NodePointer;
        RightChild     :NodePointer
END;

VAR
    TreePointer    :NodePointer;
    DiskFile       :TEXT;

{ ---------------------- Procedure BuildBT ---------------------- }
PROCEDURE BuildBT(VAR Node :NodePointer);
{ This procedure reads a data file and builds a binary search tree (BST). Each
    node contains one number, and two pointers, LeftChild and RightChild. Two
    pointers, Current and Previous, are used to point to the current and previous
    nodes. }

VAR
```

```
   Current, Previous :NodePointer;
   Number           :INTEGER;
BEGIN
{ Read the first number and insert it into a node to start the root of
a tree. }
   Node := NIL;
   NEW(Node);
   READLN(DiskFile, Node^.DataKey);
   Node^.LeftChild  := NIL;
   Node^.RightChild := NIL;
   Current  := Node;
   Previous := Node;
{ Read the rest of the numbers until the EOF is encountered. }
   WHILE NOT EOF(DiskFile) DO
       BEGIN
          Current := Node;
          READLN(DiskFile, Number);
{ Traverse the tree to find the proper location to insert the number.}
          WHILE (Number <> Previous^.DataKey) and (Current <> NIL)  DO
             BEGIN
                Previous := Current;
                IF Number < Previous^.DataKey THEN
                    Current := Previous^.LeftChild
                ELSE
                    Current := Previous^.RightChild
             END;
{ Check if the number is previously inserted in the tree. }
          IF Number = Previous^.DataKey THEN
             WRITELN('Warning: The number ', Number, ' already exists. ',
             'Record skipped.')
          ELSE
             BEGIN
{ Insert the number.}
                New(Current);
                Current^.DataKey    := Number;
                Current^.LeftChild  := NIL;
                Current^.RightChild := NIL;
{ Add the new node to the tree. }
                IF Number < Previous^.DataKey THEN
                    Previous^.LeftChild  := Current
                ELSE
                    Previous^.RightChild := Current
             END
       END
END;


{ --------------------- Procedure ReadLNR ---------------------- }
PROCEDURE ReadLNR(Node: NodePointer);
{ This procedure reads the tree according to the sequence: Left-Node-Right,
  and prints the contents of each data field. }
```

```
BEGIN
   IF Node <> NIL THEN
      BEGIN
         ReadLNR(Node^.LeftChild);
         WRITELN(Node^.DataKey);
         ReadLNR(Node^.RightChild)
      END
END;
{ ----------------------- Main Program -------------------------- }
BEGIN
{ Open the disk file }
   ASSIGN(DiskFile, FileName);
   RESET(DiskFile);
{ Build the BST }
   BuildBT(TreePointer);
{ Close the file }
   CLOSE(DiskFile);
{ List the data fields in the tree }
   WRITELN('The contents of the binary tree are:');
   ReadLNR(TreePointer);
   WRITELN('Press <ENTER> to go back...');
   READLN
END.
{ --------------------------------------------------------------- }
```

The Data File TREE.TXT:

```
5
11
4
88
66
5
110
60
1
60
55
71
125
198
```

Sample Run:

```
Warning: The number 5 already exists. Record skipped.
Warning: The number 60 already exists. Record skipped.
The contents of the binary tree are:
1
4
5
11
```

```
             55
             60
             66
             71
             88
             110
             125
             198
             Press <ENTER> to go back...
```

Drill 12-7

Modify the previous program to make it read and sort names.

12-11 Application: Searching a Data File Using Binary Trees

In order to search a data file for a specific item, you only need to add one new module to the previous program (Example 12-5), the search module. This time, the module will be a function that returns a pointer to the sought item.

The Search Function

The following is the code of a function that searches a binary tree for a specific number. If the sought item is not found, the function returns NIL. Otherwise, it returns a pointer (NodePointer) to the sought item. The function is built using a recursive algorithm in which the search is done either in the left child or in the right child depending on whether the sought item is greater or less than the data in the current node.

```
{ ----------------- Function RecursiveSearchBT ------------------ }
FUNCTION RecursiveSearchBT(Node: NodePointer; Item: INTEGER) :NodePointer;
{ This function searches a binary tree recursively and returns a pointer to
  the node that contains the sought item. }

BEGIN
   IF Node = NIL THEN
      RecursiveSearchBT := NIL
   ELSE
      IF Item < Node^.DataKey THEN
         RecursiveSearchBT :=
               RecursiveSearchBT (Node^.LeftChild, Item)
      ELSE
         IF Item > Node^.DataKey THEN
         RecursiveSearchBT :=
```

```
                    RecursiveSearchBT (Node^.RightChild, Item)
            ELSE
            RecursiveSearchBT := Node
END;
{ ------------------------------------------------------------- }
```

The Search Program

In the following program, you are going to read a data file, store its contents into a binary search tree, and search the tree for a specific item. Now that you have already built many procedures to process binary search trees, you don't need to write a completely new program. You simply reuse the existing code by putting modules together and adding the new function as one of the building blocks. At the end of this program, the data in the binary tree are displayed only for demonstration.

```
{ --------------------- Example 12-6 ------------------------- }
Program BuildaTreeFromFile(INPUT, OUTPUT, DiskFile);
{ This program reads a data file that contains numbers, builds a tree
of the numbers, and searches the tree for the item entered from the
keyboard. }

CONST
    FileName = 'Tree.txt';              { The data file name }

TYPE
    NodePointer       = ^TreeRecord;
    TreeRecord        = record
        DataKey       :INTEGER;
        LeftChild     :NodePointer;
        RightChild    :NodePointer
END;

VAR
    TreePointer  :NodePointer;
    DiskFile     :TEXT;
    Item         :INTEGER;
{ --------------------- Procedure BuildBT ----------------------- }
PROCEDURE BuildBT(VAR Node :NodePointer);
{ This procedure reads a data file and builds a binary search tree
BST. Each node contains one number, and two pointers, LeftChild and
RightChild. Two pointers, Current and Previous, are used to point to
the current and previous nodes. }

VAR
    Current, Previous :NodePointer;
    Number            :INTEGER;
BEGIN
{ Read the first number and insert it into a node to start the root
of a tree. }
```

```
        Node := NIL;
        NEW(Node);
        READLN(DiskFile, Node^.DataKey);
        Node^.LeftChild  := NIL;
        Node^.RightChild := NIL;
        Current  := Node;
        Previous := Node;
{ Read the rest of the numbers until the EOF is encountered. }
    WHILE NOT EOF(DiskFile) DO
        BEGIN
            Current := Node;
            READLN(DiskFile, Number);
{ Traverse the tree to find the proper location to insert the number.}
        WHILE (Number <> Previous^.DataKey) and (Current <> NIL)  DO
            BEGIN
                Previous := Current;
                IF Number < Previous^.DataKey THEN
                    Current := Previous^.LeftChild
                ELSE
                    Current := Previous^.RightChild
            END;
{ Check if the number is previously inserted in the tree. }
        IF Number = Previous^.DataKey THEN
            WRITELN('Warning: The number ', Number, ' already exists. ',
              'Record skipped.')
        ELSE
            BEGIN
{ Insert the number.}
                New(Current);
                Current^.DataKey    := Number;
                Current^.LeftChild  := NIL;
                Current^.RightChild := NIL;
{ Add the new node to the tree. }
                IF Number < Previous^.DataKey THEN
                    Previous^.LeftChild  := Current
                ELSE
                    Previous^.RightChild := Current
            END
      END
END;
{ --------------------- Procedure ReadLNR ----------------------- }
PROCEDURE ReadLNR(Node: NodePointer);
{ This procedure reads the tree according to the sequence Left-Node-Right,
  and prints the contents of each data field. }

BEGIN
    IF Node <> NIL THEN
      BEGIN
        ReadLNR(Node^.LeftChild);
        WRITELN(Node^.DataKey);
```

```
            ReadLNR(Node^.RightChild)
        END
END;
{ ------------------ Function RecursiveSearchBT ------------------- }
FUNCTION RecursiveSearchBT(Node: NodePointer; Item: INTEGER):NodePointer;
{ This function searches a binary tree recursively and returns
a pointer to the node that contains the sought item. }

BEGIN
   IF Node = NIL THEN
      RecursiveSearchBT := NIL
   ELSE
      IF Item < Node^.DataKey THEN
         RecursiveSearchBT  :=
              RecursiveSearchBT (Node^.LeftChild, Item)
      ELSE
         IF Item > Node^.DataKey THEN
         RecursiveSearchBT  :=
            RecursiveSearchBT (Node^.RightChild, Item)
         ELSE
         RecursiveSearchBT := Node
END;
{ ---------------------- Main Program ------------------------- }
BEGIN
{ Open the disk file }
   ASSIGN(DiskFile, FileName);
   RESET(DiskFile);
{ Build the BST }
   BuildBT(TreePointer);
{ Close the file }
   CLOSE(DiskFile);
{ List the data fields in the tree }
   WRITE('Please enter the number you are searching for: ');
   READLN(Item);
{ Search the tree }
   IF (RecursiveSearchBT(TreePointer, Item))<> NIL THEN
      WRITELN('Item ', Item, ' found in the list')
   ELSE
        WRITELN('Item not found, sorry.');
   WRITELN('The contents of the binary tree are:');
   ReadLNR(TreePointer);
   WRITELN('Press <ENTER> to go back...');
   READLN
END.
{ ------------------------------------------------------------- }
```

The Data File TREE1.TXT

```
5
11
4
```

```
88
66
110
1
60
55
71
125
198
```

Sample Run:

```
Please enter the number you are searching for: 60
Item 60 found in the list
The contents of the binary tree are:
1
4
5
11
55
60
66
71
88
110
125
198
Press <ENTER> to go back...
```

Summary

In this chapter, you learned some advanced programming tools and algorithms.

1. You learned how to sort data by using the bubble sort and the quicksort method. You should also keep in mind that the latter is faster and more efficient, especially with large databases.

2. You also learned the different methods to search a file or a list for a specific item, and that the binary search algorithm is faster than the linear search algorithm. However, the binary search works with sorted data only.

3. You learned how to sort data by storing them into a binary search tree, whose declaration takes the following form:

```
TYPE
    Data-Type = type-definition;
    NodePointer = ^TreeRecord;
    TreeRecord = record
        DataKey  :Data-Type;
```

LeftChild :NodePointer;
RightChild:NodePointer
END;

4. Finally, you learned how to traverse a binary tree using different methods, and how to apply the binary search algorithm to search the tree for data items.

Exercises

1. Write a program to read text strings from the keyboard and store them into a binary search tree. The strings in the tree must be unique; in other words, if you enter the same text twice, it should be ignored.

2. Write a program to read text strings from a text file and store them into a binary search tree. You may use the file NAMES.TXT on the companion CD to test your program.

3. One of the popular classic computer games is a guessing game known as Animal. In this game, the program asks you to think of an animal, and tries to guess the name of this animal by asking you some questions, which can be answered by either Yes or No. If the program gives up, it asks you to provide the name of the animal, and a suitable question that distinguishes this animal from others. Here is how it works (the player's responses are bolded):

```
Welcome to the animal Game.
I will try to guess the name of the animal you are thinking of.
Are you ready to play (Y/N)? y
Is it domestic? y
Is it a cat? n
I give up! Please tell me the name of the animal: a dog
Thanks...
Please type a question that tells the difference between a dog and a cat:
Does it bark?
For a dog, is the answer to this question Yes or No (Y/N)? y
Are you ready to play (Y/N)?
```

If you play again, you will find that the program learned the new information about the dog:

```
Is it domestic? y
Does it bark? y
Is it a dog? y
```

The more you play the more the computer learns about new animals. The following are some tips to help you write this program:

1. The knowledge base behind this program is a binary search tree. It is initialized with three elements only:

- The question Is it domestic, which is the root of the tree. The two pointers coming out from the node are Yes and No.

- ■ The name cat on the Yes side.
- ■ The name lion on the No side.

2. Each time you enter a new animal, you add to the tree a new question node and a new animal node either on the Yes side or on the No side.

The Next Step

You should now have enough tools to write solid code in Pascal and create good application programs. However, you may want to read about the following compiler-specific topics that are not covered in this book:

- ■ Direct/Random access files
- ■ Graphics

Although this book does not cover Windows programming, mastering the standard Pascal language is necessary before you step into Windows programming.

The ASCII Character Set

The Printable Characters

Decimal	Octal	Hexadecimal	Character
32	40	20	space
33	41	21	!
34	42	22	"
35	43	23	#
36	44	24	$
37	45	25	%
38	46	26	&
39	47	27	'
40	50	28	(
41	51	29	)
42	52	2a	*
43	53	2b	+
44	54	2c	,
45	55	2d	-
46	56	2e	.
47	57	2f	/
48	60	30	0
49	61	31	1
50	62	32	2
51	63	33	3
52	64	34	4

Decimal	Octal	Hexadecimal	Character
53	65	35	5
54	66	36	6
55	67	37	7
56	70	38	8
57	71	39	9
58	72	3a	:
59	73	3b	;
60	74	3c	<
61	75	3d	=
62	76	3e	>
63	77	3f	?
64	100	40	@
65	101	41	A
66	102	42	B
67	103	43	C
68	104	44	D
69	105	45	E
70	106	46	F
71	107	47	G
72	110	48	H
73	111	49	I
74	112	4a	J
75	113	4b	K
76	114	4c	L
77	115	4d	M
78	116	4e	N
79	117	4f	O
80	120	50	P
81	121	51	Q
82	122	52	R
83	123	53	S
84	124	54	T
85	125	55	U
86	126	56	V
87	127	57	W
88	130	58	X

Decimal	Octal	Hexadecimal	Character
89	131	59	Y
90	132	5a	Z
91	133	5b	[
92	134	5c	\
93	135	5d	]
94	136	5e	^
95	137	5f	_
96	140	60	`
97	141	61	a
98	142	62	b
99	143	63	c
100	144	64	d
101	145	65	e
102	146	66	f
103	147	67	g
104	150	68	h
105	151	69	i
106	152	6a	j
107	153	6b	k
108	154	6c	l
109	155	6d	m
110	156	6e	n
111	157	6f	o
112	160	70	p
113	161	71	q
114	162	72	r
115	163	73	s
116	164	74	t
117	165	75	u
118	166	76	v
119	167	77	w
120	170	78	x
121	171	79	y
122	172	7a	z
123	173	7b	{
124	174	7c		

Decimal	Octal	Hexadecimal	Character
125	175	7d	}
126	176	7e	~

The Control Characters

Decimal	Octal	Hexadecimal	Key	Mnemonic Code
0	0	0	^@	NUL
1	1	1	^A	SOH
2	2	2	^B	STX
3	3	3	^C	ETX
4	4	4	^D	EOT
5	5	5	^E	ENQ
6	6	6	^F	ACK
7	7	7	^G	BEL
8	10	8	^H	BS
9	11	9	^I	HT
10	12	a	^J	LF
11	13	b	^K	VT
12	14	c	^L	FF
13	15	d	^M	CR
14	16	e	^N	SO
15	17	f	^O	SI
16	20	10	^P	DLE
17	21	11	^Q	DC1
18	22	12	^R	DC2
19	23	13	^S	DC3
20	24	14	^T	DC4
21	25	15	^U	NAK
22	26	16	^V	SYN
23	27	17	^W	ETB
24	30	18	^X	CAN
25	31	19	^Y	EM
26	32	1a	^Z	SUB
27	33	1b	ESC	ESC
28	34	1c		FS

Decimal	Octal	Hexadecimal	Key	Mnemonic Code
29	35	1d		GS
30	36	1e		RS
31	37	1f		US
127	177	7f	DEL	DEL

Reserved Words and Standard Identifiers

Reserved Words

AND	ARRAY	BEGIN
CASE	CONST	DIV
DO	DOWNTO	ELSE
END	FILE	FOR
FORWARD	FUNCTION	GOTO
IF	IN	LABEL
MOD	NIL	NOT
OF	OR	PACKED
PROCEDURE	PROGRAM	RECORD
REPEAT	SET	THEN
TO	TYPE	UNTIL
VAR	WHILE	WITH

Additional words reserved in Turbo Pascal:

ABSOLUTE	EXTERNAL	IMPLEMENTATION
INLINE	INTERFACE	INTERRUPT
SHL	SHR	STRING
UNIT	USES	XOR

Standard Identifiers

Constants

FALSE	MAXINT	TRUE

Types

BOOLEAN	CHAR	INTEGER
REAL	TEXT	

Files

INPUT	OUTPUT

Functions

ABS	ARCTAN	CHR
COS	EOF	EOLN
EXP	LN	ODD
ORD	PRED	ROUND
SIN	SQR	SQRT
SUCC	TRUNC	

Procedures

DISPOSE	GET	NEW
PACK	PAGE	PUT
READ	READLN	RESET
REWRITE	UNPACK	WRITE
WRITELN		

Additional identifiers predefined in Turbo Pascal:

Constants

MAXLONGINT	PI

Types

BYTE	COMP	DOUBLE
EXTENDED	LONGINT	SHORTINT
SINGLE	WORD	

Functions (discussed in this book)

CONCAT	COPY	LENGTH
PI	POS	RANDOM

Procedures (discussed in this book)

APPEND	ASSIGN	CLOSE
DELETE	EXIT	INSERT

Note: The standard procedures GET, PUT, PACK, UNPACK, and PAGE are not defined in Turbo Pascal.

Operators

Arithmetic Operators

Operator	Arithmetic Operation	Operands	Result
+	Addition	REAL/INTEGER	REAL/INTEGER
−	Subtraction	REAL/INTEGER	REAL/INTEGER
*	Multiplication	REAL/INTEGER	REAL/INTEGER
/	Real division	REAL/INTEGER	REAL
DIV	Integer division	INTEGER	INTEGER
MOD	Remainder of integer division	INTEGER	INTEGER

Relational Operators

Operator	Meaning
>	Greater than
<	Less than
>=	Greater than or equal
<=	Less than or equal
=	Equal
<>	Not equal

Set Operations

Operation	Operator
Union	+
Intersection	*
Difference	−

Set Relational Operators

Operator	Expression	Meaning
=	S1 = S2	Both S1 and S2 contain the same elements.
<>	S1 <> S2	S1 and S2 do not contain the same elements.
>=	S1 >= S2	All elements of S2 are in S1.
<=	S1 <= S2	All elements of S1 are in S2.

Precedence of Pascal Operators

Operator	Precedence
NOT	Priority 1 (highest)
* / DIV MOD AND	Priority 2
+ - OR (XOR in Turbo Pascal)	Priority 3
= > < >= <= <> IN	Priority 4 (lowest)

Index

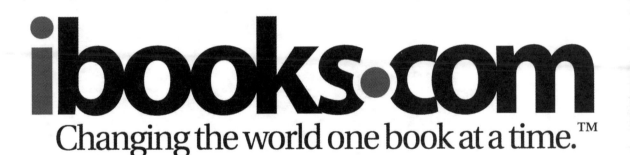

I don't have time for learning curves.

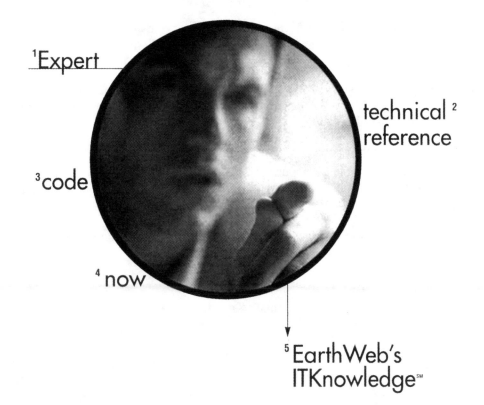

[1]Expert

technical [2]
reference

[3]code

[4] now

[5] EarthWeb's
ITKnowledge℠

They rely on you to be the ❶ expert on tough development challenges. There's no time for learning curves, so you go online for ❷ technical references from the experts who wrote the books. Find answers fast simply by clicking on our search engine. Access hundreds of online books, tutorials and even source ❸ code samples ❹ now. Go to ❺ EarthWeb's ITKnowledge, get immediate answers, and get down to it.

Get your FREE ITKnowledge trial subscription today at itkgo.com.
Use code number 026.

EARTHWEB
Go further *faster*

About the CD

The companion CD-ROM included with this book contains the examples and drills referenced throughout the text and a full retail version of Delphi 4 Standard Edition.

The examples and drills are in the Exercises folder, and are organized by chapter. For more information about these files and how to install them, see the readme.htm or readme.txt file in the Exercises folder.

When you insert the CD, a setup screen for Delphi 4 will pop up. Click on Delphi 4 to begin the installation process. The Serial Number is 100-004-2029 and the Authorization Key is 4AX35FX0.

Use Windows Explorer to access the Exercises folder.

In order to compile the programs in this book using the Delphi compiler, you must use the console mode. You do this by adding the following directive to your program:

```
{$APPTYPE CONSOLE}
```

To compile a console program, for example P1.PAS, use the command line:

```
DCC32 P1
```

This will create the executable file P1.EXE.

To run the program, use the command line:

```
P1
```

Notice that your path must include the Delphi\Bin directory. For more information on using console applications, see "A simple console application" in the Delphi Help.

 Caution: Opening the CD package makes this book nonreturnable.